One Hundred and Four Men

The William Pit Disaster, 1947

William Pit, Whitehaven, Cumberland, August 1947
Photograph courtesy of *The Yorkshire Post*

ONE HUNDRED AND FOUR MEN

THE WILLIAM PIT DISASTER, 1947

Amanda M. Garraway

HAYLOFT PUBLISHING LTD

First published 2007

Hayloft Publishing Ltd, Kirkby Stephen,
Cumbria, CA17 4DJ

tel: + 44 (0) 17683) 42300
fax. + 44 (0) 17683) 41568
e-mail: books@hayloft.eu
web: www.hayloft.eu

ISBN 1 904524 52 4

A catalogue record for this book is available
from the British Library

Printed and bound in the EU

Papers used by Hayloft are natural, recyclable products made from wood grown in sustainable forests. The manufacturing processes conform to the environmental regulations of the country of origin.

Cover design Sean Duffy

For
Mr. Thomas Unthank,
Pitman from Whitehaven
1788-1847

"A lover of justice, truth, and equity between man and man"
and the sole inspiration for the work that has become
One Hundred and Four Men

...but if from local situation, or any other impediment, it be found impossible to ventilate William Pit, so as to enable the men to work with a greater degree of safety, then I say that such a pit ought not to be worked at all. Signed 'X'

From *The Whitehaven Gazette,* Monday, 10 November 1823, following an explosion at William Pit that killed 32 miners and 17 horses

CONTENTS

ACKNOWLEDGEMENTS

The compilation of *One Hundred and Four Men*, faced two major stumbling blocks — the passage of time, and a vast body of water. How would it be possible to memorialise the lives of one hundred and four pitmen, when each had been in his grave for more than a half century? And furthermore, how would such an endeavour come to pass when the principle author was separated from her hometown by a great expanse of land and sea, at a distance of over 4,000 miles?

I am forever grateful to the team of men and women sent my way, each with a pivotal role to play in the fulfilment of this work; the majority of whom I have never laid eyes upon.

I begin with two children, Miss Joyce Hewer and her cousin Master Frank Hewer, shown here in 1948 while on holiday at Skegness with the orphans and widows of William Pit's disaster victims.

Fifty three years later, Joyce, now Mrs. Haile, stood at the newly dedicated William Pit memorial and in honour of her father, Joseph Wilson Hewer and uncle, Ronald William Hewer, laid two red roses of remembrance. I thank Joyce for the flowers that inspired the front cover, for giving me beauty among the ashes.

Joyce Hewer and cousin Frank Hewer, Skegness, 1948

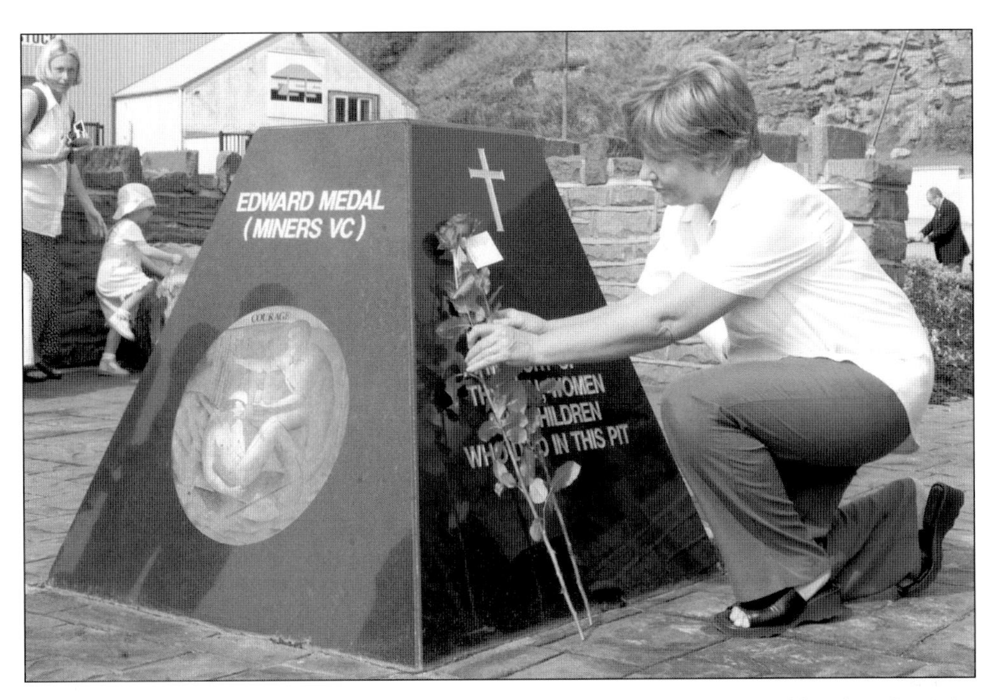

Joyce Haile at the William Pit Memorial, with daughter, Alison, and granddaughter Rosie in the background: descendants of one coal miner. Photograph courtesy of The News and Star.

In 2002, after appealing to *The Whitehaven News* for the then out of print book, *The Most Dangerous Pit in the Kingdom*, I received a mysterious email from an unidentified source: *"I read your letter in the marras' bible, The Whitehaven News. Father, uncle and great-uncle killed in 1947 disaster. Dark days."*

What followed were a series of letters and photographs detailing the lives of three coal miners. The little boy in the flannel suit had brought forth the first story. I thank Frank for introducing me to the world of a pit family, for his humour and his humility, and not least of all, his friendship. Ronnie would have been proud.

The project made significant advances after Colin Edgar of *The Whitehaven News* willingly agreed to publish all appeal and update letters to the reading public. Editors of *The News and Star, The Times and Star, The North West Evening Mail, The Yorkshire Post, The Lanarkshire Gazette,* and *The Lancashire Evening Post* followed suit. In December 2006 BBC Radio Cumbria aired a live interview and created a website page. I extend my gratitude to each and every one for allowing my voice to be heard.

In the early days of the appeal, a letter came from Mr Joseph Ritson, a keen researcher, with not only an interest in genealogy, but also Cumberland's military history in both the first and second world wars. His name was not unknown to me as I had previously read his many contributions on the BBC's *People's War* website. Joseph Ritson became my right hand man. His focus, knowledge, guidance, discipline and wisdom, kept me grounded. He transcribed documents and letters, and willingly interviewed contributors who had no idea where to start. A class act. I thank Joseph for his most welcome assistance.

I am indebted to 'the brotherhood' - the pitmen who took a girl by the hand and gave her the sights, sounds, and smells of a coal mine, and offered the truth about pit disasters: Daz Beattie, the smooth voice from Yorkshire, who taught me about the loader end and coal dust.

The delightful Ronnie Calvin who wrote the foreword and kept me entertained. Raymond Devlin for *The Most Dangerous Pit in the Kingdom*, for *The Cost of Coal*, for photographs, advice and geography lessons (the sun rises in the east and sets in the west). My dear friend and confidante, Joseph Loy, who was there in 1947, for hand drawn colliery maps, books, tapes, and secrets shared. Tom Scott who knocked on doors and handed me the fruits of his labour. True pitmen each and every one.

Mr Reliable, Sean Duffy of Cleator Moor, who was among the very first to offer me support and encouragement. Sean designed web pages, taped the interview, emailed letters to papers and mailing lists, visited contributors, compiled the video, cropped photographs, and from my written vision, designed the front cover.

Geoff Everitt, master of the genealogical lookups, who at my beck and call, researched the family trees of many of the William Pit miners.

Jim Patterson of Lowestoft, who one day, out of the blue, sent me an email and offered me the Pitmen website. I am still in awe!

I thank my family – my parents John and Brenda Garraway for keeping the faith that it would all come to pass; my husband David for ensuring the children were clothed and fed and on occasion, bathed; my daughters Madison and Presley who allowed me my time with my magnificent obsession; and my five-year-old son, Noah, who made me laugh after he glanced at a photo of actor Brad Pitt and asked if he was a coal miner.

To the many letter writers in England and Scotland, who offered assistance and wished me well – thank you so very much, your generosity was overwhelming.

And lastly, but by no means least, I thank the storytellers, the men, women and children who came forth, and in writing, offered me the lifeblood of their loved ones. Here, words fail me.

Amanda Garraway, Canada, 2007.

Some of the letters sent to the author about the 104 men and their families.

FOREWORD

For many years mining was a way of life in Whitehaven and West Cumberland. The miners, their wives, and families, were a special breed who helped each other in many different ways at times of gladness, times of grief and times of need. The sorrow that is mirrored in the hearts of the womenfolk and families of the 104 miners who died in William Pit, Whitehaven on 15 August 1947 must never be forgotten, nor the sacrifice of the miners.

There have been many times when I have wondered about all the men who lost their lives in William Pit on that fateful day and how best to remember them. Radio, television and newspaper reporters have often asked me to talk about my Dad, Herbert Calvin, but I have always said he was just one of the 104 men. They should all be remembered for who they were.

The people of Whitehaven have already helped pay for a Memorial Stone on top of William Pit to remember all the miners who lost their lives over the years. Now, Amanda Garraway has given me the chance to put in this book my own loving memories of my Dad alongside those of the families and friends of the other men who lost their lives that August day.

This book will help remember how those miners lived, who they were, and how important they were to their families and friends. Let us never forget these 104 men who made the greatest sacrifice of all to win coal from underground. They gave their lives for us all while earning their daily bread.

Ronnie Calvin, R.M.,
Cumbria County Councillor,
and son of disaster victim Herbert Calvin,
June 2007

PROLOGUE

I believe there is a God in Heaven, and that He remembers the lives of men long after they have gone the way of their forefathers; I believe that He raised up the unwitting descendant of a long-suffering coal mining family, and led her to a special place, and there showed her a great mystery that would take over 34 years to unravel.

As a child I used to dream of fanciful things, of fame and fortune as a great actress. I would never have imagined in my lust for grandeur, that such lofty ideas would plummet from the high places, and not only to the green grass at my feet, but to the depths of black caverns below it. In the summer of my ninth year, God is His infinite wisdom, gave me the coal miners of Whitehaven, and in doing so re-directed the desires of my heart and allowed me to dream a bigger dream.

On a childhood excursion to Whitey Rock in 1973, I accompanied my mother, my sister, my aunt, and my cousins along a stretch of asphalt known as the wagon road. It was our intent to spend the day with a well-stocked picnic basket, with bathing suits, and orange arm bands for a paddle in the Irish Sea. The road seemed long, and we voiced our complaints, until we were led to an old field, and there we flew like the wind to reach the steps that would take us to the shore. I finished last, for in my flight came a diversion, a hole in the ground barricaded by a fence and barbed wire. Across the brickwork and among the long weeds that thrived there, was a rotting plank of wood, which offered a warning: 'KEEP OUT.'

I still hear the seagulls and feel the warmth of the sun on my sandaled feet, my stand-still moment, when time seemed ceased to matter, and the cries of my cousins to hurry were ignored. Only my aunt remained, as I asked, 'What is this?'

'Oh lass,' she answered, 'ah think it has summat ta dee wid old William pit.'

Author back centre with family on Whitey Rock, August 1973. William Pit field behind great wall

And then I was gone, my day at the beach recorded in a single photo. We emigrated to Canada the following year. Except for a brief stint writing poetry about William Pit in 1983, I rarely thought of my trek through the field, but neither had I forgotten how I had felt in the midst of it. I call it my haunting. My significance.

****

There has been much weeping and wailing and gnashing of teeth, in the little community on the West Cumbrian coast. That Whitehaven has been a town with a murderous coal mining past is displayed in the pages of record books and old newspapers. Beneath manicured church gardens and cemetery plots are hundreds of unmarked resting places of men, women, and children who laboured in the dark places to make a living. They were burned, maimed, crushed, suffocated, dismembered, oppressed by owners and authorities, blamed at inquests, and classed as the common folk, who lived just a brief short time, before their lives were extinguished.

On 15 August 1947, at approximately 5.40pm, an explosion occurred in William Pit that took the lives of fathers, husbands, sons, uncles, brothers and cousins working the afternoon shift. Of one hundred and seven trapped behind roof falls, one hundred and four lost their lives within twenty minutes.

It is twilight, and I insist that the legacy left by our pitmen in our documented history should not be their deaths, but their lives and how they lived them.

I have compiled this book for the generations, for those who came before, and for those who come after. While they represent only a handful of Whitehaven's lost, I pray they be your pride, your joy.

These are the one hundred and four men…

A NOTE ON SOURCES

Above and beyond the contributions received from families and friends, that truly are the heart and soul of this compilation, other sources of information about the one hundred and four lives, include newspaper reports, memoriam notices, and various documents relating to the 1947 William Pit Disaster, which have been transcribed and reproduced with the kind permission of the Cumbria Record Office and Local Studies Library (Whitehaven) and the *Whitehaven News.*

A number of the 104 pitmen, despite the broad appeal, have not received a memorial letter. I will always wonder about them, their names are etched in my mind, and as a result my contact details will be kept up to date with both the publisher and local newspapers.

These relatives are the children of Joseph Norman - Josephine, Victor and Joe - at the William Pit memorial stone in 2001. Photograph courtesy of the 'News and Star.'

ANDREW AGNEW

Andy
Son-in-law of Isaac McAllister
Brother-in-law of Edward McAllister

Andy Agnew was 36 years old when he lost his life in the disaster. Employed as a brusher, Andrew lived at 17 Todhunters Buildings, Queen Street, with his wife formerly Bridget McAllister, and their two young sons, Howard and Peter. At 2.50pm on the afternoon of 19 August 1947, Mr Agnew was raised to the surface of William Pit and later identified by his brother-in-law, Isaac McAllister of 86 Scotch Street, Whitehaven. Andrew was the 86th man located by recovery teams. He was laid to rest at Whitehaven Cemetery.

Two memoriams placed in *The Whitehaven News* one year later, reveal that both Andrew Agnew's father-in-law and brother-in-law also lost their lives in the disaster.

In loving memory of my dear husband
Andrew Agnew,
killed in the William Pit disaster 15 August 1947
aged 36 years
He lived for those he loved
And those he loved will remember
Eternal rest give unto him, O Lord
Remembered always by his loving Wife and sons,
Howard and Peter

Also of my dear father and brother,
Isaac and Edward McAllister
also killed in the disaster
O, sacred heart of Jesus
Have mercy on them
R.I.P.
All so sadly missed

Andy Agnew and son, 1941.

****

In loving memory of a very dear son and brother
Andrew (Andy),
killed in the William Pit disaster, 15 August 1947.
A better son and brother never lived
A heart of gold his last would give
A loving smile a welcome face
No one can fill his vacant place
From his Dad, sister Lizzie, brothers Tom, Frank and sister-in-law Peggy

JOHN DOUGLAS ALLAN
and his son
HENRY TROHEAR ALLAN

Jack Allan and his son Harry

John Douglas Allan was 59-years-old and a contract employee at William Pit. Known as Jack, he lived at 5 Buttermere Avenue, Seacliffe, Whitehaven, with his wife Agnes. At 4.40am on the morning of 17 August 1947, Jack was brought to the surface of William Pit and later identified by his son Norman Allan, of 60 Crummock Avenue, Woodhouse. Mr Allan was the 54th man located by rescue team members.

Henry Trohear Allan was a 39-year-old brusher, and lived at 45 Hill Top Road, Arrowthwaite, Whitehaven. He was survived by his wife Annie, and two children, Jean and John. Annie was expecting their third baby. On 17 August 1947, Norman Allan also identified his brother, after Harry was brought to the surface of William Pit at 7.15 am, two and a half hours after his father. Harry Allan was the 61st man recovered.

****

My memories of my Dad and Granda never fade, I can still picture them. My Granda was very special to me. When I was a little girl he would come to our house on Hill Top Road every weekend, and ask my Mam if she would let him take me to the pictures. It was as though he was a boyfriend and we would go to the Queen's Cinema, have the best seats in the house and he would buy me a lovely box of my favourite chocolates – I used to feel like a princess! I also remember that he kept a beautiful garden at his house on Buttermere Avenue.

Granda was very experienced at his job and was good at 'finding' coal – he seemed to know where the best places were to dig for it. When I was small (about four-years-old and John was two-years-old), we all moved from Whitehaven to 'Water Gin', a small place near the village of Oughterside (near Prospect/Aspatria) so that Dad and Granda could develop a small opencast mine which was called 'Slowly On'. However, this didn't work out very well as the locals enjoyed helping themselves to the coal, and after a short while Granda was made manager at a pit at Prospect. We all moved to the mine manager's house and Dad was made a deputy at the same mine. By the time I was ready for starting school we had all moved back to Kells and the men went to work at William Pit.

My Dad was a very good looking man and had a lovely singing voice – but only for family occasions. My friends at school used to comment on how he looked like a film star! I was at Whitehaven Grammar School when we found out that Mam was expecting a baby. He went to ask for permission for me to leave to help look after her and the baby as she wasn't very well. He would have been surprised to know that she was to have twins. When the twins were born Uncle Norman (Dad's brother), and Auntie Betty came up with the great idea (ha,ha) that they should be named Henrietta and Harriet after Dad. Mam said that she wouldn't dare, because the girls would grow up and 'kick her legs off!' They settled on Norma after our uncle, but we don't know where Barbara came from (the name means strange or foreign and despite many jokes she's neither!)

When Dad left school he trained to be a butcher as his family were related to the Partingtons who were well-known farmers and butchers. However, he gave up the profession before very long as he couldn't bear the thought of slaughtering animals.

Mam and Dad met playing tennis at the Welfare at Kells and they also loved walking. They would often walk along the cliffs to St Bees, Saltom or Whitehaven.

Dad also loved dogs and had a wire-haired fox terrier called Vic. After Vic died, Mam decided that was the end of dogs in the house, but a friend bred greyhounds and Dad rescued the runt of the litter who was going to be put to sleep. He persuaded Mam to let him keep 'Lady' and she was a lovely natured animal – we all loved her. On the day of the disaster she lay on the lawn and wouldn't eat, drink, or come inside despite the fact that it was a very hot day. Even though Mam wasn't a dog person, she wouldn't let anyone else have Lady. Uncle Norman knew that Dad had been training her to run the November Handicap race at Workington, so we took her along and, running under her proper name of 'Quaker Girl', she won the race – we were all so pleased and Dad would have been delighted too.

I vividly remember that terrible day. Usually Granda Jack, and his two sons Harry and Norman didn't work together, they used to take a shift each. One would be on first shift, another on back shift, and the other on night shift. Unfortunately on 15 August, my grandfather asked Dad to give him a hand. My mother Hannah, my brother John and I spent a horrible day worrying as soon as we heard there was something wrong at the pit. When eventually we found out the result of this horrific day, my mother, was put to bed and we had to be very careful with her. The family also lost two other members – Thomas Allan and Albert Tweddle.

My Mam's family were also involved in mining and her father John Quayle was presented with the King Edward Gold Medal for mine rescue after the Wellington Pit disaster in 1910. His medal was given by the family to the Whitehaven Museum collection and we can make arrangements to see it at The Beacon.

Jean Trohear Hughes, Barbara Nesbitt, Norma Hall and John Allan (in spirit)

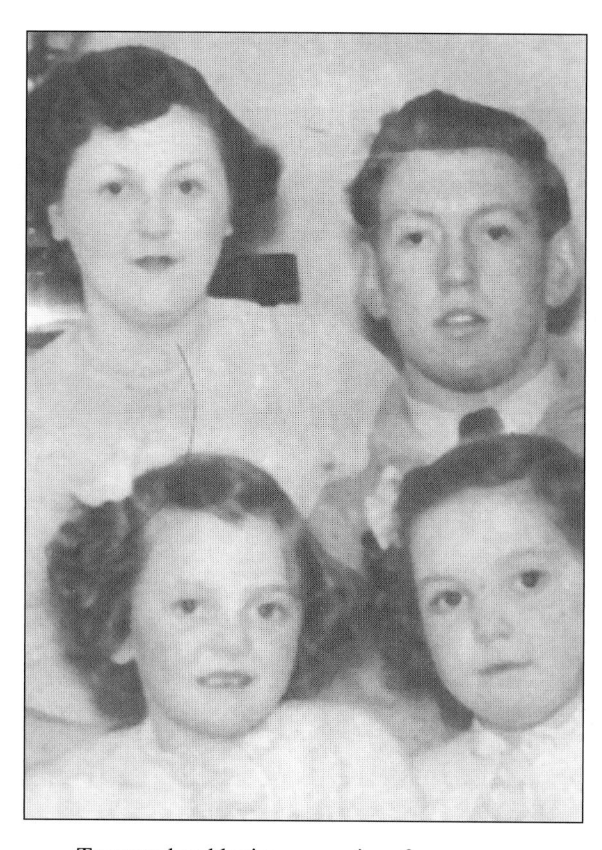

The Allan Children: Jean, John, Norma, Barbara

Treasured memories of a dear
father-in-law and Granda,
John (Jack) Douglas
who passed into eternal life at
William Pit, August 15, 1947
You left a beautiful memory
A sorrow too great to be told
But to us who have loved and lost
you
Your memory will never grow old.
Fondly remembered by his
daughter-in-law Annie and grand-
children Jean and John

Treasured and loving memories of a
dear husband and Dad,
Henry Trohear (Harry) who passed
into eternal life
at William Pit August 15, 1947,
Beautiful memories treasured ever
Of those days when we were together
Life is eternal love will remain
In God's own time, we will meet again
Sadly missed and longed for by his loving
wife and children

Treasured and loving memories of
my dearly loved son
Henry Trohear (Harry) Allan who
passed into eternal life
at William Pit August 15, 1947.
Lord take this message to my son above
Tell him I miss him and give him my love
Sweet is his memory, dear is his name
God bless you my son, until we meet again
Too dearly loved to ever be forgotten
by his loving Mother

In loving memory of a dear
brother and uncle, Harry
who departed this life on August 15, 1947
in the William Pit
a loving brother true and kind
Few in this world his equal to find
Deep in our hearts his memory is kept
We who loved you will never forget
Lovingly remembered by Norman, Betty,
Margaret, Thelma and Harry

In loving memory of a dear
Dad and Granda,
who departed this life on August 15, 1947
in the William Pit
Deep in our hearts a memory is kept
Of a Dad we loved and never forget
God took him from us without farewell
How deep is our sorrow no one can tell
Lovingly remembered by his son Norman,
Betty, Margaret Thelma and Harry

THOMAS ALLAN

Tommy

Nephew of Jack Allan
Cousin of Harry Allan
Brother-in-law of Albert Tweddle

Tommy Allan was 33-years-old and a stoneworker at William Pit. He lived at 26 Buttermere Avenue, Seacliffe Whitehaven, with his wife Isabel and young daughters Mildred and Frances. At 10.15am, on 16 August 1947, just over sixteen hours after the explosion, Tommy was brought to the surface of William Pit and identified by his brother-in-law John Bird of 82 Main Street, Distington. He was the third man located of the 104 who perished.

****

My Dad, Thomas (Tommy) Allan was 33-years-old when he was killed in the William Pit disaster. As a young man he lived at Parton with his Dad Harry, mother Frances, and his two sisters Jinnie and Frances. My Mam, Isabel (Bell) Bird lived at Lowca with her four sisters and three brothers and she met my Dad at a dance in Parton. They were married in 1938 and moved to a house in Queen Street, Whitehaven. They had two daughters Mildred born in 1940 and me, Frances, born in 1942. My Dad's parents ran a public house in Parton for many years but eventually moved to live at Fleswick Avenue, Woodhouse. Jinnie married Albert Tweddle and also moved to Fleswick Avenue where they lived next door to her parents, and Frances moved to Carlisle. My Mam and Dad moved from Queen Street to Buttermere Avenue at Seacliffe in 1943.

On the day of the disaster Mildred and I had been taken for a day out to Lowca with our cousins. Later a message came to our aunt that we had to go home straight away. When we arrived the house was full of people. I can remember there were lots of people crying. My Mam's brother, Adam, was in the police force in Dewsbury and borrowed a motor bike as soon as he got the news and was in Whitehaven by 7pm to be with my Mam.

Harry Allan, senior, who survived the disaster and his wife, Frances.

My grandfather, Harry Allan, was working at the pit bottom on the day of the explosion. He was injured, carried out and taken home and from that day on he was house bound, as he never recovered from the loss of so many of his family. On that day he lost his son Tommy, his brother Jack Allan, his nephew Harry Allan and his son-in-law Albert Tweddle (Jinnie and Albert had no family).

Dad was the third body to be brought up the pit but by some mistake he was taken to a house at Frizington. My Mam's brothers waited at the pit for his body and when the last men were brought up everyone realised that there had been a mistake and my Dad's body was brought home from Frizington. Dad and Albert were buried next to each other in Moresby church yard where some years later my Mam and Jinnie were buried with them.

Frances Sirkett (née Allan),
daughter of Thomas Allan

In memory of a loving husband and daddy
Thomas Allan
killed in William Pit disaster August 15, 1947
Sadly missed by his loving wife and daughters, Mildred and Frances

In loving memory of our dear son Thomas Allan;
also our dear son-in-law Albert Tweddle
Who were killed in William Pit explosion August 15, 1947
One by one our loved ones leave us
And we often wonder why
But they are waiting for our coming
We shall meet them by and by
Ever remembered by Father and Mother

Jennie Tweddle (nee Allan), Frances Allan, Bell Allan (nee Bird), Mildred Allan at Skegness 1948

In loving memory of our dear brother Tommy;
also our dear brother-in-law Albert
who were killed in William Pit Disaster, August 15, 1947
God took them from us without farewell
So deep is our sorrow no one can tell
The tragic way in which they died
Will always make us wonder why
Always remembered by Frances and Isaac, Carlisle

****

JOHN ANDERSON

John Anderson was 50-years-old and employed as a pan-puller at William Pit. He was a resident of 29 Buttermere Avenue, Whitehaven, and was survived by his wife Sarah and seven children. Brought to the surface at 11.15pm on 16 August 1947, John was later identified by his nephew, Edward Ackerley of the same address. Mr. Anderson was the ninth man located.

My name is Sarah Murray (née Anderson) the daughter of John Anderson. Just to set the record straight, my Dad had seven children .

Anne is 85, at the time she was 26
John is 80, at the time he was 21
Helen is 76, at the time she was 17
Sarah is 68, at the time she was 9
Ronnie is 66, at the time he was 7
William is 64, at the time he was 5
Elizabeth is 60, she was about 9 months.

The day of the explosion I was on the golden sands beach at Whitehaven with my brothers Ronnie and Billy , and cousins who were on up holiday. I remember hearing a loud explosion and seeing a cloud of smoke. I remember someone telling us to go home and wait. We found out later what had happened.

At the time of the disaster Helen was at work at The Gaiety Picture House. She remembers someone running in shouting that the pit had blown up. She was told to go home but she went to the pit top, were she found our Mam. They stayed there for days till they gave up hope of any more survivors. John was in the merchant navy at the time. He found out weeks later when one of his friends received a newspaper from home giving details about the disaster. *Sarah Murray*

****

In loving memory of my dear husband, John,
who was killed in the William Pit explosion August 15, 1947
The blow was hard, the shock severe
We little thought that death was near
Only those who have lost can tell
The loss of a loved one without farewell
Always remembered by his loving wife and family, also his son-in-law Ron

JAMES ATKINSON

James Atkinson aged 45 years, was employed as a brusher in William Pit. He was survived by his wife Ada Mary Atkinson and four children. He lived at 4 Gameriggs Road, Whitehaven. In the afternoon hours of 19 August 1947 at 1.20pm, Mr. Atkinson was brought to the surface of William Pit and identified by his son William James Atkinson of the same address. He was the 85th man located.

****

In loving memory of my dear husband, James Atkinson
who died in the William Pit Disaster August 15th, 1947
What would I give to clasp his hand
His cheery face to see
To hear his voice to see him smile
That meant so much to me
He did not fail to do his best
His heart was true and tender
He did work hard for those he left
That's something to remember
From his loving Wife, and family, Greenbank.

Treasured Memories of my dear brother James
Killed William Pit August 15, 1947
Not a day do we forget you
In our hearts you are always near
God alone knows how much we miss you
Bringing many a silent tear
From his loving sister Louisa and family

Treasured memories of my dear Uncle James,
killed William Pit, August 15, 1947
Not just today but every day in silence we remember
Ever remembered by James, Elizabeth and Sandra

RICHARD ATKINSON

Brother-in-law of George Hutchinson

Employed as a pipe-fitter, Richard Atkinson was 28-years-old when he died in the 1947 disaster. He lived at Ladypit Cottages, Sunnyhill, Whitehaven with his wife Millicent Lucilla Atkinson and little son Malcolm. Mr. Atkinson was identified by his brother, John McKenzie Atkinson, of 6 York Terrace, Sunnyhill, after he was brought to the pit surface on 17 August 1947. He was the 66th miner located. Richard Atkinson was the brother of Margaret Hutchinson, who also lost her husband George, in the disaster.

In loving memory of a dear husband and father, Richard,
killed August 15, 1947 in the William Pit explosion,
No more to see his smiling face
Or hear him say hello
It came as a shock we didn't expect
A hard and bitter blow.
Always in the thoughts of his loving wife, Milly and son Malcolm

****

Loving memories of Richard a dear son-in-law
killed August 15, 1947 in the William Pit explosion
When last I saw your smiling face
You looked so bright and well
Little did I dream that day
Would be or last farewell
Always with you every day
From Mam and Dad-in-law

****

Treasured memories of our dear brother Richard Atkinson;
also of George Hutchinson our brother-in-law,
both lost in William Pit Disaster 1947
Loved and longed for always by brother and sisters

In fond and loving memory of my two brothers Richard and George,
who lost their lives in William Pit disaster August 15, 1947
A smile for all, a heart of gold
Two of the best this world did hold
Loved in life treasured in death
Ours to remember when others forget
Always remembered by their loving sister, Agnes, Harry and children, Liverpool.

HENRY BARKER

Henry Barker, aged 34 years, was a coal hewer at William Pit, and lived at 4 Ehen Road, Cleator Moor. Mr Barker was the father of five children, three girls and two boys. On the evening of 17 August 1947, Henry was brought to the surface and later identified by his wife Isabel Louisa Barker. Due to employment circumstances Mr. and Mrs. Barker had not lived together for six months at the time of the disaster. His wife requested that his body be taken to her address in Aspatria. Henry Barker was the 67th man located.

Henry and Louisa Barker.

I had an uncle who was killed in the William pit. His name was Henry Barker. He was about 34-years-old when he died. My mother, whose maiden name was Rachel Barker, was Henry's sister. He was married to Louisa, they had five children Richard, Martha, Edith, Henry and Rachel. Only Edith survives today.

At the time of the disaster Louise and the children were living at Hayton, near Maryport, but Henry was living at Cleator Moor. I think he worked on a farm before the William Pit; he had not worked in the pit for very long. I can remember my Mum saying to me that she stood on the pit bank all night with Louise and my grandma (Henry's mother Martha Barker). My mother also told me when she said a prayer over his coffin she heard his voice say, 'Don't cry for me. I'm not in there (the coffin) I am still in the pit.'

My Mum and Dad named my brother after him. That's all I know about my uncle Henry, as I was not born until 1950.

Edith was only seven-years-old when her Dad died and the only memory she has is of walking with her Dad along the railway line from Aspatria to Bullgill to her Grandma Martha Barker. She remembers that her Dad loved to play cards. Edith also has a photo of her Dad with three other men who she says worked down the pit.

*Rachel Langstaff, n*iece of Henry Barker

JAMES RICHARDSON BARWISE

Jim

James Barwise, aged 49 years, was a brusher at William Pit. He lived at 5 Low Harras Moor, Whitehaven, with his wife Elizabeth and two children under sixteen years, Gwendoline and Bernard. Mr. Barwise was brought to the surface of William Pit on 17 August 1947 at 1.50pm, and identified by his father, Jerry Barwise, of 5 James Pit, Whitehaven. James Barwise was the 50th man located.

In August 1947 James Richardson Barwise, lived with his wife Elizabeth Barwise (née Parkinson) and children Bernard and Gwen at Harras Moor, Whitehaven. James was among the many miners who died in the 1947 William Pit explosion who had previously served with the Border Regiment.

James R. Barwise had been in the 5th Battalion of the Border Regiment, the Territorial Battalion that recruited mainly in West Cumberland. Following the William Pit Disaster, James was remembered by the Border Regiment and was mentioned in the regimental magazine. A copy of this is retained in the Regimental Archives at Carlisle Castle.

As a young man, James Richardson Barwise had also been in the army during the First World War, serving as a driver in the Royal Field Artillery (R.F.A). James was one of the many townsfolk recognised as having served in that war by his home town of Whitehaven in the official 'Borough of Whitehaven Roll of Honour, European War 1914-1918.' A reference copy of this can be found in the County Records Office, Whitehaven (Ref. DH 7/2). This Roll of Honour lists James's WW1 service number as 270240 and his address in 1919 as 18 Gore's Buildings, Whitehaven.

These two periods of James's life whilst he was in the army have been officially - even if only briefly - recorded. Undoubtedly other things - such as home and family, friendship and work - were more important to him. These more personal aspects of life are not as readily recorded for posterity. But at least as his military service has been recorded he can be remembered for giving some years of his life to the service of his country.

Joseph Ritson

****

In loving and affectionate remembrance
of my dearest husband, Jim,
killed in the William Pit disaster
August 15, 1947 aged 49 years.
To be remembered by those he loved
Would be all he would ever ask
From his Wife and children,
Low Harras Moor

In loving remembrance of James P. Barwise
killed in the William Pit disaster,
August 15, 1947
Always in the thoughts of his loving Father.

Treasured memories of Jim, killed in the
William Pit Disaster August 15 1947
Not past today but every day
In silence I remember
From his brother Sam

****

Acknowledgements: The KORBR & Border Regiment Museum, Carlisle and the Cumbria County Records Office, Whitehaven.

JAMES M. BOWES

Jinkie

James Murray Bowes was a 34-year-old coal cutter at William Pit. He was survived by his wife Mary and three children. The family lived at 5 Garfield Place, Parton, Cumberland. James Bowes was raised to the surface of William Pit on 18 August 1947. He was the 73rd miner reached by search and recovery teams. Mr. Bowes was laid to rest at St. Bridget's Churchyard, Moresby on 19 August 1947.

****

In loving memory of my dear husband
James M. Bowes
killed in William Pit Disaster
August 15, 1947.
When last I saw your smiling face
You looked so bright and well
Little did I think dear Jinkie
It was our last farewell
Inserted by his loving wife and family

JOSEPH BRANNON

Joe

Joseph Brannon was 45-years-old and a brusher at William Pit. He lived at 21 Greenbank Avenue, Greenbank, Whitehaven. Mr. Brannon was survived by his wife Susannah and three children. In the early morning hours of 17 August 1947 just after midnight, Joseph Brannon was brought to the pit top and identified by his oldest son, John Brannon of the same address. Joseph had been a member of the King's Own Royal Border Regiment's 2nd Battalion.

****

I am writing to you about my grandfather Joseph Brannon. This information has been provided by my mother Isabel Parr (née Brannon).

Joseph Brannon was born on the 26 October 1902. Joseph was married to Susannah (née Walsh) known to her friends as 'Shanna'. Susannah was two years older that Joseph. They lived at 21 Greenbank Avenue, Whitehaven. Joe and Shanna had three children — John born in 1923, my mother Isabel born in 1924 and the youngest, Joseph, born in 1926. Of these three children, Isabel and Joseph still survive today.

Joseph Brannon was originally employed as a miner at Haig pit, but at some point was laid off and had to find employment elsewhere. He couldn't get any mining work at that time and my mother recalls him working down in Barrow doing demolition work.

She remembers that during the Second World War he had to fill in enlistment forms. She remembers that on the forms he cited his occupation as a labourer and not a miner. This inevitably led to him being called up into the armed forces. My mother said he did his basic training at Catterick and on completion of training was later posted to North Africa where he served his country for two years. When the war was over Joseph returned home to his family. He attempted to get mining work at Haig pit but was unsuccessful, but managed to find employment at William pit.

My mother's recollection of the day of the disaster is that it was a sunny August day. It was a Friday and a Holy day of obligation 'The Feast of the Assumption'. My mother was still living at home and said that on that morning she attended mass at St Begh's Roman Catholic Church with her parents and her Aunt Lizzie, who was visiting the family from Lancaster.

Joe Brannon's widow, Shanna, is pictured with their three children, John, Isabel and Joseph.

My granddad was a devout catholic and never missed mass. She vividly recalls walking back from church after the service to their home at Greenbank. On the way back my mother said Aunt Lizzie tried to persuade Joseph to take the day off work and travel down with the family for a short break at her home in Lancaster. She remembers Joseph saying to Aunt Lizzie that he couldn't take time off as he would lose two days' pay and he couldn't afford to lose that amount of money so he had to go work.

At some point on the walk back Joseph hurried ahead as he needed to get home and changed out of his best clothes and into his work clothes as he was due on the afternoon shift. My mother said they half expected him to be sitting on the front step when they got back because he didn't have a key to get into the house. When they finally got back, he was waiting at the front door dressed in his work clothes, as he had climbed in through an open window pane. He was that determined not to be late for work. Shortly after that my mother said granddad left for work.

The last family member to see my granddad before he went down the mine was his youngest son Joseph, who had just finished the first shift at William Pit. My granddad had picked up his wage packet and before going down the mine had given it to Joseph and asked him to take it home and give it to his mother, Shanna. They then said their goodbyes and my granddad went down the mine to start his shift. After news of the explosion, the family suffered through the dreaded wait for news as to the fate of Dad and the other miners. My mother told me that it was my Uncle John who identified my Grandad's body. She said that John later told the family that when he identified his Dad he only had one slight mark on his face where he had fallen and was otherwise unmarked from the explosion.

My mother remembers her Dad with great fondness and love. She said he was a good honest man who didn't deserve the fate that was dealt to him or the other 103 men who lost their lives on that sunny Friday August afternoon.

Susannah Brannon, wife of Joseph Brannon known as Shanna.

My grandmother Susannah never remarried and remained living on Greenbank. Susannah's son Joseph never married and remained living at home until my grandmother passed away on the 24 July 1983 at the age of 83. My mother Isabel is now 82 years of age and Joseph is 80 years of age. They both now live on the Mirehouse estate in Whitehaven.

I hope this information is of use and helps you get a bit better insight into Joseph Brannon. My mother, due to her age, can get a little confused from time to time but her recollection of that day, although a bit vague in parts, is how she remembers the events leading up to the disaster.

Robert Parr, grandson

****

In loving memory of a dear husband and father, Joseph
who lost his life in the William Pit
Explosion August 15, 1947
The shock was great, the blow severe
To part with one we loved so dear
To a beautiful life came a sudden end
He died as he lived, everyone's friend
On whose soul Sweet Jesus have mercy
R.I.P.
From his loving wife, sons and daughter

In loving memory of Joe
killed In William Pit Disaster August 15, 1947
No more to see your smiling face
Or hear you say hello
It came as a shock we didn't expect
A hard and bitter blow
St. Theresa pray for him
From his loving sister Catherine, James and family

In loving memory of a dear brother Joseph (Joe)
who lost his life in William Pit
August 15, 1947
Your end was sudden Joe dear
You made me weep and cry
But, Oh, the saddest part of all
You never said goodbye
R.I.P.
Always remembered by
Bella, Bridget and families

THOMAS BRANNON

Tommy

Thomas Brannon was 57-years-old and a chocker at William Pit. He lived at 55 Haig Avenue, Bransty, with his wife Mary Ann and was the father of four sons. Brought to the surface at 10.50am on 19 August 1947, Tommy was identified by his son, T. Brannon of 111 Park Gate, Frizington. He was the 83rd miner located. His brother Robert was a member of the rescue squad.

The Brannon Men.
Back Row: Thomas Brannon (cousin), unknown, William James Brannon (brother), Joe Brannon (brother), Robert Brannon (cousin), Gerald Brannon (cousin).
Middle Row: ***Tom Brannon*** *(died William Pit 1947), Robert Brannon (uncle), William James Brannon (father of Thomas Brannon), John Brannon (uncle).*
Front Row: ***Robert Brannon (brother),*** *Harold Brannon (nephew), Tom Brannon (nephew)*

Thomas Brannon, 1890-1947, was the oldest of nine children born to William James and Mary Ann. They were a large coal mining family. Thomas' grandfather and father, along with many other Brannon relatives were already working the mines in the Whitehaven area when he was born. His uncle Tom Brannon, was a well known figure at William Pit, where he was the miners' delegate for over 30 years and worked at the pit for more than half a century.

Thomas Brannon perished in the 1947 disaster along with his niece's husband Ronald Hewer. Tragedy continued to strike the family.

His brother William James died from injuries sustained in a pit accident at Bolton, and his younger brother Joe died the year previous from yet another accident at William Pit. Another brother, Robert, died in a railway accident.

Thomas Brannon married Mary Ann (Polly) Metcalf, and fathered six children, two of whom died young. Another son, Jack Brannon, died in 1942 in the RAF during the war, from an infected needle. *Chris Drake,* great nephew of Thomas Brannon

****

I remember the disaster well, being eighteen-years-old at the time and living at Bransty Road. My friend Billy Brannon lived at 55 Haig Avenue, Bransty. My other pal John Ennis lived at the Close, Bransty behind Billy.

I had called round for John Ennis and then went for Billy Brannon. We were going to the pictures. We walked down to the bottom of Bransty Brow and saw all the activity and asked what was going on. We were told there had been an explosion at William Pit.

Billy said to me, 'My Dad's down today.'

I then went to my grandmother's on George Street to tell them what had happened. My Aunt Florrie was also there from America. They were shocked but as yet not aware of the casualties. Later that evening we went to the top of Bransty Cliff, above the pit, everyone was waiting for news.

Sad to say Billy's Dad, Thomas, was killed, also our neighbour's son Vincent McSherry. A day never to be forgotten.

My Dad had worked at William as a blacksmith but he was not there that day. Billy Brannon and his brothers have all since died, he had no sisters. *Frank Lewthwaite*

****

Treasured memories of a dear husband and Dad, Thomas,
who was killed in William Pit disaster, August 15, 1947
'Tis not the tears of the moment shed
That tell of hearts that are torn
But the lonely grief of the after years
Remembrance silently borne
Oh Jesus open wide Thy arms
And let him rest therein
From his loving wife and sons and daughter-in-law and grandchildren, also Nancy

JACOB E. BRIDGES

Jakey

Jacob Bridges, was a resident of 85 Grasmere Road, Woodhouse, Whitehaven. He was survived by his wife Mary Edith, and their three young children, Caroline (Carol), Mary Edith (Edie) and Philip. Employed as a coal cutter at William Pit, Jacob was 37-years-old when he was killed in the disaster. At 8.50am on the morning of 17 August 1947, Mr. Bridges was brought to the surface of William Pit and later identified by his brother-in-law William Brown of 97 Grasmere Avenue, Woodhouse, Whitehaven. Jacob Bridges was the nineteenth man located.

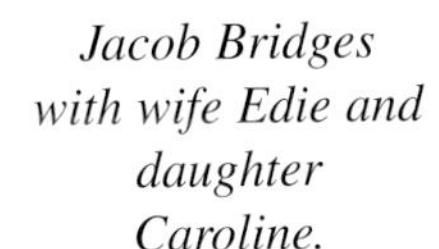

Jacob Bridges with wife Edie and daughter Caroline.

I will never forget the day when William Pit went up. I am Edie Wells, née Bridges. My father was Jacob Edward Bridges. He was 37-years-old and the most wonderful and loving husband and father. Mam was 32, and she was left with three small children. My sister Carol was nine, I was seven, and my baby brother was three-months-old.

It had been a bad day. My baby brother had been sleeping on the settee and somehow rolled off. He had a big bump on his head and we could not get him to stop crying. My Mam's friend, Ada Hooper, who lived opposite had been standing at her gate when a woman came scurrying up the road saying William Pit had gone up.

It was a few minutes before it dawned on her that my Dad was down the pit. She ran over with the news. Never for a moment did we think my Dad wouldn't be coming home. Everyone was making their way to the pit but Mam started to clean the house from top to bottom.

She stripped their bed, putting white sheets and clean covers on. She was crying all the time. She said we must have the bed nice when they bring him home wounded. Then we waited, and waited, and waited.

I was seven and the apple of my Dad's eye. I was nine-weeks-old before my Dad saw me. He was at Dunkirk in the war. He was one of the men who made it home from the beaches of Dunkirk. He made it home to die in the pit.

Mam said he was so proud when he got a son. But he never had time to get to know him. I remember when we were bathed and had our clean nighties on he would give my sister and I a few minutes start, and then he would chase us to bed. My sister and I used to kill each other trying to get up the stairs. We used to scream hysterically pulling each other down the stairs. I remember him singing to us *The Three Little Fishes* song, not that he could sing, and we used to plead and plead for him to sing it.

Down in the meadow in a little bitty pool
Swam three little fishes and a mama fishy too
"Swim," said the mama fishie, "Swim if you can,"
And they swam, and they swam, all over the dam

Mary Edith Wells, daughter

****

In loving memory of my dear
husband Jacob Edward Bridges,
killed in William Pit August 15th, 1947
We had a father with a heart of gold
He was more to us than wealth untold
Kind and unselfish a father so true
Our proudest possessions
are memories of you
Ever remembered by his loving wife,
Sons and daughters

****

In loving memory of Jacob E. Bridges
accidentally killed in William Pit
August 15, 1947
aged 37 years
We never heard his last faint sigh
We never saw him die
We only knew he passed away
And could not say goodbye
Always in our thoughts
From Aunties Ann, Jean and Alice,
Uncles Jack and Eddie and cousins at
home and away, also Phil with M.E.L.F

Pictured above, Carol, Edie, and Mary Edith at Skegness 1948 and right, Carol, Edie and Philip Bridges.

HARTLEY BYERS

Pat

Hartley Byers was a 35-year-old brusher at William Pit. He lived at 13 James Street, Whitehaven, with his wife Mary, who was expecting a baby, and their four children - William James, Alan, Mary and Brian. Raised to the surface at 7.50am 17 August 1947, Hartley Byers was later identified by his brother, Stanley Byers, of 36 Springfield Road, Bigrigg. Mr. Byers was the 59th miner located.

My name is Bill Byers and my Father was one of the men killed in the William Pit Disaster in 1947. At the time I was seven-years-old with two younger brothers and a sister all under five-years-old.

There are many things that I recall especially the terrible hardship that families like ours had to endure, a result of which was that my mother lost the baby she was carrying at the time. Over the years minor errors to some of the details have crept in and I should like you to correct these when you publish your book.

We lived at 13 James Street and not 15 which has often been quoted. You don't forget unlucky 13 when something as awful as this happens. The youngest son is called Brian. Sister Mary passed away some seven years ago after a long hard life looking after Mam as well as raising her own family. When my mother lost the baby she was carrying at the time, she had to undergo surgery and unfortunately became a paraplegic and as a result she had to have constant care for the rest of her days.

There are no photographs to hand of my Father, the only one being placed alongside my mother when she passed away some years ago. I am 71-years-old now but the events of that Friday evening are still as fresh today as they were when it happened. I was out horse riding with others on the hills above Whitehaven when a pit siren started blowing, that being the sign that something serious had occurred. There were only the two pits, Haig and William, and alas it was William.

The sons of Hartley 'Pat' Byers - Allan, Brian and Bill

When the rest of the pit sirens joined in, you became aware that a major accident had happened and as we know the results were very tragic for a lot of people.

Dad's nick-name was Pat - Hartley Pat Byers - he was quite proud of it actually. If you said Hartley Byers no one knew who you were talking about, but say Pat and everybody knew him by that name. Looking at your original e-mail you seem to have the rest correct. As you know, I am the eldest, then there is Allan, and Brian who is in his sixties now but is still regarded as the baby of the family. We meet most Monday nights in the local Veterans Club which is a great way to have a couple of drinks, a good old fashioned crack, it keeps the family in touch and we can bring each other up to date.

****

In loving memory of a loving husband and father,
Hartley (Pat) Byers
who was killed in the William Pit Disaster August 15, 1947.
We miss your smile your happy ways
With you we spent our happiest days
'Tis sad but true we wonder why
The best are always the first to die
Loved and longed for always by his loving wife and children.

****

In loving memory of Hartley,
the beloved son of Mr. and Mrs. R Byers,
accidentally killed in William Pit Disaster August 15, 1947
No more to see his smiling face
Or hear him say hello
It came as a shock we didn't expect
A hard and bitter blow
Lovingly remembered by Mother, Father and family

HERBERT CALVIN

Herbert Calvin was 40-years-old, and employed as a brusher at William Pit. He lived at 67 Peter Street, Whitehaven, with his wife Mabel and their three children, Vera, Ronald and Sydney. On the morning of 19 August 1947 Herbert Calvin was raised to the surface of William Pit and identified by his brother, James Calvin, of 1 Laburnum Crescent, Easington Village, Co. Durham. He was the 80th man located. Herbert Calvin had served his nation in the King's Own Royal Border Regiment's 5th *Battalion during the Second World War.*

Four years later, in 1951, James Calvin also lost his life in a disaster at Easington Colliery County Durham — another Whitehaven pitman who paid the ultimate price.

My Dad goes off to war

I was just under five years of age when in 1939, our family, along with other families, went through the big wooden gates at William Pit and on to the Wagon Road to wave goodbye to all the T.A. (Territorial Army) soldiers leaving by train from Whitehaven to go to war. That was the last time we saw our Dad until late in 1945 when we all went to see him at Bransty Station. Dad had been a prisoner of war in Germany and had spent over 5½ years behind barbed wire as a guest of the Germans.

It was great having your Dad back with you. But he had to go away again for six weeks rehabilitation and treatment to help him recover from his years as a prisoner of war. But what we did not know then, was that we would have our Dad again for such a short time for in 1947, William Pit would take him from us forever. The short time he was with us was a wonderful time, especially to have someone to teach you new things.

Memories of time spent with my Dad

I remember going with Dad to the Whitehaven Drill Hall and picking garden mint to take back home for Mam to use with our Sunday dinner. When I joined the T.A. in the 1960s the first thing I did was to go out to the rear of the Halland where there was this big clump of mint growing. I often think of that time with Dad, and ever since have had mint in my own garden.

One of the first things my Dad made when he came back home was a leather tool bag to keep his tools in. He would repair our clogs and shoes. One of the tools he had was a rasp. Dad would work on a length of greenheart wood, working with the rasp and shaping it into a fishing rod. I know we could not have bought a better fishing rod. Without my Dad's guidance showing me how to repair and make things out of wood I don't think I would have been able to enjoy doing it myself in later life. I still have a rasp in my tool box.

After Dad came back from the war he used to take me fishing. He always went to dig up rag worm for his bait. At first, Dad would not let me go fishing until I got used to handling the big green, blue and red rag worms. He once put one of these rag worms into my hand and it nipped me! I dropped it right away and he had a good laugh and said, 'Get used to handling them and I'll take you fishing.' So I soon learned the right way to hold and use rag worm.

One day when we were fishing on the North Pier, me using a hand line and Dad his long rod he caught a very large codfish. The only way for Dad to land this big fish was for him to guide his long rod and fish back along the pier to the steps that went down off William Pit Beach. When he got his fish out he slung it over his shoulder and I got the big rod and walked behind my Dad with great pride watching this big cod hanging down his back. In all my years of sea fishing I have never caught a codfish even a quarter of the size my Dad caught that day.

Memories of Beaches and 'Bacca'

There were days when we all went as a family on to Wellington Pit Beach from where we lived on Peter Street. All our neighbours, cousins, uncles and aunties would spend lovely summer days down there playing in the rock pools and trying to fish. All the men folk would gather coal and wood and get a good fire going and when you saw the Billy cans of water hung over the fire you knew it was time for tea.

Our beaches at Whitehaven were named after the beach where the coal mines dumped their spoil on to them. So the tides would wash it out to sea and along the shoreline. Today our beaches still have mine spoil on them, but little or no coal and they are a lot cleaner.

When schools were on holiday I would be sent to buy my Dad's chewing tobacco. Coal miners would chew this 'bacca' to help keep the coal and stone dust out of their mouths and I did the same thing myself for most of the years I worked down the mines. One day when I was coming back home over the playing field I took a small piece of Dad's 'bacca' out of the paper it was wrapped in and put it into my mouth. But I wish I had never done this for it burnt my mouth and I swallowed some of it.

So I had to run as fast as I could to the tap up the passage next to our house to wash my mouth out. It took a long time to get rid of this nasty taste in my mouth so I never tried it again until I started work down William Pit in 1950. Even though I was older it still took time to get used to chewing 'bacca' down the pit.

My Dad at William Pit

On Fridays when the schools were on holiday I would go with my Dad to bring his pay back home for Mam. Dad and his workmates - the Smiths - worked the back shift. They were brushers: that means enlarging the roadway after the first shift had taken the coal out, and set the supports. It was great standing outside the lamp room as all the miners got their cap lamps and oil lamps.

Dad used to let me hold his oil lamp and walk part of the way with them to the top of the pit shaft. I used to watch the cages going down the shaft from the pit yard. There was always a great smell about the pit top with all the grease and oil.

My Dad took me down to William Pit on Vesting Day in January 1947 when the coal mines changed over from being owned by private companies to 'belong to the people'. Not that it made a big difference at first for the old owners were part of the N.C.B. (National Coal Board). It was much later that things changed as those of the 'old school' passed on.

Dad was a great player of the accordion and he would put a chair outside our house and play for the whole street. On Sundays he would play hymns. Dad did not read music: he just played it by ear.

Herbert Calvin, accordion player

A few short but happy years

These are just a few memories of my Dad, for I only knew him for too short a time. But they were very happy times. When Dad was killed in William Pit in 1947 along with his mates the best Mam in the world took over.

Mam got a job at the National School so we would not starve or 'want for owt'. Our Mam taught us manners and to be kind and <u>*courteous*</u> to other people. Mam did not drink, smoke or swear. I was very lucky to have had a Mam and Dad like these. *Memories of Ronnie Calvin, transcribed by Joseph Ritson, April 2007*

SOME BIOGRAPHICAL DETAILS

Date of Birth - 10/12/1906

Marriage - 26/12/1931 to Miss Mabel Murphy at Holy Trinity Parish Church (C. of E.) by the Reverend Frederick Knowles Fell. The witnesses at the wedding were Joseph Mitchell Murphy and Margaret Spence.

Army Service number 3597973. Originally served with the 5th Battalion T.A. The Border Regiment, transferred to 170 Tunnelling Company, Royal Engineers on 29/11/1939. In June 1940, 3597973 L/C Herbert Calvin was captured by the Germans and became a POW. On 14/06/1940 3597973 L/C Herbert Calvin was interned in POW Camp Stalag XX A(5) [International Red Cross Reference No RBO 5851, 22/06]

Date of Death - 15/08/1947 (Died in William Pit, Whitehaven).

Buried in Whitehaven Cemetery.

Ref. Nº RBO 5851 212 b-bis

Geneva, 22.6.4o.

Dear Madam, (Sir)

We beg to inform you that we have received a card dated 14.6.4o. from the STALAG XX A (5) Germany advising us that C a l v i n, Herbert L/C 17oth Coy R.Es. born 1o.12.19o6 is interned in that camp.

From now on you can send letters to the above mentioned prisoner of war to the address given, adding the following : "Kriegsgefangenenpost" (prisoners of war post) and "Gebührenfrei" (free of postal charges).

He is well.

Yours faithfully.

Comité International de la Croix Rouge
Agence centrale des prisonniers de guerre
GENÈVE

The card of notice sent to Mabel Calvin about Herbert's POW status

****

In loving memory of my dear husband,
Herbert Calvin
killed in William Pit disaster
August 15, 1947
Though his smiles have gone forever
And his hands we cannot touch
We shall never lose sweet memories
Of the one we loved so much
Always remembered by his loving wife Mabel, and his children, Vera, Ronald and Sidney all at Peter Street; also Maggie and John at Newtown

JAMES CAMPBELL

Jock

James Campbell was employed as a machine-man, and was 40 years of age, when he was killed in the 1947 disaster. His home was at 81 Woodhouse Avenue, Whitehaven, with his wife Sarah E. Campbell and their nineteen-year-old daughter. On the afternoon of 17 August 1947 at 1.50pm, Mr. Campbell was brought to the surface and later identified by his father, James Campbell of 3 Montgomery Place, Newtown, Scotland. He was the 42nd man located.

****

In loving memory of my dear husband James
who was killed in the William Pit explosion, August 15, 1947
We never heard his last faint sigh
We never saw him die
We only knew he passed away
And could not say goodbye
Ever remembered by his loving Wife, daughter and son-in-law
and all at Scotland and Hill Top.

****

In loving memory of a dear son and brother James (Jock)
Who was accidentally killed in the William Pit disaster
August 15 1947
Quick and sudden was his call
Only those who have lost can tell
The pain of parting without farewell
Fondly remembered by his Father, Mother,
brothers and sisters in Glasgow

HAROLD J. CARR

Twenty-two year old Harold John Carr was a single man and employed as a shift-hand at William Pit. He lived at 9 Jane Street, Frizington, with his parents. Harold was brought to the surface on 17 August 1947 at 10.10pm and identified by his brother-in-law Henry Coates of 1 Ladypit Cottages, Sunnyhill, Whitehaven. Further details reveal that Harold Carr was supporting his five-year-old niece Pauline.

I have been reading in *The Whitehaven News* about your forthcoming book *104 Men*, and could not let this opportunity pass to inform you of my uncle who died in this disaster – although I have very little information of him. The disaster occurred some years before I was born, so I am only able to pass on what my mother told me.

His name was Harold Carr, and I think, at the time of the disaster he was only 22-years-old. He was the only son born to John and Dora Carr, although he had several sisters – Emma (my mother), Annie, Matilda, Kathleen, Teresa and Rene.

According to my mother, who is now sadly deceased, Harold should have been on the first shift but had overslept. Having arranged a day trip to Blackpool for the following day, he felt he could not take another day off and went in on the back (afternoon) shift instead. Tragically, that decision was to cost him his life in the explosion. He was a bachelor when he died so there were no descendants.

I am so sorry I cannot furnish you with any further information or photographs – I wish I could. However I wish you well with your book and I feel sure it will be a very worthy tribute to those who lost their lives. *Mrs. Sandra Ludlow,* niece of Harold J. Carr

****

In loving memory of our dear son, Harold,
killed in William Pit disaster
August 15, 1947
There's an open gate at the end of the road
Through each must go alone
And there in a light we cannot see
Our Father claims His own
Beyond the gate our loved ones find
Happiness and rest
And there is comfort in the thought
A loving God knows best
Always remembered by his loving
Mother and Father, also little Pauline

In loving memory of Harold Carr,
Killed in William Pit August 15, 1947
Not just today but every day
In silence I remember
Always remembered by his loving sister,
Matilda, South Shields.

In loving memory of my
dear brother, Harold,
killed in William Pit disaster
August 15, 1947
Christ will clasp the broken chain
Closer when we meet again
Remembered always by his sister
Emma, Harry, and family
48 South View Road, Bransty

****

RICHARD CARTMELL

Dicky

Richard Cartmell was a 25-year-old shift- hand at the pit. He lived at 59 Valley View Road, Greenbank, Whitehaven, with his widowed mother, Susannah Cartmell. He was formally identified by his brother Wallace Cartmell of 9 Bowness Road, Greenbank after being brought to the surface at 3.25pm on 16 August 1947. Records indicate that Richard Cartmell supported his niece, the five year old daughter of his deceased sister.

****

I was seventeen-years-old at the time of the William Pit Disaster but remember it as if it was yesterday. My uncle, Richard Cartmell, was 25-years-old when he was killed. He was more like a big brother to me. Dick, as he was known, served four years in Burma with the Border Regiment, but would never talk of his experiences of that time. He was a lovely young man with a ready smile. He enjoyed dancing at the Empress Ballroom and a pint with his mates. The week previous to the disaster he and his friend Tommy Fox, who was also killed, had spent a week's holiday at my aunt's in Ulverston, which they enjoyed and said they were going back for another holiday whenever possible. Dick was one of the first few men to be brought to the surface and his funeral was the first, it was pictured in all the daily newspapers.

It seems ironic that the war in the Far East ended on the 15 August 1945 and he was killed on the 15 August 1947. He was at home two years. It was a terrible time for Whitehaven. Some families lost husbands *and* sons and everyone felt the sorrow because it is a small town and everyone knows everyone else.

Eunice Domigan (née Cartmell), niece of Richard Cartmell

I knew Dick Cartmell quite well, we often met in town. Tall, thin, with a cheery apple cheeked face, always smiling, nearly everyone called him Juicy. We used to meet him in town at the weekend, he always stopped for a chat, the main topic: if he had a chance of getting a coal hewer's job. *A friend and co-worker*

****

Treasured memories of a dear son,
Richard
who was killed in the William Pit disaster August 15, 1947;
also Margaret his sister who died August 22, 1943
Though their smiles have gone forever
And their hands we cannot touch
We shall never lose sweet memories
Of the ones we loved so much
Loving remembered by their mother and family at Greenbank

WILLIAM CLARK

Billie

Mr. William Clark was 46-years-old and employed as a brusher at William Pit. He lived at 15 The Square, Parton, with his wife Florence and daughter. Raised to the surface on 17 August 1947, at 10.15 am, William Clark was formally identified by his brother-in-law, John Bell of 105 Foundry Road, Parton. He was the 34th miner found by rescue workers. Mr. Clark was laid to rest at Moresby Churchyard on 20 August 1947.

****

In loving memory of my dear husband
Billie,
who died in William Pit disaster August 15, 1947.
No one stood beside you
To bid you a last farewell
No word of comfort could you leave
To one who loved you well
Ever remembered by his loving wife

****

Treasured memories of my dear Dad,
who died in William Pit Disaster August 15, 1947
No one knows how much I miss you
In my thoughts you're ever near
Loved, remembered, longed for always
Bringing many a silent tear.
Remembered always, Mavis

JAMES CLIFFORD

Jimmy

James Clifford was a 26-year-old brusher at William Pit. He lived at 72 Frizington Road, Frizington, with his wife Lilian and two young daughters, Susan and Barbara. At 9.30pm on 16 August 1947, Jimmy Clifford was brought to the pit surface and identified by his father, William Henry Clifford, of 5 Nook Street, Frizington. He was the seventh miner located by rescue workers.

Jimmy Clifford with his daughter Susan.

My Dad went by the name of Jimmy. I have no recollection of him but I will have a long think about him and try to remember things my Mam used to tell us about him. Unfortunately she passed away in June 2005. It's sad as she would have been very proud to have read a book all about this devastating disaster.

I do remember one significant thing about Jimmy - that is that he saved some people from a burning house on 15 August 1942. I have the certificate on the wall in front of me as I do this email, as well as a newspaper report of it all. It is in a very delicate condition so may not copy too well.

My sister Susan was in touch this week and like me, she has no memories of Jimmy. No one really talked about him. As she said, it's as though it was a case of 'least said, soonest mended.' So I will fill you in on what little we know. He was the second born child and second son of William Henry and Violet Clifford. There were nine more children born after him - five boys and four girls. One boy died aged fourteen of meningitis, and another aged about six of diphtheria. So my grandparents certainly knew tragedy.

I recall my mother saying Jimmy was a very quiet man and a good father. Apparently Susan (as young as she was) would walk a few houses up the street to meet the bus every time he came off shift and continued to do so even after his death until one day she rushed up to another miner shouting 'Daddy! Daddy!' then realised it wasn't Daddy. Mam said that the miner was so upset that from then on he got off the bus at a different stop.

My mother remarried in 1951, and had a set of twins in 1952. Then we went to my mother's home town of Millom to live until we emigrated to Australia in 1963. So I'm afraid that is all we know of Jimmy. Rather sad isn't it? Susan and I only have one photo each of him. I have his certificate of commendation for the fire rescue and the paper cutting and also his cigarette case. Very little to show for the short 26 years he lived! *Barbara Brown, daughter*

****

In loving memory of Jimmy
killed in the William pit disaster August 15, 1947
Always remembered by his wife and children

****

The following article was transcribed by Joseph Ritson from *The Whitehaven News* of Thursday, 20 August, 1942, with the kind permission of the Whitehaven Records Office and details James Clifford's gallantry on 15 August 1942, five years to the day before the William Pit Disaster.

FRIZINGTON HOUSE GUTTED

Mother and Two Children Suffocated

HUSBAND GALLANTLY RESCUED BY HOME GUARD CORPORAL

A small house, No 13, Nook Street, Frizington was the scene of a grim sight in the early hours of Saturday when a young mother and two children lost their lives, and the head of the family was removed to Whitehaven Hospital suffering from severe burns to the face, neck and arm.

The dead are Margery Jordan (23), Eric Jordan (3), and Patricia Jordan (2). The injured man is Frederick William Jordan (26), a labourer. He was gallantly rescued by a Home Guard Corporal, James Clifford (21), a neighbour, and was treated by Dr Sharp, Frizington, before being moved to hospital.

Other occupants of the house at the time were Mr and Mrs John Watson, the parents of Mrs Jordan, and their nine-year-old daughter, who were sleeping in the front bedroom, and a son, Alexander Watson (19), who was sleeping in the kitchen where the fire originated. They all escaped unhurt. The Jordans were occupying the back bedroom directly over the kitchen.

The Whitehaven Fire Brigade was summoned at 1.40am and arrived at 1.55am. By then the house was doomed, but though hampered by a poor water supply the Brigade succeeded in preventing the flames from spreading to adjoining houses. The fire was under control about 3.00am and about 4.00am the charred bodies of the victims were recovered from the debris in the kitchen. The fire was finally extinguished at 5am. The house was gutted. The Whitehaven Brigade was under Company Officer Hall. The police on duty were Sergt. Hindson and PCs Reay, Wilson and Backhouse.

The inquest was held on Saturday afternoon by Mr R. W. Marley, Deputy Coroner. Among those present were Police Inspector J. Bell, Cleator Moor, and Company Officer Hall of the N.F.S.

SUFFOCATION CAUSED DEATH

Dr Sharp, Frizington, said the cause of death in all cases was suffocation due to smoke fumes.

John Watson, a general labourer at the Whitehaven Institution, identified the bodies and was then informed by the Coroner that he could give his evidence later. Alexander Watson, farm labourer at Lamplugh, said he entered the house at 12.30am after attending a dance. He went there in order to change his clothes and decided to lie down on the couch in the kitchen before returning to work next morning. The kitchen fire was out. There was a certain amount of linen hanging above the fireplace. The gas mantle was damaged and the flame was protruding through it. There was a quilt almost underneath the gas bracket for airing purposes. His brother, Thomas, who was in the kitchen before him, left the house at 12.45am, and he lay down on the couch. He left the gas burning.

The Coroner asked, 'Why did you do that?'

'I forgot about it.'

"I WAS FLUSTERED"

Continuing, witness said that neither he nor his brother smoked in the room and he noticed nothing unusual when he lay down. After going to sleep he awakened feeling hot and then noticed that the quilt and the clothes in front of the fireplace were well alight, but at that time the linen had not caught fire. He did not notice the gas. He went to the foot of the stairs and shouted for his father. His mother came downstairs and shouted first, followed by his father: then on his mother's instructions, he ran for the police and to arouse the neighbours.

The Coroner, 'Don't you think you could have got this fire out by pushing the quilt up the chimney?'

'I was flustered and didn't think of putting the fire out. I didn't go upstairs and I don't know what happened afterwards.'

Recalled John Watson, who was awakened by his wife, who said the house was on fire. He went downstairs and found the kitchen full of smoke and everything well alight. He got his wife downstairs and then returned and brought down his nine-year-old daughter, who was in the same room as themselves. As he got into the lobby James Clifford came in the front door and asked if there was anybody else upstairs. When he told Clifford that his son-in-law and daughter and two children were still there Clifford ran up the stairs which were burning at the time. He was convinced that the fire started in the kitchen. Witness went back to the back of the house to see if Clifford had got out there but could not see anyone. He did not see Clifford again until later. They had no sand or water in the house but they tried and failed to get in the back door to the water tap.

Inspector Bell said, 'Did you notice exactly where the worst of the fire was in the kitchen?'

'In the corner near the gas bracket.'

'When did you last see your son-in-law?'

'At the stair-head putting on his trousers.'

RESCUER'S STORY

James Clifford, 5 Nook Street, miner's helper at Ullcoats Mine, said he was awakened about 1.30am by his mother saying, 'Get up and help the Watsons, their house is on fire.' He was there in two or three minutes and met Mr Watson at the door. When Watson told him about the four people in the back door he fastened a handkerchief round his mouth and nose and ran up the burning stairs. He got in the back room, which was thick with smoke, with flames already creeping along the floorboards. He bumped into Jordan, who was standing in the room and seemed to be trying to tie the sheets together.

'I asked Jordan if the back window was open. He said 'yes'. I pushed him towards it and he collapsed on the window frame. I returned and felt all round the room and on the bed but could not find anyone. As the fumes were then affecting me I returned to the window, climbed over to Jordan on to the kitchen shed, and pulled him on to the roof after me.' Jordan was wearing a shirt and trousers.

'A VERY BRAVE MAN'

The Coroner complimented Clifford on his conduct, which was that of a very brave man. It was possible, added Mr Marley, that if greater efforts had been made at the outset to the fire this might have been achieved and the terrible tragedy averted. As it was, there was certainly no evidence of negligence and therefore he was bound to return a verdict of 'Accidental Death.' He extended his sympathy to the Watson family and to the injured Mr Jordan in the great loss they had sustained.

Inspector Bell associated himself with the Coroner's vote of confidence, and with his remarks regarding the gallant conduct of James Clifford.

RELIEF FUND OPENED

A relief fund for the relatives of the victims has been opened by the Ennerdale Rural District Council.

ROBERT CONKEY

Robert Conkey was a 43-year-old brusher at William Pit. He was survived by his wife Annie Conkey and their two daughters Jean and Mary Dorothy. The family lived at 29 Smihfield, Egremont. Mr Conkey was brought to the pit surface at 5.00am on 19 August 1947, and identified by his brother, Joseph Conkey Williamson of 13 Park View, Castle Croft, Egremont. He was the 78th man located by rescue workers.

****

When Robert was tragically killed in the William Pit disaster, mum (Jean) was only fifteen-years-old and my aunt (Dorothy) was only five-years-old. Sadly, Nanna (Annie) died fourteen years ago (aged 89 years) and unfortunately there are not many photographs around, but mum has found a locket with a photograph of each of them which I will send to you. In the pictures Granda was 43 years and Nanna was 42 years. One memory of Granda was that he loved being in his garden.

Mum has also written something which she would like included in your memorial with the photographs. *Lynne Eastwood, granddaughter.*

****

A Father is precious
And so is his name
Without one to love
Life is never the same.
Jean Mitchell (née Conkey).

****

In loving memory of my dear
and only brother, Robert
Who lost his life in the William Pit disaster
August 15, 1947
Ever remembered by his loving brother Joe,
and all at Park View, Castle Croft, Egremont

****

Robert and Annie Conkey.

Treasured memories of Robert,
the dearly loved husband of Annie Conkey
and dear Dad of Jean and Dorothy
who died in the William Pit disaster August 15, 1947.
'Tis not the tears of the moment shed
That tell of hearts that are torn
But the lonely grief of the after years
Remembrance silently borne
Oh Jesus, open wide thy arms
And let him rest therein
Sadly missed by his loving wife and two daughters at Smithfield, Egremont.

The locket photographs as they were sent.

****

WILLIAM CROFTS

Bill

Brother-in-law of Thomas Richardson

William Henry Crofts was survived by his wife Millie and four children. The family lived at 111 Queen Street, Whitehaven. Mr. Crofts was formally identified by his brother-in-law James Hughes of the same address, after he was brought to the surface of William Pit at 7.55am on 17 August 1947. He was the 26th miner found by rescue workers.

According to an article that appeared in *The People* newspaper of 17 August 1947, William Crofts had been scarred in three previous mining disasters.

****

SAMUEL DEVLIN

Sammy

Samuel Devlin was 27-years-old and a haulage hand at William Pit. He lived at 9 Union Buildings, Low Road, Whitehaven, with his wife Mary and two children. At the time of the disaster Mary was expecting the couple's third child. Sammy Devlin was brought to the surface of William Pit at 3.40am on 17 August and identified by his brother William Devlin, of 12 Woodhouse Road, Greenbank, Whitehaven. He was the 53rd miner found by rescue workers. Mr. Devlin was interred at Whitehaven cemetery on 22 August 1947.

In October of 1947, Mary Devlin gave birth to a daughter, Sambra. Baby Sambra lived only a few short months and was laid to rest with her Daddy in Whitehaven Cemetery. Mr. Devlin was another William Pit miner who served his country in the Second World War as a member of the King's Own Royal Border Regiment 5th battalion. *AGR*

Sammy Devlin worked at Main End Brow top, detaching setts as they came up and re-assembling them, ready to go outbye in the morning. It was a lonely job, seldom seeing anyone during his shift. If there was no coal coming out, he walked down to the Junction to join in the "crack" until coal re-started, and rode the first full sett out to the top. *A co-worker*

****

In loving memories of a dear husband and Daddy
killed in William Pit disaster August 15, 1947
What would I give to clasp his hand
His cheery face to see
To hear his voice, to see him smile
That meant so much to me
He did not fail to do his best
His heart was true and tender
He did work hard for those he loved
That's something to remember
Ever remembered by his loving wife and children, Charlie and Yvonne

In loving memory of my son, Samuel Devlin
killed in William Pit explosion August 15, 1947
At night when all is silent
And sleep forsakes my eyes
My thoughts are in the silent grave
Where my dear son lies
And when the tears steal to my eyes
I seem to hear him say
Don't fret for me dear mother
God will help you each day
Never one day forgotten by Mother, Sisters and Brothers

JOSEPH G. DIAMOND

Joe

Joseph Gerald Diamond was 33-years-old and employed as a brusher at William Pit. He lived at 8 Grasmere Avenue with his wife Isobel and four children. He was brought to the surface of William Pit at 2.20pm on 17 August 1947 and formally identified by his brother-in-law Robert Johnston of 7 College Street, Whitehaven. Joe Diamond was the 45th miner found by rescue workers.

My Dad and Mam were eighteen and seventeen-years-old respectively when they married. Mam had five children and two miscarriages. Their third child, Robert, died in infancy. My earlier memories of Dad as a miner's son was that he always tried to dress smartly when going out, other than to work, but he had very coarse hands with dirty and broken nails. His eyes in my memory were black rimmed which he tried to clean with Vaseline or something similar (silly things to remember). His job was as a Brusher though even until this day I never understood what that was.

My relationship to him was no different I assume, than what it is today between any young teenage boy and his Dad. He is someone who is always there when needed. Though, my sisters used to tell a different story. They told of him sitting them on his knee and either singing or telling them stories (I enjoyed his ghost stories). I have early memories of his 'hobbies' i.e. gambling, snooker and the 1947 Grand National race which in those days, I think, ran on a Wednesday. He had picked a horse, small, but an excellent jumper of repute. So he gave my mother £1 to bet to win at Wim Hornsby a bookie who lived round the corner on Loweswater Avenue. Bookies and gambling was against the law but I think the police turned a blind eye. Dad was on the afternoon shift which was, I think, 12 or 1pm until 8 or 9pm. After he had left Mam could not believe putting £1 against a lot of other good horses, so she bet each way. Mam, listening on the radio, and the horse leading up to the near finish was beaten into second place to my mother's considerable relief. Dad came home and she could not contain herself to tell him of his luck. He exploded and repeated very angrily, 'When I bet to win, I bet to win! Don't ever change it again!' Though I believe he took the money.

During the weekend on a patch of ground known as the Brows where Edgards factory, then latterly Kwik-Save, and now Netto supermarkets are, there was very serious gambling known as Pitch and Toss with men posted on the hillside watching out for a police raid.

On the Saturday (I think) of the Pit holidays, Dad came in and asked about Mam, who was at St. Bees with my brothers and sisters. He stated he had been told by one of my teachers (a snooker friend) that I was a clever lad, then he began pulling pound notes out of his pockets. I counted it into stacks total £110 in total of which he gave me £1 (if he had given me 3d or 6d I would have been over the moon).

He went to bed and I set off and ran to meet my mother and family returning. I met them at the Whitehouse (at a junction of High Road, Wilson Pit Road and Sandwith Road). When Mam asked what was up I told her about the pound note and it promptly disappeared, never to be seen again. Then came the inquisition as to why he had given it to me. After initially not saying, or refusing, threats and fear took over, and I confessed all (fancy these days single mothers instilling fear into a fourteen-year-old lad - no chance!) As I said it went to pay for his dinner when he got up. *(Here Hughie told me that his Dad offered his Mother a mere £5 from his winnings which resulted in him being hit by the flying roast of dinner).*

You are right about the £5 and its after effects. Correct too about his snooker ability. I had heard he was good but the only time I saw him play was in the old snooker and billiard hall in King Street where Woolworths is now and he lost. Walking home with him, I asked about his ability and then losing. 'But I won the money!!' was his reply. Mother told me tales about his playing, years after his death, and how during the war he worked in Doncaster. Of course the local snooker hall attracted him. Sitting watching, a local invited him to play. He agreed but then was invited to make it interesting, to play for 'half a dollar.' (2s 6d or 12½p in present coinage). He played and scraped a win. The opponent asked how about another game this time ten bob, (10 shillings or 50p now). Again he scraped a win. A further request, a chance to get his money back, play for a pound. All pretences went out of the window. Dad won again! His opponent a local, renowned Shark realized Dad's talent. The 'shark' then invited Dad to go to various clubs in the area to play like a duffer and lose money given him. Then the 'shark' would incite the best players to a challenge whilst he would play with this CLOD (Dad) who could not hit a straight ball. Within three months they were banned out of everywhere in the area around Doncaster.

Oh! I have just remembered about his ghost stories. He told a vivid one about the Newtown 'Boogle' a supposed ghost-dog haunting the area. A girl opposite in the street was scared after listening to his tale. She was Marion Kennedy (married name Lewthwaite). Dad told her not to worry, it never came unless someone whistled for it. Terrified going back home, as she reached her gate he whistled, and she screamed and ran all the way back. This he did a few times to her, though she came back other days to hear his tales again (who needs T.V. when you have a good imagination?)

Relating to hard times, my parents never locked their doors - suppose a neighbour needed something like a 'masting of tea' or a drop of milk, etc. They had nothing but small amounts of money which usually was gone after Monday morning if that late. There was nothing to steal!! Perish the thought of stealing from a neighbour!!

My school days were interrupted by his death. I should have left school at Christmas 1946 (school leaving age rose to fifteen after 1 January 1947) but my Dad listening to his teacher friends, I mentioned earlier, insisted I stay on in Mr. Hurley's class for he wanted his son to go, hopefully into mine management. In fact I had an interview arranged in Workington on the day and time of his burial, a major change to my life. It would have been a great achievement for an ordinary collier's son in those days.

You were correct about Mam remarrying in 1953 (I think September). Jim on reflection was good for Mam, but who loves a stepfather when you're twenty years old? John Birkett came to see my mother, in fact I think he visited Edie Bridges across the street and Mrs. Milburn further along the street. They lost their husbands too. Three men within 25 yards- lost. No doubt a sad time. He told Mam that he had asked Joe to go with them but they had disagreed on tactics; my Dad said he had to get out for his wife and kids sake.

My grandfather moved to West Cumberland with a son and daughter. He left other children behind. I never found out any reason. My mother was rather bitter about none of the Diamond family getting in touch afterward, but no doubt they were like everyone else, they had nothing to give and in 1947 it would be a long and expensive journey from Stirling in Scotland.

My Dad I believe was born in Bannockburn, a celebrated place in Scottish history- not Dad's birth though! His sister Margaret married locally but moved to Fife in Scotland.

A matter of interest, when Dad died, in his pocket he left a note with initials on e.g. H.D

12/6; J.S 1/12/6; W.D. 2, etc. Mam did not understand it. In the weeks following H.D would come to her and say he owed Joe 12s.6d. W.D. came and said he owed £2. There were several initials of men who she reckon had died but she estimated there were a few still living who did not come forward. When he won money he had been generous to his friends and loaned them money. *Hugh Diamond, son*

****

In loving memory of a dear husband and father
who lost his life in William Pit Disaster August 15, 1947
I lost my life's companion
A life linked with my own
And every day I miss you
As I walk through life alone
God gave me strength to fight the blow
But what it meant to lose you Joe
No one will ever know
Loved and remembered always by his wife and children

****

In loving memory of my dear son-in-law, Joe,
who lost his life in William Pit Disaster August 15, 1947.
Eternal rest give unto him O' Lord
And to those who lost their lives with him
From Mam and all at College Street and Barrow

****

THOMAS G. DIXON

Thomas Gladstone Dixon was 55-years-old and a brusher at William Pit. He was a resident of 23 Yeathouse Road, Frizington, Cumberland. Mr. Dixon was the father of three children over sixteen years of age, and had been separated from his wife for over fifteen years. On the afternoon of 17 August 1947, Thomas Dixon was brought to the surface of William Pit at 3.50pm, and identified by his brother, James Dixon, of 2 Trafalgar Square, Frizington. Thomas Dixon was the 48th miner recovered by rescue teams.

****

Treasured memories of Thomas Gladstone,
beloved son of the late John and Sarah Dixon
who lost his life in the William Pit explosion August 15, 1947
Fondly remembered by sisters and brothers at home and away.

A newspaper photograph of the widows and children on a trip to Czechoslovakia in 1956. The trip was paid for by Czech miners. At that time Czechoslovakia was behind the Iron Curtain.

JOHN HENRY DORAN M.M.

Duffy

John Henry Doran M.M., known as Duffy, was a 50-year-old brusher at William Pit. He lived at 8 Low Harras Moor, Whitehaven, with his wife Eleanor. John Henry and Eleanor were the parents of eight children: John Henry Jr., Billy, Arthur, Raymond, Charlie, Joseph, Esther, Iris, and Geoffrey. On 22 August 1947 at 10.30pm Duffy was brought to the surface of William Pit and identified by his son William Doran of 33 Lakeland Avenue, Woodhouse. John Henry Doran M.M., was the 103rd man located by the rescue workers. His identification number was Special 4. John Henry Doran was laid to rest at Whitehaven Cemetery on 23 August 1947.

I read your request in *The Whitehaven News* for recollections about the men who died in the William Pit explosion on 15 August 1947. If it is any use to you for your project, you are welcome to use some or all of the following information about John Henry Doran M.M. I am not sure how relevant it is for your particular project, because I was researching a different subject when I came across this information. It is mainly based on original documents held at the Border Regiment Museum Archives, Carlisle and the Cumbria County Archives, Whitehaven. In 1947, Mr. Doran was 50-years-old, married with eight children and at that time living at 8 Low Harras Moor, Whitehaven. I was born after the 1947 William Pit explosion so I have no personal recollection of the time. However, the following information is about his earlier life.

John Henry Doran, M.M.

During the Great War, John Henry Doran signed up at Whitehaven Drill Hall on the same day as many of his 'Whitehaven Marras' (Pals). He was given Service Number 240745. John Henry Doran and his 'Pals' served in the 5th Battalion The Border Regiment, a part of the 150th Infantry Brigade. In April 1917, during the Battle of Arras, 5th Border as part of the 150th Infantry Brigade made two major assaults on the German lines: on 23 April and 24 April, with 5th Border sustaining heavy casualties. One of the 'A Company' 5th Border 'Pals' who died of wounds on 25 April 1917 following the Battle of Arras, who had signed up on the same day as John Henry Doran, was 240733 Private Walter Pepper. Walter Pepper was originally from Keswick and in 1917 he was a 22-year-old married man. The Pepper family home was at 3 Charles Street, Whitehaven, not far from the Doran residence.

After the Battle of Arras, the then 20-year-old John Henry Doran was nominated for the Military Medal by the Commanding Officer of 5th Border, Lt Col John Ralph Hedley DSO. The award of the Military Medal to 240745 Private John Henry Doran was announced in the 'London Gazette' on 9 July 1917 (page 6828), and referred to in 'The Whitehaven News' on 12 July 1917. Unfortunately, the written citations as to exactly why John Henry Doran and some others from 5th Border were nominated for the Military Medal were lost. Lt Col Hedley received a slight reprimand from his superior officers for this. In fact, shortly afterwards, on 14 July 1917 Lt Col Hedley died of a heart attack, perhaps as a result of the stress he was under at the time. Sadly, the written citation for John Henry Doran MM now seems to be permanently lost.

Whatever the actual reason for winning the Military Medal, it indicates that John Henry Doran M.M. was an outstandingly courageous individual. Afterwards, he very rarely talked about being awarded the Military Medal, and apparently his Great War medals were sold during the Miners' Strike to help the family finances. Indeed, the name of John Henry Doran M.M. and details of his high honour are missing from the 'Borough of Whitehaven Roll of Honour'. This was published by Whitehaven Town Council in 1919 in an attempt to recognise the townsfolk who had served, and in some cases, died in the 1914-1918 War.

If servicemen, their relatives, friends or clergyman did not send in the personal details of someone who served they were not entered in the 'Roll of Honour'. According to Councillor J. R. Musgrave, Mayor of Whitehaven in 1919 "...those who most willingly offered their services are the most unwilling to pose as heroes or claim recognition." John Henry Doran MM was one those who appeared unwilling to put his name forward as the hero he really was. Only once, and even then it was for a very good reason, was he ever known to give his name as 'John Henry Doran MM'.

During the Second World War, John Henry Doran served in the William Pit Home Guard, which was connected to the Border Regiment. Other members of the William Pit Home Guard Company were among the twelve miners who lost their lives in a pit explosion on 3 June 1941. John Henry Doran MM was one of the 104 brave miners who lost their lives in the William Pit explosion of 15 August 1947.

For about a year, I was researching stories for the BBC *People's War* project, dealing with World War Two. Because it was a WW2 project, a few of the accounts I posted to the BBC *People's War* website concern the 1941 William Pit explosion or other aspects of mining in West Cumberland. I referred to the 1947 explosion in passing, but not in much detail, as it

Back row, left to right: John Henry Doran M.M., Arthur Doran, Billy Doran, Jenny Wrape, Betty Kelly, Esther Doran, Martin Wrape. Front row, left to right: Eleanor Doran, Ellen Wrape, Iris Doran and Florence Wrape.

fell outside the core years of WW2. I also happened to research some First World War Border Regiment stories during the times I visited the Regimental Museum at Carlisle Castle and John Henry Doran MM and Walter Pepper were two of these. *Joseph Ritson.*

John Henry Doran was my father-in-law. All the Doran men were known as Duffy Doran, but he was known as Duffy Doran M.M., because as a very young man in the 1914 war, he won the military medal for bravery. He never talked about it.

During the week of the disaster, when people were coming and going to the house, the medal was stolen from the mantelpiece where my husband's mother had always kept it. My late husband Billy and I tried pawn shops, and even the Carlisle Castle Barracks but it was never found.

John Henry was a real character and very well known. He loved a gamble and a drink, but when we was married he became teetotal, and at our wedding he only had lemonade. He was also known as a poacher and often in those hard times it was a way of feeding a large family.

The day of the disaster, Duffy was late for work on that last shift and it was my mother-in-law's last memory of him – hurrying off to work. Billy and I were out walking in a beautiful placed called Barrow Mouth when we met someone who told us the terrible news. We were only married in March of that year. It was a dreadful time.

My husband and his brother went down the pit with the rescuers, but were sent up immediately, when it was discovered their Dad was one of the victims.

In addition to Billy's Dad, his mother also lost sons John Henry Jr., and Arthur in the pits. Son Raymond lost an arm, and another son Charlie lost fingers. My mother-in-law, who had a big family, was left with young children to bring up on her own, and she raised them to be a family to be proud of. She died on the 6 April 1988 at almost 90 years of age.

I have enclosed a photograph showing John Henry. I think it was the only photo ever taken of him. It is our wedding picture, and he is at the end on the left hand side.

Jennie Doran, daughter-in-law

****

In loving memory of John Henry Doran M.M. aged 50,
Killed in the William Pit Disaster, August 15, 1947;
Also John Henry Doran, son of the above, died February 4, 1939
Until the day dawns
R.I.P.
From his wife, sons and daughters, daughter-in-law and all at Ryhope

In loving memory of my dear brother John Henry Doran,
killed in William Pit, August 15, 1947
Not just today but every day
In silence we remember
From his loving sister Elizabeth and all at 48 Greenbank

In loving memory of our dear Father, died August 15, 1947
We never thought that afternoon that you were going to die
You left us all so suddenly
You never said goodbye
From Billy and Jennie

WILFRED FARRER

Wilf

Wilfred Farrer was 34-years-old and employed as a pan-puller when he lost his life in the 1947 William Pit disaster. He lived at 66 Windermere Road, Woodhouse, Whitehaven, with his wife Jane (born 16 March 1910) and their two sons, Albert born 9 February 1936, and Wilfred born 28 February 1940. At 5.30 on the morning of 20 August 1947, Wilfred Farrer was brought to the surface of William Pit and later identified by his brother, Stanley Farrer of 78 Windermere Road, Woodhouse. Of the 104 men lost in the disaster, Mr. Farrer was the 98th located.

****

My grandfather, Wilfred Farrer, was one of the men tragically killed in the disaster. I wasn't born until 1971, so sadly, I didn't know him. My own Dad passed away four years ago and I don't really have a lot of information to give to you, but would love for him to be remembered in your book. My Dad was only seven-years-old when his father was killed, and never really talked about that time in his life. There was one occasion when we were both looking at some old photographs and came across one of Dad with his Mam, Jenny, and his brother Albert (who was killed in Haig Pit in Whitehaven two days after his wife had given birth to their third child). This is probably why Dad didn't open up to us, he found it so painful to talk about the pits after losing both his father and his brother. When I questioned him about the picture he told me it was taken when they had been invited to Skegness after the pit disaster.

I do remember my Dad taking me down to the William beach on numerous occasions and just walking. He never really said why we were there, and as I was so young I didn't question him, but looking back now, I suddenly realise why. I was playing bakery shop with the old well-washed Whitehaven bricks (they just looked like loaves of bread) and he was visiting the place where he lost his Dad. Isn't it funny what brings back memories?

RESIDENCE: 19, SANDHILLS LANE. 19, SANDHILLS LANE.
WHITEHAVEN, Aug. 1947
Mrs J. Farrer.
To JOSEPH FEARON & SONS, Dr.
(PROPRIETOR: GEORGE FEARON)
JOINERS, CABINET MAKERS AND UNDERTAKERS.
447 FUNERALS FURNISHED. PHONE 272.

Date	Particulars	£	s.	d.
Aug 22nd	To making Arrangements & Attendance Lettering Plate & Conducting Funeral of the late Wilfred Farrer	1	10	0
	Cemetery Fees	5	18	0
	Messrs Bue & Conways A/c (Cars)	9	10	0
	St Marys Church Fees		10	0
	1 Solid Cast Nickel Crucifix		7	6
		17	5	6

Settled Sept 2nd 1947
J. Fearon & Sons

The invoice for Wilfred Farrer's funeral expenses

11 Raby Gardens
West Hartlepool
Durham

my Dear Jenny and Kiddies
Just a few lines hoping to find you all in the best of health as it leaves us all well at time well Jenny I hope the two boys are being good boys and looking after their mother
Jenny I know it will be a hard Xmas for you and the boys you will miss Wilf and the boys will miss the daddy but you will have to keep up for their sakes and be Father and mother to them and I know they will pay you back in time so good luck to you Jenny and God Bless you all and dont forget if you want to come to West Hartlepool this summer you are always welcome so I will close with love from Aunt Amy and Alf and all at Raby Gardens

Letter sent to Jenny Farrer, Christmas, 1947

Widows and children at Skegness, 1948.

Wilfie and Albert Farrer with friend James Curwen

I have been sifting through my late father's papers, and came across some photographs and a whole pile of news cuttings from the time and receipts for things like compensation - £571.18d which my grandmother received from the National Coal Board. I also found a sympathy letter from someone (can't make the name out) willing her to be strong for the boys sake and stating it would be a sad Christmas with the boys missing their Daddy. I never knew these letters and receipts existed until now. I'm not sure if any of this is relevant to you as I'm not sure of the content of your book but you are welcome to have a look if you wish, anyway just a small mention of my grandfather would be appreciated and I'm sure my father would have been proud.

Wendy Farrar, granddaughter

In loving memory of my brother
Wilfred Farrer,
who was killed in William Pit disaster August 15, 1947.
Your end was sudden dear brother
As oft times we sit and talk of you
Of things you used to say and do
And wonder why you had to die
Without a chance to say goodbye
From your sister Maggie and kiddies,
also Winnie, Violet, Frances and Stanley and John

To the Registrar of the WHITEHAVEN AND MILLOM COUNTY COURT

IN THE MATTER OF THE WORKMEN'S COMPENSATION ACTS, 1925 to 1943.

AND

IN THE MATTER OF AN ORDER MADE UNDER PAR. 16 OF SCHEDULE II. OF THE WORKMEN'S COMPENSATION ACT, 1906, BY THE SECRETARY OF STATE, ON THE 24TH APRIL, 1920,

AND

IN THE MATTER OF AN ARBITRATION BETWEEN

JANE FARRER, ALBERT FARRER, WILFRED PATRICK FARRER, of 66, Windermere Road, Woodhouse, Whitehaven, in the County of Cumberland, Dependants of Wilfred Farrer, deceased.

APPLICANTS

AND

THE NATIONAL COAL BOARD, Whitehaven Unit, Solway Colliery Office, Moss Bay, Workington, in the said County.

RESPONDENTS.

Be it remembered that on the 15th day of August 1947 personal injury was caused at William Colliery to WILFRED FARRER late of Whitehaven deceased, by accident arising out of and in the course of his employment, and that on the 15th day of August 1947 the said Wilfred Farrer died as the result of such injury.

And that on the 3rd day of April 1948 the following decision was given by a Committee representative of the said National Coal Board and their workmen, having power to settle matters under the above-mentioned Acts in the case of the said National Coal Board and their workmen, that is to say:—

1.—We declare that the Respondents, the National Coal Board are liable to pay the sum of £571 - 18 - 0d. as compensation to the dependants of .... Wilfred Farrer late of 66, Windermere Road, Woodhouse, Whitehaven, in respect of the death of the said Wilfred Farrer which took place on the 15th day of August 1947 from injury caused by accident arising out of and in the course of his employment as a workman employed by the said respondents as a Pan Puller at William Colliery

2.—And we order that the Respondents do within one calendar month from the date of this award pay the said sum of £571 - 18 - 0d. to Isaac Scott and James Martin (hereinafter called the Trustees) to be dealt with by them for the benefit of the dependants of the above-named deceased as hereinafter ordered by paragraph 4 of this Award, and we apoint them Trustees for such purposes accordingly, and we order that the receipt of the Trustees shall be a sufficient discharge to the respondents and that the power of appointing new Trustees of the said moneys shall be vested in the National Coal Board and the National Union of Mineworkers.

3.—We declare that the persons hereinafter named are entitled to share in such compensation as dependants of the said Wilfred Farrer, deceased, and that the said sum of £571 - 18- 0d. shall be apportioned between such dependants in the shares and proportions following that is to say:—

£		
400 - 0 - 0	for the benefit of	Jane Farrer, Widow, Age 37
54 - 6 - 0	do.	Albert Farrer, Son, Born 9-
117 -12 - 0	do.	Wilfred Patrick Farrer, Born 28-2-1940.
£571 18 - 0		

Jenny Farrer with Albert and Wilf, Skegness, 1948.

In loving memory of
my dear husband,
killed in William Pit Disaster
August 15, 1947
The dearest Dad
this world could hold
A loving smile and
a heart of gold
Dearer to us than
words can tell
Was the Dad we lost
and loved so well
Ever remembered by his Wife
and two sons,
Albert and Wilfie

WILLIAM FISHER

Billy

*William (Billy) Fisher was 39-years-old and employed as a brusher. He lived at 12 Gores Buildings, Whitehaven, with his wife Ginny and four children - Sheila, William, Stella and Janice. On the afternoon of 17 August 1947, at 1.00pm, Billy was brought to the surface of William Pit and later identified by his brother, Wilson Fisher, of 51 Church Street, Whitehaven. Mr. Fisher was the 39*th *man located by rescue teams.*

Family Associations with the Infamous Colliery

August 15th 1947 will long be associated with the terrible disaster that struck West Cumberland and the mining community in particular. William Pit exploded and, together with the 'after-damp' — the highly poisonous carbon monoxide, 104 precious lives were lost — almost all of the personnel down the pit on that Friday afternoon shift. The detail of the mine's story is recorded elsewhere. However, for the sake of generations to come, our family associations are recorded here.

My name is Bob Matthews and I was born in Whitehaven in 1945 at the home of Mary and Henry Poss (in West Cumberland, Postlethwaite as a surname was almost always abbreviated to Poss). Aunty Mary is my mother's sister, whilst Uncle Henry was their cousin. They lived, at the time of my arrival, at 39 Cambridge Road, Hensingham.

During my earliest years, I was blissfully unaware of the pit disasters that dogged our community. However, I do recall visiting my other Uncle Henry Smith (my mother's brother), and seeing him laid up with a serious collection of shoulder and arm injuries, as a result of a colliery accident. I can see him now, after nearly 50 years, with both arms heavily bandaged, strapped up like a mummy and being given a drink by Aunty Marion from a baby's cup. This was only one of many 'scrapes' that he had during his working life - many of which could easily have cost him that life.

My most direct connection with the 1947 William Pit Disaster is through Stella, my wife, whose Dad was one of the victims.

William (Bill) Fisher

Billy Fisher was one of the 'Parton Fishers', the large family originating in that generation from the village of Parton, on the northern outskirts of Whitehaven. Born in 1908, he was three years older than the girl he married, Jane Davis (Ginny), eldest daughter of Martha and Ted Davis. Bill followed after so many local lads whose biggest employment opportunities were in the coalfields. The Great Depression of the 1930s was a desperate time, seared into the memories of anyone who lived through them. Any economic downturns, which have been experienced during the second half of the 20th century, are slight shadows of those times. Desperate times were about to be left behind in 1947 for the Fisher family of four

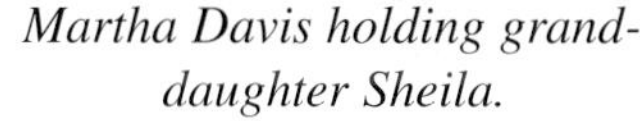

Martha Davis holding grand-daughter Sheila.

William Davis (known as Ted or Ned)

children — Sheila, age twelve; Billy, ten; Stella, four, and Janice, two. Stella, my wife, has few memories of her Dad — although they all involve him singing and dancing around the room with her, this, almost always, after his return from work and having had his bath — a necessity of those days, when no provision was made at old pitheads for cleansing workaday grime. One of the favourite songs was *She's a big girl now*. By all accounts, from inside and outside the family, Bill was entirely devoted to his family, providing for them and their welfare. He was no drinker and spent all of his free time with his youngsters, out walking and playing whenever possible. One memory is of carrying toddler Stella, small but hefty, from visiting relatives at Parton, home to 12 Gore's Buildings, near St. James Church.

Bill had sisters — Ginny, Hannah, Lizzie and brothers Anthony, Wilson and Harry (who had a son, Michael, who was killed by a bus whilst he was playing cowboys and indians in Parton). Their mother, was a hard working lady who kept a beautiful home.

Ginny Davis, on the other hand, came from a poor home. Her mother, Martha (née Sewell), had ten children, with eight dying in babyhood. Only the eldest, Ginny (Jane) and Stella, the youngest, survived to adulthood. Aunty Stella, now Steele, née Davis, lives in Carlisle (1997). Their father, Ted Davis, was a farm worker — labourer in those days — long hours and poverty line wages being the norm. How did Britain avoid bloody revolution? Ironically, after we were married in 1966, we bought a house next door to the Watson family, for whom Stella's grandfather had worked all those years previously. They testified to his hard work and diligence.

Bill and Ginny Fisher, then, from different backgrounds, worked hard to set up and support a lovely household — he, to maintain what he was brought up to, she to give her children what she had lacked. Sadly, it was not to continue. On the 'back' shift, of Friday 15 August 1947, at 5.30pm, a shot was fired into the roof of a worked out area — a cuckoo shot — and the resulting catastrophic explosion killed many in the immediate area. One of the inherent problems of deep mining is the ventilation system, which sustains a gas free atmosphere; in case of fire and/or explosion, the combustion products are swept through the rest of the workings.

This was the terrible consequence of that fateful afternoon — the resultant and lethal carbon monoxide, was drawn around the inbye workings catching the rest of the personnel although they were far away from the explosion site.

Ginny Fisher holding daughter Sheila, Stella Davis, and Bill Fisher.

The official report records evidence, which seems to indicate that the immediate area of blast damage was along about 2,000 yards of tunnel. Many of the 104 fatalities were caused by the afterdamp poisoning. Indeed, the men in the rest of the workings did not feel any blast or hear sound as such but, as is the wont of these occurrences, they detected a major alteration in the airflow and sought to determine the extent and nature of the problem. They knew that something 'big' had happened, as the phone system failed and several were heard to ring continuously, indicating severe problems.

Bill Fisher was one of the 45 men who survived the explosion unscathed but succumbed to gas poisoning in the aftermath. These men were deployed in the area further inbye and on the opposite side of the main haulage road to the explosion site. It is shown on the official plans as the No. 2 Rise.

The plan, copies of which are in my possession, labels Bill Fisher as No.39. It is ironic that the three men, who were sole survivors, were in the same vicinity as Bill. It is certain that he would have been one of those encouraged to join the older and experienced Birkett, who wanted to go deeper into the mine to avoid the expected gas. Birkett, Hinde and Weighman went into 'Skelly's Heading' for a few hours, only just surviving the carbon monoxide but were, at least, able to walk out after 20 hours, meeting rescue teams who were working their way through roof-falls and the like. Indeed, the rescuers mistook the three for fellow team members.

I have not been able to verify that oral account heard from others, that on their way to comparative safety, a dark shadowy figure passed them. This was reported as 'the angel of death'. However, on occasions of this sort, rumour and legend grow substantively. My hypothesis of this story's origin is that on first emerging from the workings, Bob Brannon, a rescuer and also Miners' Lodge Secretary, suggested to his team-mate who saw 'shadows' that he was 'seeing things'. I rest my case.

One dramatic, long-standing misgiving over Bill's death is dispelled, in that the 45 of whom he was numbered, had no marks of violence on them whatsoever. They had clearly been gassed and would fall asleep without any pain or suffering. Of course, for those who were severely burned but not killed outright, unconsciousness must have brought blessed relief from agony. The official list shows that of the 104 deaths, 90 were as a result of monoxide poisoning.

In the relative safety of 'Skelly's Heading', Birkett, Hinde and Weighman felt the effects of gas. They were only some 130yards from the first of 30 victims. If his workmates had followed Birkett's coercing, would they all have survived? This bitter question must be prefaced by the knowledge that, had they all crowded into the lower area, the 'good' air would have almost certainly have been used up. As it is, there remains the haunting, abiding recall, that the general feeling expressed to the 'three' was that 'they' would 'come to get us' before long. Eternity will provide us with the full answer. We may only speculate.

Accounts are recorded of miners found clasped in a final embrace; of some who had wept at the approach of the end — coal dust had been washed away in tell tale clear streaks. As Christians, we can only trust that those who were certain of their eternal welfare were able to minister to others in their own extreme moments. We also trust that those who had no such chance, recalled their own basic and rudimentary introduction to eternal things.

The desperate task of victim recovery went on until the last body was recovered at 9pm on Saturday evening of the following week, the 23 August. They were sent home, in the time-honoured fashion. Bill Fisher's body was brought to the surface at 1pm. On Sunday, 17th, he was identified by his brother, Wilson Fisher. There had been no shortage of volunteers for underground rescue and recovery work. Now, there was a similar response to the urgent need to perform a final duty to fallen 'marras' — digging the graves for the 104 victims. The weather was warm and summery.

Bill Fisher was laid to rest in a new plot in Moresby Churchyard. His grave is along by a group of victims from the 1941 explosion at Lowca Pit. His grieving widow, Ginny, was herself laid there following her passing at the age of 80 years in 1992.

The Enquiry

This was subsequently held in the Methodist Church Schoolroom from 7-10 October. Expert witness evidence showed that the cause of the initial explosion was as a result of an inadequate safety check of shot firing. It is likely, because the bored hole was not checked for any breaks, that a cavity containing dangerous levels and quantities of methane-natural gas was broken into and that the resultant shot of sheathed explosive ignited the gas and other 'fuels' causing the devastating firestorm along the workings. The big quantities ensured that lethal amounts of combustion products were circulated through the workings. The area that was the scene of the explosion was worked out and the roof was being caved in, in a controlled way by the use of this 'cuckoo shot'. It is ironic that the shot should be described in this way as it led to those deaths. Cuckoo shots were banned forthwith.

Family Matters

Victim's families were awarded the sum of £600. A disaster fund was set up and eventually Ginny was granted twelve shillings (60p) per week.

My Dad, Bob Matthews (senior) worked for the Prudential Assurance Company. We lived, then, at 8 Lakeland Avenue, Seacliffe, generally known in the town as 'Wudduss' — Woodhouse, on the map! Dad was out working his agency of Kells and Wudduss, when news of the tragedy spread rapidly. Dad immediately recognised the possible consequences and, although offices were closed for Friday evening, he managed to contact his seniors and made arrangements for emergency payments to be made to cover urgent needs. Friday was payday and most of the victims would have had their pay, in cash, with them in the pit.

Two other points to bear in mind (i) the scale of the toll was not yet apparent; (ii) almost none of Dad's customers had bank accounts. Consequently, on Saturday morning, a clerk was despatched from the Carlisle Prudential Office, with a suitcase full of cash. My Father met him at the station and, on instruction from way above, paid out, in cash, the 'sums assured' to families as their loved ones were confirmed as victims. Such action by any company must be applauded in like circumstance. Dad remained at the pit gates until after midnight. As an elder in our local assembly, he was well known by the community and he spent his time with anxious relatives.

Hannah Scott was cousin to Ginny and about ten years older. Alf, her husband, had worked in mines overseas, particularly in African goldmines. Ida, their daughter still lives in Whitehaven - she is the widow of Kingsley Parrish, former Clerk to the Harbour Commissioners. Hannah's father was a well-known rope maker - a craft in big demand in mining and shipping localities. They made a lot of money by travelling off around rural mines and to the North East.

On the afternoon of the explosion, Hannah had not spoken to Ginny for some months over some unremembered rift, involving other family members and Ginny was amazed to answer the door and find Hannah on the step. Her words were, 'Let's put bygones behind us lass, there's been an explosion in William - isn't your Bill on t' back shift?' Ginny's world, like so many others, was about to fall apart.

Sister Sheila recalls an incident from that awful day: she was sent to the fish shop and returned with a piece of news gleaned from the shop and which she blurted out, 'Here, they are saying that our Daddy's pit has blown up.' She was told by Grandma to stop talking silly and go out of the room. Sheila is now not sure whether this was the first news or an attempt to ease pain. My own family's anxiety was ameliorated somewhat, when it was realised that my two Uncles Henry, were not at work — Poss was on a different shift, whilst Harry Smith was on holiday at Morecambe. These two men were highly regarded by both men and management for their total integrity and honesty. They were both bible teachers and their workaday example was testimony to their beliefs and practices — John Skelly was one of their ilk.

Henry Smith

Known as Harry, it was his shift that was caught in the explosion. He had volunteered to work during the main holiday on refurbishment and was having 'time off in lieu'. He had many tales to tell of deliverance from dangerous situations. One concerned a previous holiday refurbishment episode. They were installing a new fan underground and the parts had to be taken down the shaft. One part of the casing was extremely large and Uncle Henry was to ride down with it. He was at this time a 'deputy', a job carrying with it the responsibility of prime safety. As the cage began its descent, the rig was just disappearing below, when 'something' spoke to Uncle Henry and told him to stop and get out. Calling loudly to Tom Banks, the 'banksman' - in total charge of the winding gear, the brake was slammed on and the cage was returned to the surface. In response to Tom's frantic, 'What's wrang 'arry?' my uncle quipped, 'Ah've forgot me bait - let t' cage ga' and he walked away. Tom, a fellow Christian, called him a 'daft faggot' and sent the cage on its way down. Moments later, the fan case slipped off its anchorage and jammed in the shaft. Had Uncle Henry been in there, he would have been thrown down the shaft to certain death. *Try explaining that!*

On the day of the 1947 disaster, Uncle Henry and Aunty Marion, on holiday in Morecambe, heard the news as they were eating in their hotel. They left immediately, catching the next train and Uncle Henry, on arrival at Bransty Station, went straight to William Pit and, in his best suit, got into the cage for rescue work — he knew every man who was lost. The man who covered for his holiday, Lawrence Murtagh, was a victim.

Uncle Henry knew Stella's Dad, Bill Fisher, very well. I would like to think that the special fondness which Uncle Henry had for Stella and I, was partly due to his recollection of his old marra and the horrors and loss of that day. It was Uncle Henry who jumped at the chance to perform our marriage ceremony. On that day, as he greeted us once more in the Civic Hall at our reception, he actually kissed not only Stella but me as well — something unknown to a previous generation, except in special circumstances.

A story recounted by Jack Mullen at Uncle Henry's funeral concerned the high regard in

The widow and children of Billy Fisher: Sheila, Stella, Ginny holding Janice, and Billy Jr.

which he was held by his men. His mission statement was, 'Don't ask anyone to do anything that you are not prepared to do yourself.'

A big rugby match was to be held in Whitehaven. To ensure a lack of the expected absenteeism on the day of the match, Uncle Henry promised to let them go early as long as the full tasks were carried out for that shift. Everything completed, they duly left early. This was then frowned upon by the manager who, on the following day, sent home the 'errant' Harry — suspended. On learning of this, his shift walked out to a man in support of him, their highly respected boss who had honoured his word to them.

Czechoslovakian Involvement

As may be imagined, the effect of the tragedy was felt by mining communities worldwide. Many of these responded to the Disaster Fund. By October, this had reached £80,000 and then came a cheque from the Czechs — all of the Bata shoe workers in Czechoslovakia worked overtime to donate £5,000. Bata had a shoe factory in West Cumberland — at Maryport. A little time before, the National Union of Mineworkers had sent £32,500 to a Czech village community wrecked by the Germans in the war and that generosity was not forgotten. Czech miners also worked overtime and the proceeds were used to pay for a holiday for William Pit widows and families. This was in 1956 and my wife, Stella, her sister Janice and bother Billy, were able to join dozens of others to a delightful trip to the Czech resort of Marianske Lazne. En route to the continent, they were treated to a sightseeing tour of London — for most their first to our own capital city.

Because Czechoslovakia was under Soviet Russian domination at the time, being 'behind the Iron Curtain' was an intriguing and somewhat daunting experience. One lady instructed her children not to kneel at their bedside to pray in case they were arrested for subversion. The groups were lavishly and most kindly treated by the generous Czechs and great friendships were made. They offered free educational study places to the young people but these and other generous offers were never taken up, one assumes for political reasons.

One of (William) Bill Fisher's bequests was that 'if anything ever happens to me, I don't want my lad to go down the pits' — a very common assertion of those generations. My own grandfather, Harry Smith, made a similar statement about his son, Harry, written about above, to no avail, of course. Young Billy Fisher did join the mines - Haig - and was also tragically, fatally injured in a pit accident in March 1968.

'Young' Billy Fisher

Against his mother's wishes and his deceased father's expressed sentiments, the fifteen year old school leaver, Billy Fisher, did join the mining workforce of West Cumberland. A handsome, dark haired young image of his father, Billy married Audrey Birkett of Cleator Moor and they had two little girls - Angela and Vivienne. When we married in August 1966, Billy 'gave away' Stella, as a substitute for their father. Being very shy, he was extremely nervous on the day, yet very proud of his little sister. Angela and Vivienne, along with cousin Gillian, were bridesmaids.

On Monday, 25 March 1968, I arrived home to Coronation Drive to be greeted by Ida Parrish with the terrible news that Billy had been seriously injured in a mining accident and that we should meet up with my mother-in-law at the West Cumberland Hospital. Stella arrived home shortly afterwards and her stinging words of horrified shock and anguish were seared into my memory - 'Oh NO! - it can't be! Those pits can't take our only lad!' Weeping subsided as West Cumbrian stoicism kicked into practicalities. We did not possess a car, so I went to my parent's house to tell them the news and borrow their car.

Stella and I arrived at hospital to be greeted by her mother and older sister, Sheila. They assured us that, although Billy was gravely injured and 'critical', he had stabilised and was to be transferred to Newcastle, probably by helicopter, the following morning. This was a clear indication to me that his injuries were indeed grave and that his chances of full recovery were almost negligible. However, we returned to our house with hope and prayer and had a meal together. At about 9 o'clock we returned Ginny to her home on the Valley but as we turned into Irt Avenue we saw a hatless policeman at her door - our worst fears were realised - Billy had just died without regaining consciousness. Another generation had fallen victim to the monster coal.

The Inquest

On 10th April, as reported by *Whitehaven News,* 18 April 1968.

Mr. William Fisher's address was given as 63 Ennerdale Road, Cleator Moor. Evidence of identification was given by Sidney Morton, practising solicitor, married to Billy's wife's sister. Albert Birkett of 52 Lakeland Avenue, Seacliffe, stated that he had worked with Mr. Fisher for six years. (This Birkett was nephew to the Birkett who survived the William Pit Disaster).

On the morning shift that day, he and Billy were following up the coal shearer towards the face, moving hydraulic props. Along 200 yards of the 3ft. 9in. seam, Billy noticed a forward support that was 'drunk' - not vertical. To correct this prop, a second jack should have been inserted to take the weight as the crooked prop was released. To save time, this was not done and the Witness agreed that no 'dome' was in place on top of the jack and domes are used to prevent slipping.

'We were on our knees and once the pressure was eased, I got the impression that the prop was coming towards us. As it fell, I went backwards. I fell and lost my helmet and the lamp dropped off. When I recovered, I saw Mr. Fisher lying on his back. I spoke to him but got no answer. I noticed that the forward roof bar was lying about a foot away from him. The rear prop had also come out and the support had also swivelled around.'

Chargehand faceworker, George Kelly, of High Road, Kells, was directing a force of 20 in the district, when he heard Mr. Birkett shout, 'Fisher's unconscious'. When he reached the scene, the props were lying on the floor. His belief was that one of them had hit Mr. Fisher.

Mr. Gordon Thompson, of 40 North Row, Kells, said that he was overman but that both he and the deputy had not been at work long enough to have checked the coalface left by the previous shift. 'It is mining practice to set another prop before releasing one which is out of line.' He later agreed with Mr. G. N. Worthington (representing the family) that he found the distance between some bars wider than the regulation three feet. One gap was 7 feet 6 inches and one bar had only one prop. A verdict of 'accidental death' was recorded.

The Aftermath

Billy Fisher's funeral was held at St. John's, Cleator Moor on Friday, 29 March 1968. A very large congregation overflowed the church and family and friends were joined by senior management and union representatives. As became tradition on these awful occasions, the Union Jack flew at half-mast over Haig Colliery as a sign of the fatal accident and respect for the family.

Billy's widow, Audrey, was just two months into a pregnancy - Billy had been excited about becoming a dad for the third time, although his mother-in-law did not know until after his accident. A little girl was born posthumously to him later that year. She was the most beautiful little child, with a mop of black hair and looked just like the dad who had been taken. Audrey named her 'Billinda' - to give her a name as close to her father's as possible. She was not to grow up though, because, at about six-months-old she became a victim of cot death. Deep sadness was upon our family, as one would expect, as we laid a tiny white coffin to rest forever, a few inches above that of her beloved Dad.

The prompting for these notes was the marking of the 50th anniversary of the 1947 Disaster on a warm, sunny afternoon in Whitehaven. The 50th Anniversary of the disaster was to be marked by a ceremony of remembrance in St. Nicholas' Churchyard, followed by a commemoration at the old William Pithead. There was seating for those who, as families of the deceased, wished to attend and Sheila, my sister-in-law with John Elliott her husband, Gillian their daughter and Stella and myself obtained numbered tickets for seats.

The service was moving and, after the address by the Bishop of Carlisle, Whitehaven schoolchildren, one to represent each man lost, brought forward a red carnation as a token and placed it in the memorial plaque, commissioned for the occasion and fashioned after a pit wheel — the symbol of deep mining. As the floral tributes were brought forwards, each victim's name was read from the Roll of Honour.

At the conclusion of the churchyard service, we then processed through the town to the old Pithead for a final wreath-laying. It seems to be the will and hope of all of those present and many others, that some sort of permanent memorial should be made to those lost and who paid the full price for our coal. *Bob Matthews, formerly of the Lake District National Park Centre, Brockhole, Windermere, now retired and living at Backbarrow, Ulverston.*

****

Treasured memories of a very dear husband and Daddy,
William (Bill) who was killed in William Pit Disaster August 15, 1947
A good life is often too short
But a good name endureth forever
Ever in the thoughts of his loving wife and children

In loving memory of our brother, Bill,
who was killed in William Pit explosion
August 15, 1947
We miss his smile, his cheery ways
We miss the things he used to say
When happy times we oft recall
'Tis then we miss him most of all
Always remembered by his sisters Jennie, Grace, Hannah and Lizzie

Treasured memories of our loving brother, Bill,
who lost his life in the William Pit Disaster August 15, 1947;
also our dear mother who died September 1947.
Forget them no, we never will
For in our hearts, we love them still
From Harry, Alice and Michael

Treasured Memories of our dear brother Bill
Who was killed in William Pit disaster August 15, 1947
Happy and smiling always content
Loved and respected wherever he went
Worthy of everlasting remembrance
From Anthony Ellen and Family

Memories of a dear brother, Bill
killed in the William Pit Disaster, August 15, 1947;
also a dear mother, who died September 1947.
Christ shall clasp the broken chain
Closer when we meet again
Always remembered by Wilson, Doris and Jean

In loving memory of my dear brother Bill
Who died in William Pit Disaster
August 15, 1947
A day of remembrance sad to recall
From John and Maggie

****

THOMAS FOX

Tommy

Thomas Fox was 24-years-old and a coal hewer at Wiliam Pit. He lived at 29 Bowness Road, Greenbank, Whitehaven. His next of kin was listed as his father, Samuel Fox of the same address. On 17 August 1947 at 2.35am Thomas was brought to the surface of William Pit and identified by his brother William Fox, also of the same address. Mr. Fox was the fifteenth miner recovered by search and rescue personnel. Thomas Fox, then aged eighteen, had survived the 1941 explosion at William Pit. His testimony at the subsequent inquest was greatly praised. Tommy Fox is also mentioned in the pages dedicated to Richard Cartmell, and in a memoriam from 1948 in remembrance of William McMullen and Thomas Fox.

****

In loving memory of my dear son, Thomas
who lost his life in the William Pit disaster August 15, 1947;
also his brother Joseph, who died in India, July 6, 1942
Death did to me short warning give
Therefore be careful how you live
My weeping friends I've left behind
I had not time to speak my mind
It is the Father's joy to bless
His love has found for him a dress
A robe of spotless righteousness
On whose soul sweet Jesus have mercy
R.I.P.
From his Mother, Father, Billy; also Vincent and wife, Blackpool

****

JOSEPH FOX

Joe

Joseph Fox was 35-years-old and an airways repairer at William Pit. He lived at 11 Woodhouse Road with his mother Elizabeth Fox. Brought to the surface of William Pit on 17 August 1947 at 5.10pm, Joe was identified by his cousin William Fox, of 1 Duke Pit, Rosemary Lane, Whitehaven. Search and rescue personnel gave Joseph a location number of Special 1 (brought to surface without an official number). In August of 1948, seven memoriams were inserted in the Whitehaven News for Joseph Fox.

In loving memory of my dear son Joseph,
died August 15, 1947 in William Pit explosion
Your end was sudden son dear
You made us weep and cry
But, Oh the saddest part of all Joseph
You had no time to say goodbye
From Mother, Benny and William,
Woodhouse, Greenbank, Whitehaven

In loving memory of Joseph Fox, killed in
William Pit, August 15, 1947
We were not there beside him
To hear his last faint sigh
To whisper just one loving word
Or even say goodbye
Some may think we have forgotten
When they see us smile
But little they know the heartache that lies
beneath that smile
From his loving sister, Sarah Ann,
27 Greenbank Avenue

In loving memory of our dear brother, Joseph,
who was killed in the William Pit Disaster
August 15 1947
We did not hear his last faint sigh
Nor even see him die
We only know he passed away without a
last goodbye
Dear Joseph whose soul
Sweet Jesus have mercy
Always remembered by his loving brother,
George, Kathie and family,
63 Greenbank Avenue

****

In loving memory of our dear
son and brother Joseph,
who was killed in William Pit explosion
August 15 1947
He had a nature you could not help loving
A heart that was purer than gold
And to those who knew him and loved him
His memory will never grow old
Never one day forgotten by his loving
Father, sister Evelyn, brother-in-law Harry

In loving memory of Joseph Fox,
killed in William Pit, August 15, 1947
We never thought that morning
That you were going to die
You left us all so suddenly
You never said goodbye
From Joe and May, 7 Overend

In loving memory of my dear brother Joseph,
who lost his life in the William Pit Disaster
August 15 1947
When last I saw your smiling face you
looked so bright and well
Little did I dream that day would be our
last farewell
Always remembered by his loving sister, Lizzie,
brother-in-law Edward, and Ted and Jessie

In loving memory of my dear brother, Joseph
who lost his life in William Pit Disaster
August 15, 1947
Happy and smiling, always content
Loved and respected wherever he went
Never selfish but willing and kind
What a beautiful memory to leave behind
Ever remembered by his loving brother,
Ned, Louie and family

JOHN N. GARNER

John Nelson Garner was 37-years-old and worked as a brusher at William Pit. A resident of 41 Frizington Road, Frizington, he was survived by his wife Sarah Elizabeth and two children - Thomas and Margaret. Brought to the surface at 3.30pm, 16 August 1947, Mr. Garner was identified by his wife. John was the fifth miner located out of the one hundred and four.

John Nelson Garner had served his country as a member of the King's Own Royal Border Regiment 5th Battalion.

****

In loving memory of my dear husband
John Nelson
died in William Pit explosion,
August 15, 1947
A day to remember, sad to recall
Without farewell he left us all
In memory we see him just the same
As long as we live we shall treasure his name
Ever remembered by his loving wife, son Thomas, and daughter Margaret

In loving memory of our dear son and brother,
John Nelson Garner
who lost his life in William Pit explosion August 15, 1947
Never one day forgotten
Ever remembered by Mam and Dad, brothers and sisters.

****

JAMES GIBBONS

James Gibbons was a 47-year-old brusher at William Pit. He was a resident of 60 Seven Acres, Parton, where he lived with his widower father Robert Gibbons. James contributed 35 shillings a week lodgings and paid for coals. Mr. Gibbons was brought to the surface on 19 August 1947, at 1.15am and later identified by his brother-in-law John Robert Stubbs of 155 Main Street, Parton. He was the 77th miner located. A request was made that James Gibbons' body be brought to the home of his sister and brother-in-law, Mr. and Mrs. J. R. Stubbs of 155 Main Street, Parton. James Gibbons was interred at Moresby Church on 21 August 1947.

****

In loving memory of
James
dearly beloved son of Robert, and the late Barbara Gibbons
killed in William Pit disaster, August 15, 1947;
also Barbara
dearly beloved wife of Robert Gibbons
died October 29, 1946.
Not one day forgotten
By all at 60 Seven Acres

****

HENRY GIBSON

Henry Gibson was a resident of the village of Parton, living at 17 Foundry Road with his wife Gladys and three young daughters. Employed as a shift hand, Henry was 36-years-old when he died. He was brought to the surface of William Pit at 1.10pm on the afternoon of 17 August 1947, and was later identified by his brother John William Gibson of 91 Foundry Road, Parton. Mr Gibson was the 38th man of 104 to be located.

****

I am writing in response to your appeal for information about the lives and families of the men killed in the 1947 William pit disaster.

Born in 1939 I am the eldest of three daughters born to Henry and Gladys Gibson. Our Dad was born in 1910, and Mam in 1911. My sisters are Linda, born in 1940, and Brenda, in 1944. We lived at 13 Foundry Road, Parton. Being only seven-years-old at the time of the disaster I can remember very little. On the day of the disaster I remember getting up in the morning and the house being full of relatives but I don't even remember being told our father had been killed. I do remember that he was a gentle quiet man. He was the ninth of twelve children (one died in infancy) with four brothers and six sisters. Some of his brothers and sisters lived nearby and he would pass their houses on his route to work, ringing the bell on his bike as he passed.

Soon after the disaster my grandma on my mother's side died and we moved to Kells to look after my Granda and to be closer to my Mam's family. Our Mam never remarried, remaining devoted to our Dad for 50 years until her death in 1997. They are now buried together in Moresby churchyard. *Freda Hodgson (née Gibson), daughter*

****

Henry Gibson, known as 'Harry', would have been my great uncle. I have no personal memories of him as he died before I was born, but the following information has been gathered from my late Grandmother, Mrs Edith Batty (née Gibson) and my mother, now Mrs Etta Gibson Davies.

He was the ninth of twelve children in the family of William Henry and Elizabeth Gibson of Parton. At the time of his death, he was married to Gladys (née Buchanan) and they had three daughters, Freda, Linda and Brenda, who were aged seven, six and two respectively. They lived at 17 Foundry Road, Parton, next door to his widowed mother.

My mother remembers my Grandmother saying Harry had told her that the pit was a dangerous place to work, and I recall her talking her about the 1947 explosion, and saying that

Gladys and Henry Gibson.

if only he had followed the men who moved further into the workings he could have survived. He is buried in the churchyard of St Bridget's, Moresby.

Henry Gibson was the son of William Henry Gibson (born 1.12.1872, died December 1934) and Elizabeth (née Walker, born 2.6.1872 , died March 1963); his siblings were John William (known as Jack), Edward, Agnes Hilda (known as Hilda), Isaac, Elizabeth, Walter who died in infancy, Edith, Gladys, Henry (known as Harry), Alfred, Mabel, and Eva.

Margaret Harrison,
great niece

I do know that Henry Gibson had just bought himself a new bicycle (drop handlebars, deraillier gears, etc), top gear at that time. He only had it two weeks.

Arthur Smith, neighbour

****

In loving memory of a dear husband and Daddy,
Henry Gibson
who was killed in William Pit explosion August 15, 1947
Many a lonely heartache
Many a silent tear
Never one day forgotten by his loving wife and three little daughters all at Kells

In loving memory of my dear son killed in William Pit disaster August 15, 1947
Dearly loved and sadly missed by his dear Mother

Loving memories of our dear brother, Harry, who died in William Pit on August 15, 1947
In God's garden of memories we meet every day
Will be loved always, by his sister Edith, brother-in-law Tom and niece Etta.

****

EDWARD GLAISTER

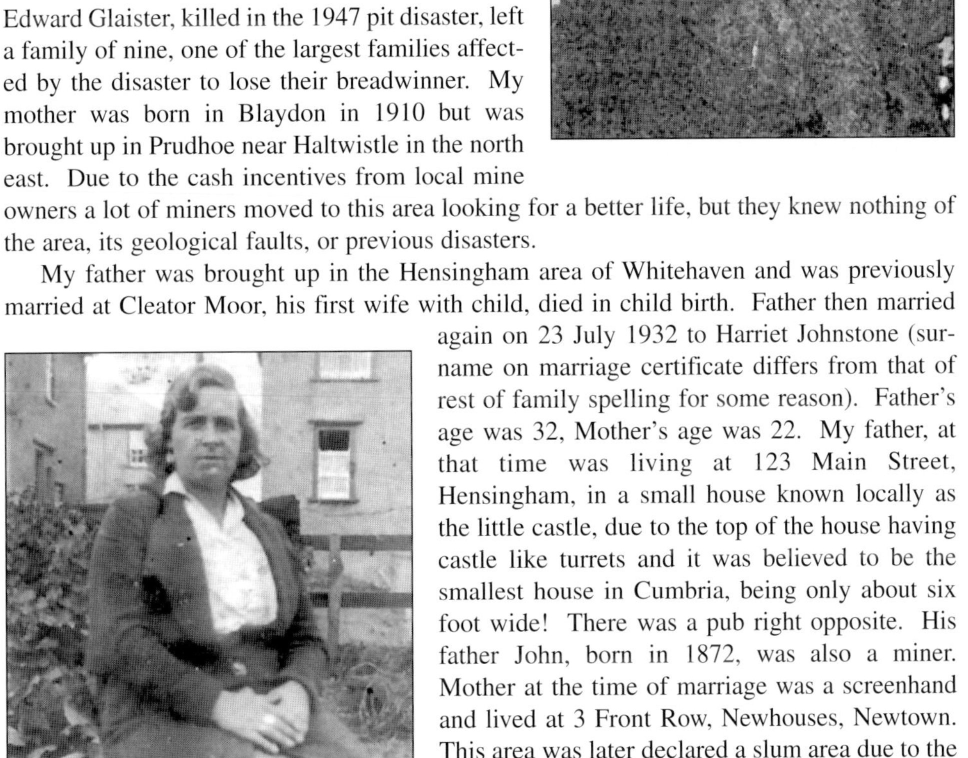

Edward Glaister was 48-years-old and employed as a brusher at William Pit. He lived at 17 Windermere Road with his wife Harriet and their nine children - Harriet, Edward, William, Joan, Gwendoline, Ruth, Gordon, Irene, Dorothy and Raymond (including two sets of twins). Mr. Glaister was brought to the surface of William Pit on 16 August 1947, and formally identified by his brother, John Glaister of 52 Main Street, Cleator. Edward Glaister was the second man to be located by search and rescue teams.

****

Edward Glaister, killed in the 1947 pit disaster, left a family of nine, one of the largest families affected by the disaster to lose their breadwinner. My mother was born in Blaydon in 1910 but was brought up in Prudhoe near Haltwistle in the north east. Due to the cash incentives from local mine owners a lot of miners moved to this area looking for a better life, but they knew nothing of the area, its geological faults, or previous disasters.

My father was brought up in the Hensingham area of Whitehaven and was previously married at Cleator Moor, his first wife with child, died in child birth. Father then married again on 23 July 1932 to Harriet Johnstone (surname on marriage certificate differs from that of rest of family spelling for some reason). Father's age was 32, Mother's age was 22. My father, at that time was living at 123 Main Street, Hensingham, in a small house known locally as the little castle, due to the top of the house having castle like turrets and it was believed to be the smallest house in Cumbria, being only about six foot wide! There was a pub right opposite. His father John, born in 1872, was also a miner. Mother at the time of marriage was a screenhand and lived at 3 Front Row, Newhouses, Newtown. This area was later declared a slum area due to the condition of the houses and open cess pits. Their first home was a one room flat in Queen Street. They also lived at Mount Steps and Mark Lane before moving to 17 Windermere Road.

Raymond Glaister, son

Edward Glaister (above right) and Harriet, his wife.

Edward Glaister's widow Harriet with their children at Skegness 1948

****

In loving memory of my dear husband Edward,
killed in William Pit Disaster August 15, 1947.
When last I saw your smiling face
You looked so bright and well
Little did I dream that day would be our last farewell
Worthy of remembrance by his wife and family

****

RICHARD E. GREARSON

Dicky

Brother of William Foulder Grearson

Molly (Mary) and Richard Grearson

Richard Edward Grearson was 47-years-old and employed as a brusher at William Pit. A resident of Parton, he lived at 173 Main Street with his wife Mary and six children - Molly, James, Richard Edward, Jonathan, Frederick and Ada. Dicky Grearson was brought to the surface of William Pit on 16 August 1947 at 11.15pm and identified by his son Richard Edward Grearson of the same address. Mr. Grearson was interred at Moresby churchyard on 19 August 1947. Other documents have the name listed as Grierson.

The photograph of Richard Grearson, with his wife Mary was found in his pocket after he was killed. The contents of his pocket also included a scrap of paper on which he had written the names of his working team - Vincent McSherry, Edward Glaister, Thomas Dixon and Joe Nicholson (not killed); a piece of coal, and two pay stubs. *Ada Egan, daughter.*

THE CUMBERLAND COAL CO. (WHITEHAVEN) LTD.
WILLIAM PIT
STANDARD EARNINGS
WAR WAGE
MINIMUM
SKILLED 1/-
TAX REFUND
DEDUCTIONS
FIXED DEDUCTIONS
RENT, LOWTHER ESTATES
PUBLIC ASSISTANCE
BOOTS
DEPOT COAL
GEAR
HELMETS
INCOME TAX
BALANCE £

One story about Richard Grearson was shortly after the wartime blackout ended and you could leave the windows uncovered, the public footpath (wagon road) to Parton runs through William pit yard. As it was black dark at night when Dicky was going through the pit yard he went to the engine house window and pressed his face hard up against the glass and then rattled on the window, you can imagine the reaction of the engine driver, he nearly freaked out. *Arthur Smith, neighbour*

I can remember Dickie Grearson making funny faces at us kids through the parlour window. He was always full of life. He used to pick me up and rub his stubbly chin on my face. I fell off his brown cow once. He gave me rides on his horses (Molly and Norah) and on this occasion on a cow. I was concussed. Dickie was beside himself with worry.

Frank Hewer.

In loving memory of my dear husband
Richard Edward,
killed in William Pit Disaster August 15, 1947,
also his beloved brother William
Your end was sudden husband dear
Our sad hearts wonder why
But oh the hardest part of all
You never said goodbye
From his loving wife, sons and daughters

In loving memory of my dear father,
Richard Edward
killed in William Pit Disaster August 15, 1947;
also dear Uncle William, brother of the above-named
A beautiful star shines over the graves
Of the ones we loved and could not save
Always in our thoughts,
Your loving daughter Molly and son-in-law Dan

****

WILLIAM F. GREARSON

William Foulder Grearson was 36-years-old and employed as a brusher at William Pit. He lived at 96 Main Street, Parton, Cumberland, with his wife Dorothy and five children - Dorothy, Frances, William, Mary, and George. At 3.40am on 17 August 1947 William Grearson was brought to the pit surface and identified by his nephew, Richard Edward Grearson of 173 Main Street, Parton. Mr. Grearson was the sixteenth miner located by rescue personnel. On 19 August 1947, William Grearson was laid to rest at Moresby Churchyard. Other sources list his name as Grierson.

Graves at Moresby Churchyard

JOSEPH W. HEWER

Joe

Brother of Ronald William Hewer

Joseph Wilson Hewer, was 40-years-old and a deputy overman at William Pit. A resident of Parton he lived at 18A Seven Acres, with his wife Margaret and five children - William, Robert, Margaret, Joyce and Joseph. Mr. Hewer was brought to the surface of William Pit on 17 August 1947 at 12.40am and later identified by his brother, Robinson Wilson Hewer of 69 Main Street, Parton. He was the eleventh miner located. Joe's brother Ronnie, also lost his life in the disaster. They were two of seven brothers.

Joseph Hewer and bride Margaret Benson

My name is Joyce Haile (née Hewer). I am the daughter of the late Joseph Wilson Hewer. I had three brothers and one sister. Sadly my two eldest brothers, Billy and Bobby have died. My sister Margaret and I can remember being on Parton shore the day of the explosion. My youngest brother, he's also Joseph Wilson, was just seven-months-old. Although I was only five years and two months at the time of the explosions, I can remember lots of sadness in my childhood. I remember the day I started Parton village school, and my Mam crying as the teachers talked to her.

I have memories of two things about my Dad. Parton being a fishing village, we were always eating crabs given to us by Mr. Curwen and Mr. Ferguson (they both had boats). Once I had poison in my foot through standing on a crab shell; my Dad put my foot in a bowl of boiling water and let the poison out with a razor blade (no antibiotics then).

I can remember Christmas when Dad would bring in the goose and we all got round the kitchen sink and plucked it, there were feathers everywhere, and the goose grease was used to rub our chests in winter. My Dad was one of the best fell-runners at the time, being mentioned in books locally as one of the three greatest.

My Mam's sister, aunt Sarah said he would come back from the fells with baskets of blueberries and we had blueberry pie.

I go to St. Bridget's churchyard regularly with my husband. Dad and Uncle Ronnie are buried side by side. My husband cuts the grass and I take flowers. We will never forget them. My grandchildren know about the explosion. We take them to the memorial at the pit top, and always take red roses on the memorial day for my Dad and Uncle Ronnie. My eldest granddaughter Rosie is seen on the left of the picture at the memorial service in 2001.

My youngest grandson is also Joseph. My son Alan takes his children to the memorial at the pit tip and Frank aged four, knows all about the men who went down the pit and died. My Dad's youngest brother was called Frank too, and he played the accordion and my Dad played the violin; they played together in the village pubs.

I keep in touch with Norman Adams who lives in New South Wales, Australia. A number of years ago he sent a letter to St. Bridget's church magazine trying to contact us and my brother and I, did write. He was from Cumbria and came to live with us in 1944 aged eighteen. He was drawn as a Bevin boy and went down the mines. He was given lodgings with us, and remembers cozy family times at our home. My Dad would play the violin and we had musical evenings. He remembers Dad and and Uncle Ronnie always walking to William Pit often in very bad weather. He said my Dad used to take us children to feed the hens and ducks on his allotment. Norman lived with us until 1947, and every year in August, he and his wife Betty take flowers to their own little cenotaph park.

Joseph Wilson Hewer

When I started courting my husband, also called Norman, he told me that his granda and two uncles were also killed in the explosion. They were Thomas B. Smith aged 62, Harold Smith aged 41 and Thomas T. Smith aged 36. We realised between us we'd lost six family members. My cousin's husband was killed too, he was Adam Raby.

My son-in-law Peter is sending on to you some photos by e-mail. The two children are myself and Frank Hewer, taken on a holiday to Skegness paid for by the miners fund after our dads were killed; my parents' wedding photo and my beloved Dad.

We will always remember all the miners, and my family tells their children about the loss of life down William Pit. I have a copy of the coroners report and have read it once and I was very upset.

Last Sunday a very wet, windy afternoon I sat in front of the fire and read *Sunset on the William.* I laughed a little, cried a little and lived all the childhood adventures we had on the beach and wagon road, and jam sandwiches definitely tasted better after being down the pit. It was just us, I think it's fantastic. I've given it to my sister to read and now my family is reading it. My copy will always be treasured. Frank mentioned about my father doing a man a favour that day by changing shifts with him. My mother always used to blame the gypsies.

A gypsy woman with a baby knocked at our door selling her wares and begging as they often did. Mam went to get something upstairs for her and caught her stealing when she came down and chased her. The gypsy woman put a curse on her (the tinker's curse). My Mam and Dad were very superstitious, and Dad would never let any of us put new shoes on the table. The pit disaster happened just a few days later. I've been in touch with Hazel, the niece of Winnie Raby. Hazel's a lovely girl and used to live near us, but now lives at Cockermouth. I've passed on your email address to her and Hazel thinks she has Adam's and Winnie's wedding photograph and will send it to you with any other information she has.

I'll write again if I can get more information about Thomas Smith, and somewhere I have a photograph taken in Czechoslovakia on a holiday paid for by the Czech miners for the widows and children of the men killed in the pit disaster. When I find it, I'll ask little brother Joe to send it to you. *Joyce Haile, daughter.*

****

Treasured and beautiful memories of
Joseph Wilson Hewer (Joe),
the dearly loved husband of Margaret
and the dear Daddy of Joyce, Margaret, and little Joe,
killed in the William Pit disaster August 15, 1947.
Life is not the same without you Joe
Nothing on this earth is the same to me
Words can never express how I miss you
How I long for your company
I weep and grieve for you always
There's a broken heart that will never heal
For there's only God in heaven knows
Just how I feel
For the tragic way you had to die
I shall always remember and wonder why

****

Treasured memories of our two dear sons and brothers,
Joe and Ron who lost their lives in the
William Pit disaster August 15, 1947
God gave us strength to bear it
Courage to fight the blow
What it cost to lose them
No one will ever know
There is no separation for those we love
No distance can divide
Every day in sunshine or shade
We still walk side by side
Father, Mother, Brothers and Sisters-in-law

****

RONALD W. HEWER

Ronnie

Brother of Joseph Wilson Hewer

Ronald William Hewer was a 38-year-old brusher at William Pit. He lived at 110 Main Street, Parton, with his wife Mary (née Blaney) and their four children - Ronald, Margaret, Frank and Joseph. On 17 August 1947 at 10.20am, Ronnie was brought to the pit surface and identified by his brother Robinson Wilson Hewer, of 69 Main Street, Parton. He was the 33rd miner located by search and rescue teams. Mary Hewer was expecting her sixth baby when her husband was killed. In March of 1948, son Neil was born.

****

Treasured memories of
my dear husband,
Ronald William,
killed in William Pit Disaster,
August 15, 1947;
also his brother Joe and Uncle Tom
He had a nature you
couldn't help loving
A heart that was purer than gold
And to us who knew and loved him
His memory will never grow old
Though the tears in my eyes
do not glisten
And my face doesn't always seems sad
There's never a night or a morning
But I think of the husband I had
From his loving wife and kiddies

****

Ronnie Hewer

SUNSET ON THE WILLIAM

by Frank Hewer

For Bethany and Aaron Jack Spedding

Widows and children of trapped miners wait for news. From the Illustrated Magazine, September 1947

As people kept vigil on the Bransty Cliffs, waiting and praying for the one hundred and four miners trapped in the William Pit below, a strange thing happened: The setting sun, sinking beyond the horizon, as if from out of the sea, rose up again, to slowly sink back down. Some saw it as a natural phenomenon. Others saw it as a sign from heaven.

Of the one hundred and seven men trapped,
three were later to make a miraculous escape,
one hundred and four perished.

****

This brief account of everyday life at the time through the eyes of
one of the victim's sons, not quite seven-years-old at the time of the disaster, is
dedicated to all mining families the world over.

****

It was a good year for the roses, but the thorns pricked deep, and still can be felt. It was a great summer as regards to the sunshine, but on Friday, 15 August 1947, dark shadows were cast. It was a tragic day for the harbour town of Whitehaven and surrounding area, but more so for the relatives, friends, and kindred spirits of the one hundred and four miners who perished in the hell hole that was the William Pit: my father, Ronald Hewer, his eldest brother Joe, and my mother's Uncle Tom included.

It is not my intent to create a sombre story, nor my intention to write an account of the William Pit its triumphs or its tragedies, far better writers than myself have done that and in graphic detail. Setting pen to paper so to speak, I merely wish to record a short period of my life and surroundings of the time.

A child's mind takes all in but, over years, can become disorientated - so much so, that places, times and events can become confused in the memory, fusing into one, giving the mind the impression that they are as one, when in truth weeks, months and even years can split them. In respect of this I will concentrate on vivid memories that I can put a time and place to. There is a great deal more I could include in these pages however this document will be brief, for to include all one's childhood memories, whether in the correct order or not, would result in a massive tome.

In America a majority of the people of the time know exactly where they were at, and what they were doing, at the time of John F Kennedy's assassination. The same could be said for those who remember the tragedy of the William Pit explosion of 1947. Though only a child at the time, I can remember exactly where I was, and what I was doing when the news of the disaster reached our door, and there this account will end.

I know little of my mother's father's family, the Blaneys, other than being told they came to Whitehaven, from the north east of England, and they were of Irish origin. My mother had been fairly young when her father died of a chest complaint (as was he), that he had endured for a while, that may or may not have been connected to the fact that he started work at the pit at twelve years of age.

My mother was no stranger to coal mining; her close relations the Brannon's of Whitehaven had been involved in coal mines since the arrival of her grandfather and grandmother's families from the County Louth, County Down, area of Ireland. They came from one poverty stricken shore line to another. Four of her mother's brothers died directly or indirectly through coal mining.

My reason for stating the above is simply to focus on my own mining links, and not to write a genealogy. I worked down the pit myself as a teenager and young man, though against my mother's wishes but, in all honesty, I enjoyed my time there; the comradeship was far superior to any I ever encountered above ground. Nonetheless, for reasons more to

The Brannon family - this photograph includes three generations - my great grand-dad, William James, centre of middle row. The man extreme left, middle row with moustache is my grandmother's brother, Tom Brannon, who was killed in the William tragedy 1947.

do with gaining myself a bigger weekly wage than any dislike I had for the pits, I left coal mining shortly before my 21st birthday, though often regretted it.

Though my mother was Roman Catholic she married my father, Ronald William Hewer who was Church of England. My father was no stranger to mining either - his father William had been a lead miner in the Lake District, indeed, so had been my father's grandfather and uncles. My father was born at Threlkeld, the family having moved from Caldbeck to Threlkeld in the latter part of the 1800s. The family can be traced back to the Castle Sowerby area in the eighteenth century. My father had six brothers, and I believe could have had seven, had not one died in childbirth.

My father, on leaving school, went to work at the coal pit. However, at the age of nineteen years, to get away from the pits, he enlisted in the army in March 1928, for seven years with the colours, and five in reserve with the Lancashire Fusiliers, duly serving in Libya, Palestine, Egypt and India. He married my mother in 1936 and was called back to the army at the outbreak of the Second World War. He served at Barnard Castle Barracks until 1942

Ronald William Hewer's grave in Moresby Church Cemetery.

when he was placed on war department reserve for coal mining, the country by then needing old miners more than old soldiers. And so, it was his lot to go to the William Pit, home guard duty and military stand by until the war's end. He received final clearance from the army in 1945, by which time he was the father of four children. A fifth child, my brother Wilson, who was two years younger than myself, died of pneumonia at eighteen-months-old. His sixth child he never saw as my mother was pregnant at the time of his death.

Our house was situated at the bottom of Parton Brow, on the corner of a tarmacked square that led round the corner past Whites Row and onwards to the old wagon road, William Pit and Whitehaven. I often wondered if our house had been built with the rubbish left over from the building of other properties, or had it been constructed by a gang of drunken teenagers playing a joke on Parton, with a couple of hours to spare before bedtime.

Diamond wedding anniversary of Frank Hewer's paternal grandparents with his father's brothers. Back row: John Hewer, Frank Hewer, Ernest Hewer, Benjamin Hewer. Front row: William Hewer grandfather, Margaret Hewer grandmother, Robinson Hewer. It is tragic that Ronald Hewer and his brother, Joe, are missing from this family group, because of an event that could have been prevented.

Grandmother Hewer, née Sisson, was born in Cumberland, but I don't know, at the time of writing, exactly where, though she did have relations living in Parton. My Grandfather, William (Bill) Hewer, having a proficient knowledge in mining, brought his family to West Cumberland presumably for a fatter wage packet in the coal mines. Their first home being an isolated mine-owned cottage on the Lowca to Harrington road near the old John Pit, known as Moor House, now long demolished, though I can still remember it prior to the demolition. They then moved to Harrington; it was there the lads went to school, before finally moving to Parton to a comparatively large house that stood next to the Ship Inn, indeed, it has been said, they were more often in it than next to it!

It would be tempting to drift into a different story than that I have set out to tell. Being from, and connected to fairly large families, so many twists and turns could be taken, however I will stick with my intentions, (though may at times reminisce on events slightly later) and compose a brief account of my time in the village of Parton before and up until the William Pit disaster of 1947.

****

The nearest our humble abode came to central heating was the black lead cast iron grate that was in the centre of the gable wall, with the oven and hot plate to one side of it leaving two alcoves - one with fitted drawers and cupboards floor to ceiling, and the other containing a shelf at waist height. Incorporated into the grate was what could have been the prototype for 'hot water on tap' - one side of the grate contained a tank with a tap on it, the downside to this ingenious innovation was that one had to go outside to the washhouse to get the gallon of water to fill it and be prepared to wait an eternity for it to reach a temperature of luke-warm. Our only water supply was in the washhouse next to the house. My mother put her faith in two large cast iron kettles that sat each side of the coal fire on two built in hobs, one to be placed on the hook that dangled above the fire to be brought to the boil when hot water was needed, and as hot water was in demand throughout the day, those two kettles had to be kept full and at the ready at all times.

The problems my mother had with that fire would have reduced many to a wreck. I have seen her covered in soot and close to tears trying to get that fire to draw air to heat the house and oven. When it was not being temperamental, it performed all its functions admirably, but when it took a funny do there was no coaxing it - the whole grate had to be cleaned out and re-laid with paper and kindling.

In the early 1940s my mother did not have an electric iron as there were no power points other than on the ceiling for light bulbs - such labour saving devices did not make an appearance in the house until a few year later. She had a wedge shaped iron 'innard' which had to be put in the hot coals and inserted into the smoother with tongs to heat it up to iron the clothes on the utility table. I use the word 'utility' flippantly as it was the only table in the house due to lack of space and was used for everything that required a flat surface, even to accommodating my father's coffin for a short while, though she did replace it after the funeral.

In keeping with tradition, my mother always laid the table for Sunday tea. There was a clean white tablecloth, the crockery and cutlery in appropriate positions, jam pot and jam spoon at the ready, buttered bread on a bread plate, various small cakes she would make, on the cake stand with one of her home made apple plate cakes taking centre stage. One Sunday we were about to start the meal when, without warning or respect for anything or anybody below, the plaster on the ceiling decided to part company from the wooden lathes that had held it in position since it had first been plastered on with something probably more akin to a coal shovel than a plastering trowel. I can remember as a child lying on the prodded rug in front of the fire gazing up at what resembled the white-washed face of the moon wondering what kept it up. That Sunday tea time brought forth the answer.

The kitchen - we called it the scullery - was positioned between the living room and the bottom of the bedroom staircase. It was about five or six feet wide and contained a concrete slab roughly three feet long and eighteen inches wide protruding from the wall. This cold slab or 'sconce', was the builder's answer to the refrigerator. Above this were two long wooden shelves, the top one used to store our Mickey Mouse gas masks and other items our parents did not want us to get our hands on. In the corner, at the bottom of the stairs, was a wall to ceiling cupboard which was our pantry. The scullery also housed the coal and wood store under the stairs. That describes our downstairs area, except there was a shelf by the front door for the radio and a picture rail around the wall about a foot below the ceiling. The house had no back door, though there was a window at the bottom of the stairs in the only place a back door could have been had the house possessed one.

In many respects we were lucky, having our own washhouse next to the house - most homes at the time did not - with our own water supply, consisting of a lead pipe rising about two foot six from the uneven cobbled floor, sporting a large brass tap fixed to the wall with what seemed to me to be two rusty spikes driven into the mortar joint through a copper clip. There was a cast iron gully complete with grid at its base.

The main feature of our washhouse was the set pot, built into a brick casing with its own fire grate and chimney. The inside walls of the washhouse, not exactly in good decorative appearance, displayed numerous patches where the lime washed plaster had parted company from the damp walls over many years. Above your head were the remains of a plaster and lathe ceiling - the washhouse cockroaches had more hiding places than Osama Bin Laden, and the spiders had a good food source, no doubt their main course being the silver fish that dwelt around the set pot grate, or the centipedes and wood lice in the damp walls.

Mary Ann Hewer
(born 1916)

I have described our downstairs pit house in the context of its absurd design and interior layout. This did not deter my mother from keeping the house neat and clean; what little furniture the living area was able to sustain was kept dusted and polished, as were the ornaments and pictures on the wall and the carpet square without the aid of a vacuum cleaner was kept in good order, the cast iron grate highly polished with 'black lead', and the brass oven dampers always carried a gleam. Her determination to keep on top of things against great odds was reflected throughout the house. Though we did not have wallpaper on the walls they were regularly painted with distemper, a powder which, when mixed with water, was similar to emulsion paint though the colour choice was very limited and it was difficult to apply without leaving brush marks.

The damp in the house was beyond my parents' control. It had been reported to the landlords a number of times, and while various attempts had been made to eradicate it, those attempts were only skin deep, and did little to solve the problem. The house, built of random stone, had no damp prevention in its foundations, and as modern day practices in dealing with damp were still in the future, little could be done about it. The washhouse, while lime washed regularly, was 'beyond the pail', as it needed a complete re-plastering job, new ceiling and floor, so in consequence, it did not get the same attention as the house.

The floors in the downstairs of the house were concrete. This was not the case with all pit houses in Parton - some had stone flag floors. Indeed my memory can point to some tenants who did not even use floor coverings, preferring to get on their hands and knees with bucket, soap and scrubbing brush. Our floors were covered with oilcloth, on top of which was a carpet square and a prodded rug in front of the fire.

William (born 1885) and Maggie Hewer (born 1887).

I well remember my Grandmother making these rugs. It fascinated me to see her create a beautiful prodded rug from a bag of coloured rags. She would wash the rags and cut them into suitable strips. Then, using a special wooden frame, with a length of hessian fixed taut into it, she would draw in chalk a design and then spend hours pegging away with her prodder, pushing the rags into the hessian. She sold the rugs to supplement their income.

Recollecting our washhouse, I remember times of hard frost when women queued up at it with their pans, buckets and kettles to get water. For some reason ours was the only tap in the area that did not freeze up. One may imagine this to have been an annoying occasion for the women but, on the contrary, I remember them, though standing half frozen to death in their turban head wear, pinnies and brats, laughing and joking with one another while awaiting their turn.

When it snowed, I remember the lorries attempting to get up Parton Brow. They were futile attempts for the most part, because, even with the chains that they fixed to the driving wheels of the vehicles, they could barely get a third of the way up slipping and sliding all over the place. More than once a lorry removed a bit of roughcast from our washhouse wall, before finally admitting defeat and retreating to the other options of Brewery Brow, Church Brow, or Lowca Brow.

As kids we would climb up onto the back of lorries going up Parton Brow. They went very slowly; I suppose they did not have the horse power of today's HGVs. Many a bottle of beer was thrown off the back of a brewery wagon and even lumps of coal were thrown off the coal wagons, to be retrieved later when the wagon was up the brow and out of sight. The drivers were too busy concentrating on the hill in front of them to notice us kids hanging on their tail boards.

My memory is fairly vivid of the big snow that hit Parton in the winter of 1947. We could still get in and out of the front door of our house, however on the opposite side of the road it had drifted completely, blocking the tenants in, to a height of half way up their front doors and ground floor windows. Communal spirit proved very much in evidence as all available hands, with all available tools, set about clearing the front doors. The feat was accomplished, until the snow plough decided to bulldoze its way through Parton and push all the snow off the road and back against the houses, including our house, only by this time the snow was not the soft powdery stuff it had been, and was more akin to pack ice.

My mother had recently bought a new brass fire side companion set, with brush, shovel and poker. Not to be outdone by the elders clearing snow, I went to help using the companion set shovel and managed to lose it. It may have been covered by snow but, even when the thaw came, the little brass shovel didn't reappear. I paid for it thought - my backside bore witness to that.

When we had torrential rain the water came down Parton Brow as if it was the River Derwent in flood. The drains could not cope with the volume of water which flowed across the gratings as if they weren't there. As kids we used to love the rain and we would float lollipop sticks down the gutter and run after them to see whose stick reached the bottom first.

We often played on the brows close to my house where a well known miner used to keep some hens. The hens didn't always use the huts to lay their eggs in, sometimes making nests in the scrub and nettles around his plot. We would go looking for eggs, often with success, but never without nettle rash. On the top of the brows was a turnip field. We called them swedes or snaggers, and often us kids sat among the bushes eating swedes - the small ones were the tasiest to eat raw.

This brings me to the greenhouse saga. The greenhouse stood near a racing pigeon loft, halfway up the brows. Inside was a well-cared for and vigorous grapevine, trained along the inside ridge, as well as tomato plants. We were trying to force the door open when a pane broke, so we managed to get in and were removing some of the delicious grapes when a voice bellowed from the brows. We panicked, dropping our ill-gotten gains and breaking some more panes in the process. Our parents had to pay the owner quite a considerable sum of money and my rear end was still sore a fortnight later. Lessons were learned the hard way.

****

Some Parton pit houses were bearable to live in, comfortable even, but the lack of amenities such as a water supply, bathroom and electricity made life a daily struggle. Other pit houses were hardly better than medieval and some were built on unstable ground. The terraced houses on the main street, improved to modern standards, would exchange hands for high prices. However, there was a lot of 'infill' housing that had been squeezed into small areas. Looking from the top of the brow, if you could see through the thick smoke from the numerous coal fires, you would see a total hodge podge of buildings.

The old village of Parton exists or existed (for much of it has now gone), on a narrow strip of land between the sea brows and the sea, protected by the coastal main line railway walls. Houses near the railway had to close their seaward facing doors and windows when there was a high tide and you could get soaked by the waves lashing over the railway line. Sometimes an extra high tide would gouge out the railway defences and I remember once a bunch of us kids running back and forth along the rear of a big house known as Beach House or Chesters, dodging the spray from waves lashing over its roof, and escaping into Lang Arch, until we were chased away by adults frantically trying to salvage the contents of the house, a task which soon became too dangerous as the waves got higher.

A large crowd had gathered to watch the spectacle. The sea was pounding the six foot high concrete sea defence walls built to protect three sides of the house. Suddenly the wall gave way, cracked, broke and disappeared below the waves, leaving the front of the building at the mercy of the sea. The waves pummelled the front of the house until, bit by bit, the fron wall was swallowed up, leaving the building looking like a doll's house, with the door open, showing the inside rooms and furniture. The sea continued to batter the house until parts of the inner walls, roof and pieces of furniture were claimed by the sea. A chest of drawers tottered precariously on the corner of one of the bedrooms and, each time a wave retreated leaving the chest of drawers still standing, a large cheer rose from the crowd. When the sea finally calmed down the chest of drawers was still there, the coast line was washed clean and the railway defences were severely damaged.

Two families were living in the house at the time - the Litts and the Lynns, I think. I don't know what happened to them afterwards. At one time the house was home to a former mayor of Whitehaven, Councillor John Boylan. I had been inside it a few times with his son John. The house was completely demolished later.

Parton beach could produce some surprises. I remember one day everyone rushing for the beach. The tide mark as far as the eye could see in both directions was strewn with whiting. Some say a massive shoal had been cornered in the shallows by sea pigs (porpoises) and could not escape. When I got out of school at lunchtime all the fish had gone - taken by the villagers and the gulls.

There were two Sumps on Parton beach. The one at the Parton Bay end was, I believe, a seventeenth century attempt to build on a natural foundation which jutted out into the sea in order to create a harbour. The plan was savagely laid to rest by a tide that had other ideas. There was a narrow guage rail track running alongside the Sumps, from the high water mark to the low water line. It was used to carry rowing boats down to the sea when the tide was out on a flanged wheeled flat bogie built for the job and also used by the kids to go whizzing down to the sea on. It had to be pushed back up though, as the rowing boat men would not take kindly to their bogie being left down at the low water line especially if the tide was coming in and the bogie was under it, indeed, if they caught us using it we had to flee double quick. T he rowing boats were brought up above the high tide line and onto Shore Green when not in use.

Calling it Shore Green was a bit of a misnomer. It was more Shore Funny Grey Colour and it was where the village lads played football, using jackets for goal posts. There were no pitch markings and often the two teams had more than fifteen players a side. It was also the place where men gathered to play pitch and toss for money. There was always a look out in case the village constable came along and the men were ready to scarper at a second's notice. The stakes were high in relation to their wages and the game was frowned on by the police.

The games used to take place on the seaward corner of the 'dead house' next door to the parish rooms. The parish rooms were used as a community hall for everything from a concert to a funeral tea. How old the mortuary was I know not and I only ever saw it used for its grisly purpose once and we were chased away on that occasion. A body had been found on the beach. It had been in the water a long time if my memory serves me right. More than one dead body was carried up from Parton beach in my twelve years in the village, but that was the only time I ever saw one myself.

Other things we found washed up on Parton beach included full tins of hard tack biscuits in square dark olive-green tins, with a circular lid in the centre, completely sealed from the water. They would have been fit to eat but we didn't try them as they would have broken our teeth. Timber was never in short supply and was often used to make henhouses or pigeon sheds. There were always one or two beach-combers out looking for anything of value.

There was no television then and, whenever the weather allowed, people would sit or stand on the front door step and chat with their next door neighbours, with passers by or with people across the road. We youngsters used to keep up with the gossip while pretending to play some game or other. We would then tell our parents the gossip but sometimes everything got in a muddle. I remember one day an old man from the bottom end of the village was declared dead by the top half, when in fact he was in the pub having a pint. It was his dog that was dead.

****

Our house had two bedrooms, or to be precise one bedroom and a box room. The bedroom was big enough for a double bed, a wardrobe, a chest of drawers, a small bedside cabinet and there was just enough room to squeeze in a bedding chest. It had good views of the main street and the terraced houses opposite. The box room was a different matter. There was just enough space for a single bed and eighteen inches away was a railed banister so that, if you fell out of bed you wouldn't fall downstairs. There was no privacy and no door. There was a good view though, of next door's garden and a hodge podge of dwellings in Garfield Place.

Some houses in Parton at the time had crude toilets. We were lucky enough to have a garden, and in it was a red brick building with two compartments - one for us and one for next door. We had flushing toilets but nowhere to wash our hands. We didn't use the toilet on a stormy night though as you would have to get out of bed, get dressed, go out of the front door, up the road a few yards, through the garden gate and to the glory hole. If you needed the 'facilities' in the night you used the Edgar Alan Poe (the chamber pot) which lived under the bed, with an enamel bucket on stand by. If we had had a back door it would have been much easier. I still remember cutting the daily newspaper into suitable sizes to thread onto a piece of string to hang up to use as toilet paper.

I remember, during the war, the black paper rolls fitted on the windows as black-out blinds. They had to be rolled down before lighting up time. The village constable patrolled the streets and, if he saw even the most minute chink of light he would knock on the door. We had a radio which ran on batteries which had to be charged up at a shop which also sold clothes, though not many, and these were paid for on the 'never, never' with a deposit and so much a week.

Make do and mend was the order of the day and you didn't get a new pair of everyday pants until both sides of your backside cheeks were on display. Good clothes were only for special occasions. We got what we were given and had to wear it whether we liked it or not. New clothes were two sizes too big so you would grow into them. Everyday footwear was clogs (shoes were kept for school). We had rubber or metal caulkers on our clogs. Most kids chose metal because then they doubled up as ice skates in the winter. Your clogs would collect snow on the bottoms until kids were hobbling about like walking on stilts. Sometimes kids would cut the holey foot part off stockings and have their feet bare, pulling the stockings up to make them look like hose. Kids would pull the long tail of a shirt up between the legs to make it look as if they were wearing underpants (though it could be plainly seen they were not by the holes in the back of their pants!)

****

My memories of Parton are of the old village and not of the estate on the top of brows known as Seven Acres. These new houses had inside bathrooms, toilets, water supplies, power points and gardens. They were the height of luxury in comparison with many of the hovels in the village below. Seven Acres, though part of the village, and home to many coalminers, was, and still is, separated from the old village by the sea brows but people in both parts of the village had the same everyday cares and financial woes.

Not all the men worked in the coal mines as there were a number of other industries nearby. However, most Parton men did work at the pits - mainly at the Harrington number ten and eleven mines. Some even worked at the Haig Pit at Kells and quite a number worked at the William Pit, Whitehaven. These men would walk along the wagon road, which is now a cycle path, that stretches from Parton to Whitehaven, between the Bransty cliffs and the coastal railway line.

I have recently discovered that the wagon road used to be in part a tunnel between Parton and Whitehaven to serve the Parton coal mines - possibly the Countess Pit, the Lamb Hill mine and, of course, the Lowca Foundry, Parton Brickworks and Tannery and other enterprises. The tunnel was removed at a later date and a rail track was laid which was used by the William Pit with main line coal wagons shunted back and forth along part of the track where a weigh bridge operated. We often played along the wagon road. I was fascinated by the different varieties of moths, bees and butterflies in the scrubby terrain. There were even slow worms and grass snakes plus gulls nesting on the cliffs as well as other birds. In some of narrow channels on the Whitehaven end there were also crested newts.

On Saturdays we were given a tanner each (six old pence) to go to the cinema at Whitehaven. There were three picture houses - the Gaiety, Empire, and the Queens. On Saturday afternoons all three would show a comedy, a cartoon, a serial and a feature film. Sixpence bought a ticket in the first four rows (the dog end), leaving two pence for the return train fair and a penny for sweets. My favourites were boiled sweets which we called cockroaches; you could four for a penny.

Anxious crowds await news at the William Pit gates, Saturday, 16 August 1947.

On warm days we would set off towards the train station and then double back and walk along the shore, or run along the wagon road, to save the two pence train fare to spend on something else - often a cheap toy from Beehive and Browns Shop in King Street. Money wasn't freely available then. There was little or no set pocket money, just a penny here and a halfpenny there. I carried messages from one end of the village to the other for a halfpenny. There weren't many telephones then and a message scribbled on a piece of paper given to a kid was one way of getting in touch with someone quickly. Mind, you got nothing off parents for running errands. If you refused you would get a 'clout across the lug' (a smack on the ear). But, on the whole, it was a good childhood - what we didn't know about we didn't miss. I was over fifteen before television entered my life and I still watch very little.

****

Often we used to spend two or three hours on the beach. Parents seemed to know where we were and worked on the principle that we would come home when we were hungry. No doubt everyone kept an eye out for us - Parton was a good place to live. We would play on the beach for many happy hours, or fish with hand lines. The fishing line had a home-made lead sinker on a separate length of cord tied onto the main line a few feet from the end. The end of the main cord had a fish hook tied to it which was baited with crab. A piece of dowel was fastened on further up the cord and the whole line would be looped out onto the fishing rock so it wouldn't get tangled. The baited and sinker end was then whirled around the head, gathering speed before being sent as far out to sea as possible in the hope of catching a cod or any other hungry fish.

Sometimes a friend of my parents would take me out in a rowing boat when the sea was calm. He would row about half a mile out and then cast his line while I got the job of bailing water out of the boat. I was led to believe this was an important job and only years later did it dawn on me that all wooden rowing boats took on water and it was just a case of him making me feel useful. Anyway I usually got a decent fish from him at the end of the day.

After the war we used to like having a bonfire on the beach. We would find a few bits of dry wood and paper, some shore coal and a box of matches and we built a fire in pyramid fashion with blackjack, a substance neither stone nor coal but somewhere in between. Soon we would have a glowing fire to sit around and cook on. It would last all day or until the tide covered it. We used an old container to boil periwinkles (cuvvins) and a sharp slither of wood or a pin was used to extract them from their shells. They tasted even better if you left them in a saucer of vinegar for a while. We cooked limpets (flidders) on an old piece of metal and occasionally we would catch edible crabs in the rocks and boil them. We used to bring cuvvins or crabs to the boil three times to ensure they were properly cooked and easy to get out of the shells.

This is not to say our mothers didn't feed us as they did provide substantial meals using only basic ingredients. The humble potato was used in tatie (potato) pies, tatie broth and tatie hash. With a couple of slices of bread and butter these made a substantial meal and the chip pan, frying pan and toasting fork were not fighting to keep themselves in employment either. The cheaper cuts of meat were used well - you can't make a good tatie pot without mutton - and these days all you get is lamb. When you think that all the cooking was done in tempermental ovens and on open fires it makes you realise what wonders those women were. What those housewives had to put up with would have today's housewife running towards Bransty cliffs with a view to ending it all. Their day from dawn to dusk often began at 4.30am and was an ongoing battle, yet they could laugh and joke as though they had not a care in the world - they took it all in their stride.

Our tin bath hung on the washhouse wall on a six inch spike driven into the mortar joint. It was brought into the house nearly every day and spent much of its time in front of the fire. There were no pit head showers at the William Pit. I remember my mother would close the curtains as the window looked out on to the main street. She would put sufficient cold water into it and when my father got home topped it up with boiling water out of the kettles, to achieve the right temperature. He would stand in the bath as he washed, while my mother would wash his back and rinse him down with tepid water she had at the ready; modesty was not in evidence. We would also use the bath and on bath nights it caused a bit of a kerfuffle as to who got in it first. In later years I would go to my Grandmother's at Bransty for the use of a proper bath.

Most women of the day wore a pinny and sometimes a brat. The brat was usually made from hessian and went from the waist to just below the knee, covering the front part of the body. It was hemmed at the waist for a piece of cord to go through and tied at the back. It was an essential part of a housewife's attire. The other essential was the turban like head wear or sometimes a headscarf to hide their curling pins. The brat was a versatile garment and had many uses such as carrying groceries from the shop, or clothes to and from the clothes line. In fact anything that required a bag was in the realms of the brat. It was also used to clean muck off kids' hands and faces, and some women even used a brat to carry coals from the beach.

Youngsters spent most of their time outdoors. The youngest were taken care of by older siblings or older kids. A favourite place to go on a warm, sunny, day was to catch minnows with fishing nets and jam jars in the crystal clear water of the Lowca Beck. Further down river the water was three shades blacker than jet from the coal washery and the pumps at Lowca Pit but upstream it was clean enough for paddling and catching the devilishly quick minnows.

Going up to big school from the infants school was an ordeal which had the bravest of the brave trembling with fear. The teacher in charge of the first class was one of the last true Victorian school ma'ams. She was highly respected by the adults of the village but even they were too scared to complain on 'little Johnny's' behalf. Little Johnny had to fend for himself. She ruled with an iron fist and a three foot bamboo cane. It was not advisable to even scratch your nose while she was teaching and it was safer, in a child's mind, to sit bolt upright and wet your pants rather than ask to go to the toilet. Her favourite punishment was to make you stand in the corner with the conical dunce's hat on your head. Today she would be convicted of child abuse but then her pupils were proud to say they were in her class. The secret was to behave yourself and get on with the lesson.

Parents worried about their kids but they never worried that a person would harm their children. Parton was a tight-knit community and everyone looked out for each other. Parents worried more about how their kids could be hurt by accidents in the beck, on the cliffs, the railway, etc. Parents did not wrap their offspring in cotton wool - the emphasis was on guiding them from a hard beginning to a possible harder future. For what were kids in working class villages in those days, if not factory fodder? Education was not directed towards gaining scholarships but more towards a job in the pit or other industrial complex.

Following dinner on that fateful day in 1947, around the time the William miners were heading to work via the Wagon Road, I was at the bottom of the black bank, a short cut from the beach up to Seven Acres, playing with a gang of other kids, when I spotted my father with a couple of other men walking towards the Wagon Road. Not wanting him to see me I attempted to hide, but his eyes were sharp, and by hand gesture and voice I was asked to go play nearer our house. I would do his bidding until he got out of sight, but I doubt that I would have gone right home.

Our days never seemed to have enough daylight hours in them, even though they seemed a lot longer as children, than they do as one gets older. We hated being called into the house for bedtime - there was always so much to do. It would be true to say I have been brought in by the scruff of the neck, for refusing to obey the parental order of, 'Git in this hoose before half past nine!!'

That reminds me of the time we were playing 'knocky nine doors' down the street. I would be about ten-years-old and our chant was, 'Me not know, me no tell, me bang knocker and run like hell.'

We were spotted by the village policeman, and scarpered, but I was the unlucky one. He walked me by my jacket collar all the way up the road, my feet barely touching the ground right up to our house at the bottom of Parton Brow, opened the front door (the Yale key was always in the lock) thrust me into the living room, his deep booming voice ringing in my ears, 'Mary get control of him.' The methods of child control were far different in those days than they are now.

We spent hours in the sea brows digging for 'howky horns' (pig nuts) ruining many of our parents' dinner forks int he process. These comical knobbly shaped edible tubers were the roots of an umbrella flowered plant we called 'scabby lips'. I never did know its real name but those howky horns were filling and tasty.

It was a pleasant sight on a late summer evening sitting on the beach and watching the sea pigs (porpoises) crossing the calm sea. If you didn't know you could thnk they were one creature and you'd seen the Loch Ness monster. They were so graceful and yet deadly as they hunted shoals of herring. On a clear day, if you stood on top of the sea brows and looked out on a calm blue sea, you could be lucky enough to see a silver shoal of herring crossing the placid waters.

We would fish from the Sumps, sometimes with a fishing line made from nothing more than a bobbin of cotton with a bent pin on the end and a bit of bread crust as bait on this improvised hook. We fished for 'bloffins' a fish about as big as a pilchard. At certain times of year there were thousands of them and they were so easy to catch. Herring fry were easy to catch too but, for them it was easiest to use a net often made with a bamboo cane and a cloth flour bag with a length of wire stitched around the edge to keep the neck open. Lying flat on the Sumps with the tide coming in it was easy to reach into the sea and scoop up herring fry. We never ate them, just caught them and then released them back into the sea.

We had standards as regards marine life. You would not take an edible crab (a Sandy) if it was below four inches in length. The standard measurement was literally rule of thumb as a bent adult thumb between tip and knuckle joint measures an inch. Many of us had homemade crab hooks which were roughly three feet long and made out of a metal rod, including 'mammy's fire poker' put into the coals until glowing red, rushed outside and bent over into a hook shape on the front step and batted with a hammer into shape. Crabs were hooked out of crevices in the rocks when the tide was out.

We played cowboys and Indians on the Wagon Road where there were large rocks to hide behind. I always wanted to be Geronimo with a couple of seagull feathers tied to my head. But, as these were the war years, 'Germans and English' took over as the favourite game. Some of us even had tin hats to make it more authentic and a lump of wood served as a rifle or Tommy gun. The trouble was trying to get two sides sorted out before the game - no one wanted to be German - so the Germans usually ended up as the lassies or kids who did as they were told, some in tears reluctantly agreeing to play the enemy.

Another favourite pastime was building a camp. We would dig out a hole in the ground, cover it with an old tin sheet and finish the top off with grass turfs to blend in with the scenery. We would leave a small hole as a door and cover the floor with dry grass to sit on. We had a candle in a jam jar for light and we would spend time telling jokes, ghost stories and general chatter, oblivious to the world around us.

It was not the done thing for a lad to play with a lass, at least not one to one, or you would be taunted with 'lassie lad' from the other boys. Mostly lads and lasses played separately however, sometimes, for a game that needed more players we would play together and it was acceptable for boys to join in at the girls' skipping rope games. Any game that included boys and girls ran the risk of a breakdown in relationships and some of those lasses had sharp fingernails as well as the ability to find the most vulnerable parts of a lad to attack! The girls would be sent packing though if they tried to join in on a 'proper' male game such as football.

Blackite (bramble) picking in early September was an essential part of those years. They made a pleasant change from apple or rhubarb cake. We also went rose hip picking. The hips were used to make syrup which was a good source of vitamins. We used to take the hips to an elderly woman's house up Brewery Brow where they would be weighed and we were paid tuppence a pound. To pick even half a pound was no mean feat at six-years-old, as you were covered head to toe with scratches from the rose bush thorns.

Then there were the seasonal games of relieve ho, tin whip, it, wall cricket, hop scotch, skippy, conkers, buttony, marbles - the list is endless. Why is it that today's youngsters are so bored with nothing to do? We were not little angels, but we were never bored. We did get up to mischief, but it was all in the best possible taste!

As mentioned earlier, my Mother's Grandfather, William James Brannon, was a coal miner and his brother Tom was union delegate for the William Pit. Her father, Charles Blaney started work at the pit when he was only twelve, dying young from a chest complaint. In fact my mother lost four uncles, her mother's brothers, directly or indirectly to coal mining. Uncle Tom died in the William Pit in the same disaster as my Dad and his brother Joe. Tom's brother, Joseph, died as a result of a roof fall in the William Pit hardly twelve months before. Willie James' brother had a leg mangled in a Bolton pit accident. The leg had to be amputated and he later died as a result. A fourth brother, Robert, was prone to blackouts in later life and was believed to have had one as he was using a short-cut crossing the Mirehouse railway line in Whitehaven and was killed by a coal train wagon.

Mining families knew the risks of their employment - accident or death was never far away - but those risks had to be taken as the greater concern was feeding their families. It was a case of work down the pit or go hungry.

Tom Brannon, former William Pit union delegate (born 1878) with his wife Theresa.

While we had our own washhouse, it was not the case for most dwellings, and at the top end of Parton there were three communal washhouses where women would go, usually on a Monday, to wash the bedding and heavy clothes. Many would wash smaller items in the house in a large enamel basin which was used for many other things such as mixing bread dough, washing dishes and washing hands and faces.

A lot of gossiping went on at the communal washhouse. There was a big table in each of the buildings, well worn with age, plus the dolly tubs, setpot and a mangle to squeeze out excess water. The mangle was five feet tall with two huge wooden rollers and a side wheel to turn the rollers as the clothes were fed through. If it had ever toppled over the result would have been fatal and many women preferred to wring out by hand. For blankets and sheets, one woman would take hold of two corners and another would take the other two, and then they would begin to twist the material as they moved backwards, squeezing out the water. There were also communal clothes lines as most houses only had small back yards.

Washing wasn't an easy task. First the setpot had to be half filled with water and the fire underneath it lit. Clothes were put into the setpot and stirred with a wooden paddle to boil the dirt out. They were then put into the dolly tub for further cleaning with a dolly stick or possy. The dolly stick was like a three-legged milking stool with a long handle. Next the clothes had to rinsed under the cold water tap, then put through the mangle before being hung up on the clothes line. On a wet day it was an ordeal getting things dry as there were no tumble driers or radiators. Pit clothes particularly had to be dry at all costs and the only thing was to put them on a wooden clothes airer, over the backs of chairs in front of the fire, or even in the oven. Some houses had a pulley airer fixed to the ceiling which could be raised and lowered when needed.

There were few cars in Parton back then. In fact it was an event to see one coming through the village. There were a few lorries though - the coal wagon, the brewery lorry, the potato wagon and, of course, the ice cream van. Kids used to take car numbers for a hobby and, on the main road might have to wait fifteen minutes or more for a car to come along. With such light traffic it was safe for kids to play on Parton Main Street.

Making trolleys was a big thing for many lads. They were constructed with any old wheels that could be found, nailed on to the underside of a short plank, and fixed in position with big nails bent over as axles. Today they would be considered lethal yet I can't remember any serious accidents. Parton Brow was steep and trolleys could gain quite a bit of speed but the worst that happened if you fell off were a few scrapes and bruises.

Milk was delivered by a four-wheeled hand cart with a T-shaped handle on the front for pulling. The cart was laden with milk churns and seasonal vegetables and people would go to the carts with jugs for their daily milk which was measured out with a copper jug. Women would use their brats or pinnies to carry potatoes and vegetables back to the house.

****

Friday 15 August 1947 was my parent's eleventh wedding anniversary and, on such a beautiful morning, my mother had begged my father to take us all to St Bees for the afternoon instead of going to work. This he would not do as, he had just started back after the pit holiday and had missed the first day of that week; he would not take two days off in the same week. He could manage on a four day week but was not willing to try it on three; nor did he want to let his workmate down by not going.

****

In those days Easter was a good time for youngsters, especially if the weather was good. On Good Fridays we did not eat meat so would go for a welcome treat at the fish and chip shop. It was a day when parents did not mind 'pushing the boat out' and buying fish, chips and 'krowklins' with salt and vinegar.

After dinner on Easter Sunday we would put on new clothes and visit uncles, aunts and grandparents, dressed in our Easter finery. With a bit of luck we would come loaded with 'pasche' or 'paste' eggs, sweets and even money. Chocolate eggs were hardly ever seen but most windows were decorated with brightly coloured pasche eggs which were hard-boiled and dyed with onion skins, tea leaves, gorse flowers, nettles and food colouring. Or they could be decorated with crayons, many with faces drawn on them. If Easter Monday was sunny we would trek to Lamb Hill quarry and have a cold tea with sandwiches. Then there would be Easter Monday egg rolling and sliding down the grassy slopes on big pieces of cardboard.

Rabbit was in common use and our house was never short of meat - rabbit pie went down very well. My father was a good rabbiter and I've heard some good tales about his coney poaching days from a man from Common End, Distington. They had some narrow escapes from gamekeepers but my father had been well trained by the army to avoid and escape detection. He kept ferrets at the top of the garden in an old stone building which had been the toilets before the new flushing ones were built. He also used to catch peewits, partridge and even pheasants. We would sometimes have pheasant or seagull eggs and it was rare my mother had to cook with dried egg which my mother hated using. I was a bit of a rabbiter myself in my teens, using a dog to catch them, but I stopped after seeing myxomatosis infected rabbits at close quarters, and have never eaten rabbit since.

In those days the only pre-packed meal was an Oxo cube and people had to live by their wits. It was not easy bringing up a family on a miner's wage. When I was older I used to visit a farm close to Parton where the farmer said he planted an extra stitch of chatties (potatoes) and an extra stitch of snaggers (swede) to make up for the ones that would be nicked by 'them lot down Parton'.

****

I was still a month off my seventh birthday on 15 August 1947, the day of the William Pit explosion. It is a day I will never forget; the events of that day are etched on my mind through trauma. The events of that day, exist in vivid mental pictures, a ghost that refuses to be exorcised.

It was probably one of the hottest days of the year, and on days like that in Parton, the beach would be full of families who would take their towels and dookers (swimming trunks or costumes), their sandwiches wrapped in newspaper, bottles of cold tea and head for the shore. Some basked on towels on the shingle with the *Whitehaven News* covering their faces, others swam and played in the sea or the dubs (rock pools). The Pussy Dub was a large rock pool, big enough to play and paddle in. Very few people had a 'proper' holiday in those days.

Environmentalists would throw their hands up in horror at Parton beach at that time. There were two main sewer pipes and industrial waste pipes all emptying their contents into the sea. It was not uncommon to see brown ovoid shaped objects in the sea when paddling or swimming. Mind you, the periwinkles and limpets near the outlet end of the sewer pipes were the biggest and tastiest!

People didn't complain then. The working class endured all manner of inconveniences and bore them with a straight back. The early 1940s were a time of restraint and shortage as the war was going on or had just ended. The country was havng a very hard time and effluent floating in the tide, or the adverse effects of industry, hardly got a second thought. Life had to be got on with, regardless of hardships which simply had to be overcome.

The worst thing on the beach though was tar and oil. Back then ships were not restricted as to what they could dump overboard and all manner of maritime junk washed up on the beach. None was worse than big dollops of tar and oil. You had to be careful not to lie in it or stand in it as it was difficult to remove. It wasn't unusual to find seabirds on the shore covered in the stuff. They weren't able to fly or even drag themselves along. Their attempts to flap their wings and their pitiful squawks are not easy to forget, nor the acts of mercy shown to them, by the only method known at the time. There was no way to clean them then and no sanctuary for them to be taken to.

Another danger posed by bathing at sea, came from jelly fish. We called them 'slobs'. There were days when the sea was teeming with them, especially when the sun was out. Swimmers had to be on their guard and, if you were stung, it was painful and I speak from personal experience. I would run screaming home to Mammy to get the blue bag out. It was the wonder of the time, the blue bag, as it used to be put in the wash to get bluey white clothes and down toilets to freshen them up, it was rubbed on boils even and, of course, it was the miracle cure for marine and insect stings. Looking back I realise it was more a placebo than a cure.

****

The local Sunday School was at the Methodist Chapel at Bank Yard, near to Black Bank. A full house of youngsters was guaranteed, all washed clean with our best clothes on. Parents were strict as regards appearance for Sunday School. I remember the teacher who was lame, standing at the front like a professional orchestra conductor, as he guided and bellowed us through renditions of classics such as *My Cup is Full.* I also went to the Congregational Chapel Sunday School. Most kids went to both, not because of any religious beliefs, but because you couldn't go on the annual outings unless you attended for a certain period first.

There was a boys and a girls school at Parton. The girls school also took the infant classes. The Joseph Williamson Boys School could be opened out into one large hall or split into three classrooms, simply by pushing partitions on tracks back and forth. Once you left infant school you stayed at the higher boys or girls school until you left school at fifteen, unless you passed the eleven plus test. I was still in the infant classes at the time of the William Pit explosion, though the disaster happened during the summer holiday.

Children started school after their fifth birthday. I can't remember my first day but my mother often recalled it. She took me down to school and left me with the teacher only to find me home again two hours later enthusing about how good school was. Apparently at first break I thought it was home time and ran off with glee, oblivious to the teacher frantically calling me back.

School was strict then, even in the infant classes, and there was no point running to your parents as they were on the teachers' side. A smack or even the cane across the backside was quite acceptable and discipline was just as much part of the teaching as the lesson itself. Not that discipline stopped us enjoying school. A good caning was something to boast about and the same teachers who gave you a caning were just as capable of being tender and caring people. There was a war on and discipline was high in all aspects of life and hard times were upon everyone.

My memories are rathered jumbled of those early years of school but I do remember having to line up in the school yard, each with a plastic beaker, to go to the milk cart to get our one third pint of milk every day. By the time I went to older boys school, the beakers had given way to third pint ready bottled milk. The school was heated by a cast iron stove; some used coke while others used coal. There was a guard around it and there was one stove in each classroom, attended to by the school caretaker.

By the time I was seven I could read and present understandable writing. I could tell the time and count way past my fingers. We used coloured beads on an abacus, parrot fasion reciting, wrote on a slate tablet, counted with beans in a matchbox and had alphabet cards with letters and pictures.

I vividly remember the toilet facilities of both schools which were medieval by today's standards. The boys' urinals had no tiles on the walls and floor, just a concrete floor and rendered walls. No matter how much disinfectant they used the toilets stank to high heaven as the porous render soaked it all in. The compartments with sit-on loos were however kept clean and had ample quantities of paper.

****

On the morning of the disaster I had been playing with some other boys in a valley, wooded on one side and scrub on the other, which cut down through the sea brows. There was a swing in the ghyll, with a rope fastened to a tree branch with a piece of wood tied on the bottom to sit on. Being the youngest of the group, I was not as good as the others at jumping off the bank onto the swing seat and used to grip the rope in my hands and swing out into fresh air with my legs dangling. I remember I played on the swing the morning of the explosion. It was a favourite place for village lads and lassies to play and we used to climb the trees, play Tarzan games, cut down wood to make camps and for bonfires, including Bonfire Night. I would be surprised if there's anything left of the wood now.

On Christmas morning we did not just get an apple, an orange or some nuts. We always had a proper wrapped up present, albeit those presents were way down the scale in value to what is handed out today. Christmas was not the long drawn out commercial rip off that it is today. We made our own decorations such as coloured paper chains. We picked our own holly (if not always legally) and the Christmas tree could be anything from a proper one to any tree branch with some sympathetic decoration. Christmas dinner would be a fresh cock chicken, carved and put on plates with roast potatoes and trimmings, though Yorkshire puddings made with dried egg powder were far from being as good as with proper eggs. It was a meal fit for a king and was followed by a sponge pudding and white sauce.

Christmas lasted only a short time. Many men worked on Christmas Eve, though they might finish early. Then there was Christmas Day and Boxing Day and then back to work. Those couple of days were probably enjoyed as much as a fortnight is now, simply because everything had to be crammed in. New Year's Eve and New Year's Day were not holidays then, though very few miners turned up for work on New Year's Day following the night before. And, of course, Christmas, like 'Jack shine a light night' (Halloween) and Guy Fawkes night, were the opportunity for us kids to make a few coppers door to door, with our renditions of Christmas carols, our hand made masks and candle in a jar, and Guy Fawkes who may have been no more than a three stone flour bag stuffed with paper and a face painted on with soot.

A hard frost saw us kids heading for Seven Acres on the top, where it was the custom to make an ice slide on the brow part of the concrete road, near my Uncle Joe's house. Buckets of water would be thrown down the hill for it to freeze over, and the kids and many adults would have a great time on that slide. This is where our metal caulkered clogs really came into their own. However I remember one occasion, through stupidity more than accident, I came a cropper on that slide. I had lost a caulker but still tried to slide down and fell flat on my face splitting my eyebrow wide open. I was carted into Aunt Maggie's and Uncle Joe's where I was treated as best could be, then taken to the doctor's surgery at Whitehaven to have it properly seen to.

I remember the children's war victory celebration party. The streets were lined with flags and bunting, the tables at the back of a terraced row, were laid with cakes and all manner of goodies I have not seen the likes of since. All the women had spent time cooking and preparing, each making some home-made contribution for the youngsters. Fruit, sweets and presents were handed out to all the kids and there were games. Later that night some of the adults sang and danced the night away on the square outside our house. Uncle Frank played the accordion and Uncle Joe the fiddle. It was late before us kids finally fell asleep as we had been hanging out of the bedroom window watching our elders.

****

My mother told me later that Uncle Joe, a pit deputy overman, made it plain to my grandfather and father that he was not happy about the dusty nature of the pit, in particular around the loader end. He said it was not acceptable. Joe duly put this in his reports. Considering it was the second 'coal dust' explosion which did the greatest damage, my mother was later to recall, that Joe's fears proved only too true.

My father often took me to his pigeon loft and to the shore green where he would talk with other men as he waited for a rowing boat to come in, to get some fish, or a conger eel which he would boil in the washhouse setpot to as feed for his greyhound. It wasn't a surprise to find a conger eel hanging from the washhouse wall, though my mother detested the things.

When dressed up my father was unmistakeable, with his trilby hat and suit. He was not tall but he was well put together and he wasn't shy. There was not a lot he hadn't seen in his days in the army and he spoke with an army twang, rather upmarket, slow and deliberate. My excursions with him though were in general short and rarely outside Parton. I do remember one day in particular when he walked me along the Wagon Road and into the William Pit yard to show me round all the buildings. I remember his banter with some of the workmen but don't know if he had gone to pick up his wages or to give me an insight into what my possible future could be. I remember him standing at what I think was the lamp cabin talkin to a group of fellows and I received a few friendly pats on the head and some of them made a fuss of me.

There is a little tale that my mother recalled, that I wanted to mention, though I only have vague recollections of the event. I was in the school Christmas play (performed on the parish room stage in front of all the parents). I was a shepherd but my mother could not get any sandals for me at the time. She had traipsed

Joe Hewer's grave in Moresby Church Cemetery.

around the shops but failed. Rather than be out done, she cut my Dad's trilby hat up and used the felt to make a pair. My mother said it was the biggest sacrifice he had ever made. His hat was his pride and joy. He was hatless and grumpy for a week but he finally got a new one. He was good with his hands at making things. He could stitch and embroider. He embroidered pictures when he was in the army, mainly with ships on them. There was one in our house for years with a ship on it and another with an elephant and trees. I do not know what happened to them; his parents also had a big one with a ship on it.

I recall my mother telling me that on the day of the disaster he went down the pit with his wages in his pocket. She never did receive them as they were probably thrown away with his work clothes.

****

Some time during the day of the William Pit disaster, a mate and myself had been poking about on the refuse tip at the top of the beach just under what we called Stanley's Arch, presumably named because Stanley Fisher's grocery shop was next to it. We chanced upon a large Oxo tin containing what we thought at the time to be very important documents. It was a long time later before I found out they were pool coupons. Nonetheless, to us two youngsters, they were the find of the century, a discovery of a life time, my peer closed the lid on the tin stuffed it up his Sloppy Joe (akin to a modern day tee-shirt) and off we sped to our garden to bury our treasure in a secret location... it could still be there yet.

There were five public houses in Parton at that time. They were the Station Inn, the Bugle Horn, the Sun Inn, the Lowther Arms and the Ship Inn - the last next door to my grandparents. Each pub had its regulars and did a good trade. There was a bookmakers nearby too. Miners, of course, frequented pubs and bookmakers, as did many working class men. My father, being no different, would place a small bet and pop into the pub for a pint, which was known as 'one for the wagon road.' The effects of a pint would have long gone before the men reached the mine.

That morning, my Dad would have been up at his racing pigeon loft on Brewery Brow. He shared the loft with his youngest brother, Frank. I often visited the loft and, so long as I sat quiet on a rickety hand-made seat until he got the birds down from an exercise flight, all was well and good. Pigeon men blamed anything and everything if their pigeons would not come down. The loft was nothing elaborate and was built from any old material that suited the purpose. Nonetheless, inside it was clean and bone dry and reguarly white-washed. Outside it was painted in stripes and looked the part from a distance, though you'd have had to go out to sea to get a good view of it. Below the pigeon loft was his 'duck pond', an old tin bath buried in the ground full of stagnant water and covered in algae. This didn't put off a pair of ducks messing about in it. Below this was his chicken run, complete with feeding troughs made out of lorry tyres split down the middle lengthways.

Before closing on my father's menagerie, I should mention his greyhound. Her pet name was Peggy or Peg and her racing name was Nettle. By all accounts anyone who backed her would have been stung. Our cocker spaniel, Nell, would have given it a good run, though I believe it was very good at catching hares. As my late mother would relate, 'He made money at the dog track, but it was not by backing his own dog. They were up to all kinds of tricks.'

As kids we often played on the wagon road and when the William Pit miners came into view, we would run to meet them but not to welcome them home - more to ask if they had any jam sandwiches left in their bait tins! Having said that, they were a welcome sight, with their black faces, bottles, knee pads and their bait tins dangling from their belts. For the most part they were happy to be nearing home and that happiness would be reflected towards us kids. They would have a bit of fun with us, passing us from one to another as though we were no more than rugby balls. They would even dangle us by the legs over the railway wall threatening to drop us when the train came along. Of course we knew they would do no such thing. Their threats were as empty as their water bottles. We would follow them into Parton stuffing curled up jam sandwiches into our mouths, needing a bath more than they did, having transferred much of their coal dust on to us.

****

We buried our treasure in a secret location at the top of our garden with the aid of a dining fork that, by the time the furtive task was complete, had taken on a shape that Uri Geller would have found impossible to achieve. I remember taking the fork, as near back to original shape as we could get it, into the house to sneak into the cutlery drawer hoping that its criminal use would not be detected and, if my mind serves me correctly cut two slices of bread with butter and jam for the two of us. All was well and normal.

****

And so it was, that I was happily playing with a playmate in the garden, with not a care in the world, life could not be better for a child touching seven years of age. Though night was fast approaching, the sun was still shining, and I knew the security of a working father, a good home and a good mother, when, from over the garden wall came a commotion of voices. One phrase I will never forget, though I did not understand at the time, someone was shouting in an excited voice, 'The William's gone up!

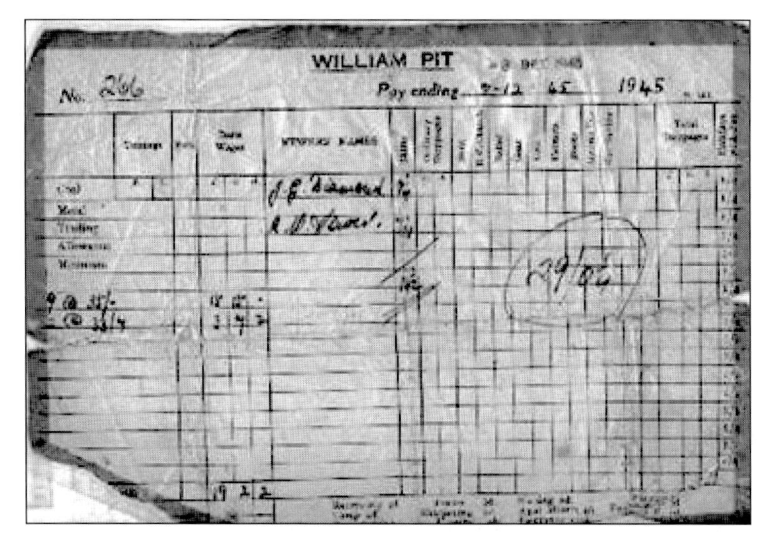
WILLIAM PIT

No. 266

Pay ending 9-12 45 1945

Ronald Hewer and his mate Joe Diamond's pay cheque for 12 December 1945. Joe was also killed that day.

EPILOGUE

Father's War Record:
Ronald William Hewer, born 1908, died 15 August 1947.
Reservist Barnard Castle Barracks. Lancashire Fusiliers, until 1942.
Placed on War Department Reserve for coal mining and home guard duty 1942-45
Dad's brother:
Joseph Wilson Hewer, born 1906, died 15 August 1947.
Home Guard, Whitehaven, William Pit.
Dad's other brothers:
Ernie Hewer, Prisoner of War, captured Calais, 1940.
Red Cross repatriation 1944 (ill health).
John Hewer, captured Calais, 1940, discharged 1945.
Benny Hewer, Prisoner of War, taken prisoner Tobruk, 1942-1945
Robert Hewer, Dunkirk and Burma Border Regiment
Frank Hewer, The youngest brother, my grandparents refused to let him sign up on grounds that they were suffering enough. Military ceded to this request.

I have listed in short my father and his brother's war records.

****

My heart is forever with the 104 men who perished down the William Pit. By August 1947 many of them had seen active service, some were discharged with the sole purpose of getting them down the pits to ease the manpower shortage.

****

Each family's celebration, and benefit from the Allied Victory was short-lived.

Joseph Wilson Hewer, with his bride Margaret.
Joe died in the William Pit disaster.

RONALD HUGHES

Ronnie

Ronnie Hughes was a twenty-year-old shift hand, at William Pit. He lived at Hospital House, Bransty, Whitehaven, with his parents and was the youngest man killed in the disaster. He was brought to the surface of William Pit on 17 August 1947 at 2.35am. Ronnie was identified by his father, John Hughes. He was the 51st miner located.

****

In loving memory of
Ronnie Hughes
Who lost his life in William Pit
August 15, 1947
We never thought that morning
That you were going to die
You left us all so suddenly
You could not say goodbye
Our memories of you are a keepsake
From which we will never part
R.I.P.
Mam, Dad, five brothers and sister,
Alice, two sisters-in-law, also Kathleen and Lorna

****

GEORGE HUTCHINSON

Brother-in-law of Richard Atkinson

George Hutchinson was 44-years-old and employed in occupations development at William Pit. He lived at 7 James Pit, Whitehaven, with his wife Margaret, and son Roland. Mr. Hutchinson was brought to the surface of William Pit at 8.55am on 17 August 1947 and later identified by his brother-in-law, John McKenzie Atkinson of 6 York Terrace, Sunnyhill, Whitehaven. He was the 20th miner found by the recovery team.

****

The fifteenth of August was a red hot day. My uncle, George Hutchinson was getting ready to go to work on the afternoon shift. His wife asked him to stay off work and take her and their son to St Bees beach. He said 'no', as they were in the middle of a heat wave and the sun and the beach would still be there at the weekend. Little did he know that he would not see his family or the beach ever again. He lived at 7 James Pit and was a face worker aged 44 years. I was on St Bees beach with my parents on that fateful day. The police came round the beach informing people that there had been an explosion at William Pit. Half of Whitehaven was at St Bees beach on that hot August day.

The only photograph I have of Uncle George is one of him when he was a child. It was taken in 1911 or 1912, after my Grandfather, John Hutchinson was killed in the 1910 Wellington disaster.

Tom Scott, nephew

Back: Uncle George Hutchinson and James Hutchinson.
Front: Sarah Hutchinson, Rose Hannah Hutchinson (my mother) and Hannah Hutchinson (my grandmother).

Treasured memories of my dear husband,
George, killed in William Pit, August 15, 1947
I lost my life's companion
A life linked with my own
And every day I miss him more
As I walk through life alone
God gave me strength to fight the blow
But what it meant to lose him
No one will ever know
Ever remembered by his loving wife and son
Also my dear brother, Dick Atkinson,
killed in William Pit disaster August 15, 1947
With sweet memories and silent tears
We will remember them

****

In loving memory of our dear brother Geordie,
who died in William Pit explosion, August 15, 1947
No more to see his smiling face
Or hear him say Hello
It came as a shock we didn't expect
A hard and bitter blow
Ever remembered by his sisters, brothers-in-law and families at home and away

In loving memory of our dear friend George,
accidentally killed in the William Pit Disaster August 15, 1947
Just sweet memories of the happy days
We all spent together
Always remembered by Sarah and children, also Kathleen and Stanley

Further memoriams for George Hutchison in the Richard Atkinson pages

****

Hutchinson/McMullen
Just a token of remembrance from his workmates
When last I saw your smiling faces
You looked so bright and well
Little did I know that day
Would be our last farewell
Rob Telfer

WILLIAM JOHNSON

William Johnson was 27-years-old and a trainee at William Pit. He lived at 43 Trumpet Road, Cleator Moor. Mr. Johnson was survived by his wife Anna May and two young daughters, Ursula and Jennifer. On the morning of 17 August 1947 at 7.35am William Johnson was brought to the surface and later identified by his mother, Norah Riley of Griffin Cottage, Frizington. May Johnson gave birth to the couple's third daughter Marjorie in the spring of 1948.

I am writing to you about my Uncle Bill Johnson who was killed in the 1947 William Pit Disaster. I remember him visiting our house in Whitehaven. He was in uniform, the RAF, and he brought me a model bi-plane which was big enough for me to sit on. So he must have seen service in the war. I know he had three daughters, my cousins who were all younger than me. I doubt very much that the youngest girls would even remember him as they would be very young. We moved to Kells shortly after, and they used to visit us there from time to time. They were at our house on the day of the disaster. It was Ursula's birthday. My Aunty May asked Bill to take the shift off and stay with us and the children, but he wouldn't. He never came back, and Aunty May was left with three little girls. The eldest would be about six. I just wanted to say that I think of my Uncle Bill now and again. I don't know what happened to that bi-plane though. I was eight-years-old when the pit disaster happened.

William Rothery, nephew

****

In loving remembrance of my dear husband, Bill
who lost his life in the William Pit explosion 1947.
No more to see his smiling face
Or hear him say hello
It came as a shock we didn't expect
A hard and bitter blow
Always remembered by his loving wife and daughters,
Mam and Dad Watson; also Mam and Frank Frizington.

****

GEORGE JOHNSON

Brother-in-law of Edward Glaister

George Johnston was a 41-year-old hewer at William Pit. A resident of 38 Lakeland Avenue, Woodhouse, Whitehaven, he was survived by his wife Mary Ann and three grown children. Mr. Johnston was brought to the surface at 8.45am on 17 August 1947 and identified by his son, William Johnston, a soldier of the same address. George Johnston was the 64th man to be located, and was also the brother of Mrs. Harriet Glaister who lost her husband, Edward, in the disaster.

In memory of a dear husband and Dad,
killed in William Pit disaster, August 15, 1947
Quickly and quietly was the call
His sudden death a shock to all
Life is eternal, love will remain
In God's own time we will meet again.
Ever remembered by his wife and family

****

JAMES W. LAMBERT

Taffy

James William Lambert was a 35-year-old brusher in William Pit. He lived at 1 Plumblands Lane, Whitehaven, with his wife Sarah Ann, and their young son and daughter. Mr. Lambert, was identified by his brother-in-law, Harold Nicholson, a boilerman of 115 Main Street, Hensingham, after being brought to the surface of William Pit at 10.18am on 16 August 1947. He was the fourth miner to be located and identified.

In loving memory of my dearest husband,
James William (Taffy),
killed in William Pit disaster August 15, 1947
When last we saw your smiling face
We were so happy and well
Little did I dream that day
I would never see you again
Will always be remembered by his loving wife and two children.

In loving remembrance of Jim (Taffy)
accidentally killed in William Pit disaster August 15, 1947.
From Harold, Ada, and all at 55 Market Place, Whitehaven

****

THOMAS LANCASTER

Tosh

Thomas Lancaster was 27-years-old, and employed as a brusher at William Pit. He lived at 33 Basket Road, Prospect, Whitehaven. Mr. Lancaster was a single man, and his next of kin is listed as his parents, John Weightman Lancaster and Jane Lancaster. In the early morning hours of 17 August 1947, at 3.40am, Thomas was brought to the surface of William Pit and later identified by his brother William Lancaster of the same address. Mr. Lancaster was the 57th man found in the William Pit disaster.

My uncle, Thomas Lancaster, nicknamed Tosh was one of the men killed in the William Pit disaster, aged 27. He was never married and as I, together with my brother, are the only remaining members of the family, adding his name to your book is my responsibility.

Tosh with his niece Betty and mam Jane.

To be killed in the 1947 explosion was really ironic, whilst the pit was closed earlier he was sent to work at Lowca No 10, a pit he really hated. As soon as William Pit opened again he went back to work there. These things are meant to be.

He was a smashing uncle, always full of fun, and a great brass band enthusiast. I still think of him each time I hear brass band music.

I must say I feel very emotional and also very guilty, you know more about Tosh than I do. My only excuse is that I was only fourteen at the time and things were never discussed in front of the young people. Also all reference to the explosion seem to have disappeared after the deaths of my grandparents.

As requested, the family names are as follows - the eldest, my mother, was Elizabeth Lancaster known as Lizzie, then there was Hannah, William known as Lanc, then Tosh, then the youngest Joseph. They also had a cousin Stanley who was brought up as their brother. He was the son of my grandfather's sister. As an after thought, my uncles were very keen pigeon racers, especially Lanc. I hope this little bit of information is of use.

Betty Cullen, niece.

Photographs, top, Tosh Lancaster, left, and his brother Lanc; bottom left, Tosh in uniform and right, Tosh and his nephew.

****

Thomas Lancaster,
beloved son of John and
Jane Lancaster
who was killed in the
William Pit,
August 15, 1947.
Hard was the blow, the
shock severe
To part with the one we
loved so dear
*Never one day forgotten
by his loving Mam, Dad,
sisters and brothers,
brother-in-law, niece and
nephew at
Fleswick Avenue*

WILLIAM HARKER LEE, M.M.

William Harker Lee, M.M., was a 27-year-old brusher at William Pit. He lived at 16 Thwaiteville, Kells, Whitehaven, and was survived by his wife, Julia Lee. Other reports have his home address as Aldby Street, Cleator Moor. On 17 August 1947 at 6.25am, Billy Lee was brought to the pit surface and later identified by his father, Jacob Lee, of the same address. William Harker Lee M.M. was the 18th man located in the William Pit disaster.

My name is Marj Nicholson, née Lee. My uncle, William Harker Lee M.M., was lost in the disaster at William Pit. He was born on 10 January 1920, and enlisted at Whitehaven 2 May 1939 and joined the Border Regiment. His army no. was 3599849. He was taken prisoner at Dunkirk, though we are not sure which camp he was taken to, but we know that he escaped, and walked through six countries to get back to England. It is believed that he brought something back with him which was a great help to the war effort, for which he was awarded the military medal. He went back to the pit after the war and the rest is history. He was 27-years-old. His family are very proud of him. My only brother was named after him.

Marj. Nicholson, niece.

Whitehaven Soldier's amazing escape from Germans

Severely wounded in battle around Dunkirk in France in June 1940, twenty-year-old Pte William Lee was taken prisoner by the Germans. Suffering from shrapnel wounds in the back and stomach, and having four machine-gun bullets in his legs, he was taken to a British Field Hospital. He was in the hospital when Dunkirk fell.

When he was fit enough to travel he was given a prison uniform and transferred to a German prison camp. He was determined to escape, and at the first opportunity he stole a key from the guard room and with a friend from Birmingham they made their escape.

They acquired some civilian clothes, money and food, and set off on foot for Switzerland. They made their way through Holland and towards Luxembourg, but with no chance of getting through German occupied Holland they turned back and headed towards Belgium. Due to the fact that all the bridges were under German guard, they had to swim over numerous canals as they journeyed south. When they reached French soil, they were helped by members of the French Resistance. They then set off towards Spain which they eventually reached after an arduous crossing of the Pyrenees. As soon as they reached Spain they were arrested and placed in a Spanish jail. They were released after 60 days and put on a ship bound for England. Altogether the journey lasted five months and covered hundreds of miles on foot before reaching England and home.

On his return home William stated, 'Now I have to go back to hospital to have the remains of the bullets and shrapnel removed; what will happen after that I don't know. I can tell you I am more than glad to be home again, but I rather miss my pals.'

For his determination to escape, and the courage that was shown during his travels through German occupied Belgium and France, he was awarded the Military Medal. In 1941, Pte William Harker Lee of the Border Regiment, travelled to Buckingham Palace to be presented with his Military Medal by King George VI. His award was reported in the *London Gazette,* 4 March 1941. On the 15 August 1947, after only ten weeks working at William Pit, William Harker Lee, aged 27, was one of the 104 miners who perished in the disaster.

Ray Devlin

****

A telephone conversation I had with a family friend, Mr. John Lowrey of Monkwray, Whitehaven, resulted in a discussion about William Harker Lee M.M, as the two had been friends in childhood as well as fellow soldiers in the King's Own Royal Border Regiment during World War II.

At Dunkirk, after Billy Lee had been wounded, his old friend John Lowrey had helped lift him in the back of a medical lorry, and watched the vehicle travel off down the road.

Back in Whitehaven, after the war, John and Billy caught up with each other. John asked Billy what had happened to him after the van had left. Billy told John that it had travelled no more that 400 yards down the way before being captured by the German unit. Billy then spent time in a prisoner of war camp, before making the heroic escape that would earn him the Military Medal.

In August 1947, John Lowrey then serving on the Haig Pit rescue squad, was asked to assist in the recovery efforts at the William Pit disaster. Standing at the fresh air base, John was called upon to bare a stretcher to the shaft, and looking down he realized he was carrying the body of his friend.

John said, 'I helped lift him into the back of that lorry at Dunkirk, and there again, I helped lift him into the daylight after the William Pit disaster. He was a great guy. A great guy.'

****

In loving memory of my dear brother,
William Harker Lee, M.M. aged 27 years,
killed in the William Pit disaster,
August 15, 1947.
Deep in our hearts his memory is kept
We loved him too dearly to ever forget
The tragic way he had to die
We shall always remember and wonder why
Evelyn, Bill and Evelyn

Treasured memories of
William Harker Lee, M.M.
Aged 27 years who was killed in
William Pit disaster
August 15, 1947
Some may forget you now you have gone
But we will remember no matter how long
Auntie Tissie and Uncle Matt
and grandmother

JAMES LEESON

James Leeson was a 48-year-old brusher at William Pit. He lived at 10 Dyke Street, Frizington, with his sister, Mrs. Bridget Henrudy and her family. Mr. Leeson was brought to the pit surface at 2.00pm on 17 August 1947 and identified by his brother Joseph Leeson of 26 Yeathouse Road, Frizington.

****

In loving memory of my
dear brother Jim
killed in the William Pit Disaster
August 15, 1947.
In the shelter of thy sacred heart
Sweet Jesus
Let him rest
Always remembered by his brothers, sisters, nephews and nieces

****

DENNIS LYONS

Dennis Lyons was a 31-year-old fan-man at William Pit. He lived at 4 Lakeland Avenue, Whitehaven. His next of kin was listed as his mother, Mrs. Bridget Lyons of 49 Butler Road, Harrow, Middlesex, a widow. Mr Lyons was raised to the surface of William Pit on 18 August 1947 at 4.55pm and identified by his brother Neil Lyons also of 49 Butler Road, Harrow. Dennis was the 71st miner located by recovery teams.

****

JOHN HENRY MADDISON

Harry

John Henry Maddison, 'Harry', was a 22-year-old hewer at William Pit. He was survived by his wife Martha Torrence Maddison and two young sons, John Henry (also known as Harry) aged two, and ten-week-old James. The family lived at 72 Fell View Avenue, Woodhouse, Whitehaven. In the early morning hours of 17 August 1947, at 3.40am, Harry Maddison was brought to the surface of William Pit and formally identified by his father, Robert Maddison of 11 Snaefell Terrace, Seacliffe, Whitehaven. Mr. Maddison was the 52nd coal miner located by the recovery team.

Five days after the William Pit disaster, the Maddison family suffered a further tragedy. Harry and Martha's infant son died on 20 August 1947 a victim of gastroenteritis. Harry Maddison and his son James were buried together at Whitehaven cemetery.

Martha Maddison, was later employed as a screen-lass at William Pit. She never remarried, and died at the age of 47 years. Mrs. Maddison was laid to rest with her husband and son. Harry Maddison served as the best man at his friend Adam Raby's wedding and can be seen on the groom's right on the photograph shown on the Raby pages.

Martha Torrence Maddison at the resting place of her beloved husband, Harry, and infant son, James.

****

In loving memory of my dear husband Harry, killed in William Pit disaster August 15, 1947; also our son, James Torrence Maddison, died August 20, 1947 aged 10 weeks.
We never heard his last faint sigh, we never saw him die
We only know he passed away
And could not say goodbye
From his wife and son Harry and all at 72 Fell View Avenue

****

Fond memories of Adam and Henry, lost in William Pit disaster, August 15, 1947
Not today but every day
In silence I remember
Always remembered by Willie at 12 Coniston Road

Photograph courtesy of Ray Devlin.

In loving memory of our dear son, Harry killed in William Pit disaster August 15, 1947; also our dear little grandson, son of above died August 20, 1947, R.I.P.
On whose soul sweet Jesus have mercy
When last we saw your smiling face
You looked so bright and well
Liilte did we think that day
Would be our last farwell
Never one day forgotten by his loving Mam, Dad and Bob

In loving memory of our dear brother, Harry killed in the William Pit disaster August 15, 1947; also my dear brother Charles, who died August 22, 1941
Their life is a beautiful memory
Their death is a silent grief
Always remembered by his sister Marjory, brother-in-law Jimmy, children Raymond and Carole

****

JOSEPH BANKS MARSHALL

Joseph Marshall was 48-years-old and a shift-hand at the William Pit. He was a widower who lived at 70 George Street, Whitehaven. He was survived by two children, a son aged seventeen, and a daughter aged nineteen, of the same address. Mr. Marshall was brought to the surface of William Pit at 5.15pm on 17 August 1947, and identified by his brother James Marshall of 69 Church Street, Whitehaven. Joseph was not given an order of location number, but was one of six William Pit miners who received a separate designation, his being Special 2. He had been working with Joseph Fox on the main intake road leading to Wellington Pit.

In loving memory of our dear father, Joseph Banks Marshall, beloved husband of the late Doris Marshall, killed William Pit disaster August 15, 1947.
We cannot tell the pain he bore
We did not see him die
We only know he passed away and did not say goodbye
Always remembered by his loving son and daughter, also Bill and Sally

In loving memory of my dear brother, Joseph Banks Marshall accidentally killed in William Pit disaster August 15, 1947.
In our home you are fondly remembered
Sweet memories cling around your name
Hearts that loved you in deepest affection
Will love you in death just the same
From Jim, Margaret, wee Margaret, Betty, Hensingham; Jimmy H.M. Forces; also all in Nanaimo, Canada.

WILLIAM MARTIN

Bill

William Martin was a 32-year-old coal cutter. He lived at 3 Wellington Row, not far from William Pit, with his wife Sarah and young son and daughter. He was formally identified by his uncle, Thomas McLaughlin a coal cutter of 5 Gores Buildings, Whitehaven, and was brought to the surface on 17 August 1947. He was the thirteenth man located. After a funeral service at St. James Church, William Martin was laid to rest at Whitehaven Cemetery on 20 August 1947.

****

In loving memory of a dear husband and Dad,
William Martin,
accidentally killed in the William Pit disaster August 15, 1947
We've many a lonely heartache
And shed many a silent tear
Just wishing with all our hearts Bill
That you were only here.
Dearly loved and sadly missed by his loving wife Sarah and children Sheila and Brian

In loving memory of a dear son and brother, William
accidentally killed in William Pit Disaster August 15, 1947
Deep in our hearts a memory is kept
Of a son we loved and never forget
God took him from us without farewell
How deep is our sorrow no one can tell
Sadly missed by Dad, Mam and Annie; also Ada, Peggy, Will and Leslie

In ever loving memory of our dear son-in-law William,
who fell asleep in William Pit disaster August 15, 1947
Always in our thoughts
Ever remembered by all at Preston Street, Ravenglass, Chingford, Barrow and Canada

Treasured memories of a dear brother, William,
accidentally killed in William Pit disaster August 15, 1947
Some may forget you as years pass on
But we will remember no matter how long
Ever remembered by Kathleen and Stanley

In loving memory of our dear friend, Billy Martin
who was killed in William Pit explosion August 15, 1947
Fondest memories of bygone days
When we were all together
Ever remembered by Maggie and Ronnie

****

ISAAC McALLISTER
and his son
EDWARD McALLISTER

Isaac McAllister, aged 54, was employed as a shift hand at William Pit. He lived at 15 Bentinks Row, Back Ginns, Whitehaven, with his wife Elizabeth Ann and two of their eight children. Isaac was brought to the pit surface at 8.15am on 17 August 1947 and identified by his son-in-law William McQuilliam of 25 Back Ginns, Whitehaven.

Edward McAllister son of Isaac, was 24-years-old and a brusher at William Pit. A resident of the Sun Inn, Parton, he was survived by his wife Mary and two young children. Mr. McAllister was identified by his brother-in-law William McQuilliam of 25 Back Ginns, Whitehaven, after he was raised to the surface of William Pit at 3.50pm on 19 August 1947.

Whitehaven Colliery Recreation Bowling Club, district bowling league winners, 1930.
Back row: J. Martin (president), Isaac McAllister (killed in William Pit 1947), I. Walker, John McAllister (Isaac's brother and father of William McAllister, the William Pit manager), J. Moore, J. Richardson and B. Finnigan.
Front row: G. Fitzsimmons, W. Hodgson, W. Jimby, R. Fitzsimmons (secretary), T. O'Pray, William Hector McAllister (Isaac's brother).

Edward McAllister.

I am the youngest of the three surviving children of Isaac McAllister. Our family lost three members in the William Pit disaster: my father, Isaac, aged 54, a father of eight; my brother Edward, aged 24, father of two; and my brother-in-law, Andrew Agnew, aged 36, and father of two.

The manager of William Pit at the time was my cousin William McAllister. Among the rescue teams were my oldest brother Isaac McAllister and my brother-in-law Bill McQuilliam, both worked down Haig Pit and came off shift at the Haig to join in the search and rescue.

My father had eight children, Bridget who married Andrew Agnew who also died in the disaster, Edna who married Bill McQuilliam, Isaac, Edward (also killed); Jinnie who married Harry Birkett (whose brother John Birkett was one of the three survivors); Tom; John, and myself.

I have a clear remembrance of my Dad taking my niece Hazel Agnew and myself (I was only 18 months older) to a little shop in the Ginns district. He lifted Hazel onto the counter and asked the lady, 'Susan, do you have anything for my lasses today?' Susan pulled out a cardboard box with Cadbury's chocolates, individually wrapped in tissue paper. It is a lovely memory. Sadly Hazel died on an Easter Saturday, when she was only three-years-old.

Our large extended family, still mostly live in the Whitehaven area and we still share many memories and anecdotes with younger members. We try to keep the memories alive. *Doreen Linton (née McAllister), daughter and sister*

Bill McQuilliam, left, and Ike McAllister, junior, right, enjoying a pint. Bill identified his father-in-law and brother-in-law. Ike, who also lost his father and brother, identified his brother-in-law, Andrew Agnew.

In loving memory of my dear husband and son,
Isaac and Edward McAllister;
also my son-in-law Andrew Agnew,
all killed in the William Pit Disaster,
August 15, 1947.
In the shelter of Thy sacred heart
sweet Jesus let them rest
R.I.P.
Always remembered by their loving wife and mother Elizabeth Ann
and all at 15 Bentinks Row

****

In loving memory of a dear husband and Daddy,
killed in William Pit disaster August 15, 1947
The dearest Dad this world could hold
A loving smile and a heart of gold
Dearer to us than words can tell
Was the Dad we lost and loved so well
Ever remembered by his loving wife and children,
also father-in-law and brother-in-law, Sun Inn, Parton

****

JAMES McMULLEN

Jimmy

Cousin of Billy McMullen and Robert Glosson Mulholland

Jimmy McMullen was a 27-year-old deputy at William Pit. He lived at 16 Sandhills Lane, Whitehaven, with his wife Ella and two little boys, James and Raymond. In the early evening of 19 August 1947 at 6.25pm, Jimmy was brought to the surface of the pit and later identified by his brother, William Thomas McMullen of Hill Top Road, Arrowthwaite, Whitehaven. James McMullen was the 93rd miner located by the rescue and recovery team.

****

Ella and James McMullen

My father James McMullen was one of the 104 men who lost their lives on that day. He was a foreman down William Pit and was 27 years of age when he was killed.

He was the son of Thomas McMullen, a coal miner, and Alice McMullen formerly Kenmare. They had two other children - a daughter Alice, and a son Thomas who was also a coal miner. My mother's name was Helen but she was better known as Ella. Her maiden name was Starkey. Her mother was Florence Starkey and her father was William Starkey.

There is not a lot I can tell you about my father as I was only five-years-old at the time and my brother Raymond was only three-months-old. One thing that I can always remember is the day Dad took me to William Pit to show me where he worked. I don't know how this was arranged, but I was allowed to ride the cage down to the bottom of the shaft, and without getting off we went back up to the surface. He said to me 'never get a job down the mines.' He took me to the canteen where I was treated to a meat and potato pie and chips.

My mother never remarried. She brought us both up on her own, with a struggle. Sadly we lost Mam eight years ago at the age of 79. I also lost my brother Raymond just after Christmas last year at the age of 59. *James McMullen, Jr, son*

Deputy James McMullen inadvertently saved the life of miner Frederick 'Geordie' Smith, after instructing him to find two tins of oil that had been sent down the pit in an empty tub. Geordie's journey through the workings of William Pit in an attempt to find the tins of oil resulted in him being on the 'right side' of the explosion. Mr. Smith's testimony was heard at the subsequent inquest.

Jimmy and Ella, wedding day, 12 April 1941.

****

Treasured memories of a dear
husband and Daddy,
James McMullen,
killed in the William Pit disaster
August 15, 1947.
In memory we see him
just the same,
As long as we live we shall
treasure his name
Deep in our hearts
he lives with us yet
We loved him too dearly
to ever forget
Always remembered by
his loving wife, and sons
Jimmy and Raymond

****

In loving memory of
my dear son James,
who died in the William Pit explosion August 15, 1947
Death is a heartache
no one can heal
Memories are keepsakes
no one can steal
Beautiful memories are
all that are left
Of one we loved dearly
and shall never forget
Never one day forgotten by his Mam, Tom, Alice,
Jean and Geordie.

WILLIAM TELFORD McMULLEN

Billy or Mac

Cousin of James McMullen and Robert Glosson Mulholland

William Telford McMullen was 22-years-old and a coal hewer at William Pit. He lived at 20a Roper Street with his wife Margaret and infant daughter Pauline. Known as Mac or Billy, he was brought to the surface on 17 August 1947 at 7.50am and identified by his father-in-law William Shrubb of 55 Valley View Road, Greenbank, Whitehaven. Billy McMullen was the 23rd man located.

His cousins James McMullen and Robert Mulholland also died, as well as his marra Thomas Fox.

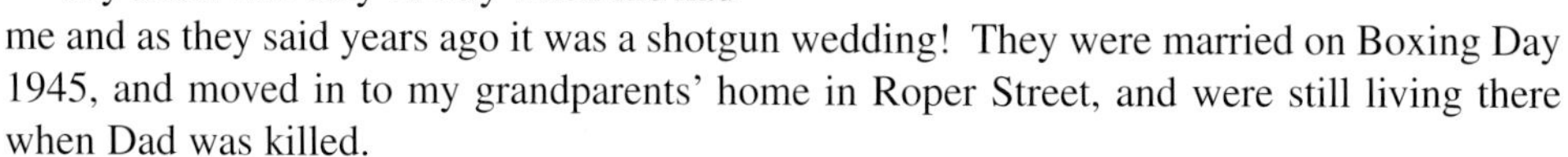

****

I am not sure how much I can help with this book but I really admire what you are doing. My Dad's sister Eliza Walker is still alive and may be able to add something more about him.

My Mam was only twenty when she had me and as they said years ago it was a shotgun wedding! They were married on Boxing Day 1945, and moved in to my grandparents' home in Roper Street, and were still living there when Dad was killed.

Apparently he wanted a little boy and told Mam if it was a girl I would be sent back! My name was going to be Terry or Billy after my Dad. Thank goodness he loved me to bits, so I am still here! Telford, my Dad's middle name is a family name and was his mother's maiden name. I think things were probably very normal in our family, although a lot of cousins and relatives all seemed to live at my grandparents' house at different times, it was very spacious. There are two definite distinct things that happened on the day of the disaster; according to my Mam I cried when my Dad went to work that day, which I had never done before, and he almost didn't go to work.

It was a nice day and my Mam tried to get him to take us to the beach, he was going to, but it was pay day and he would have had to go to pick his pay up at the office the following day, so he changed his mind. Another thing was my Grandmother was shopping in Workington and when she went to get on the train she said to my Great Aunt Agnes (her sister-in-law) that she didn't want to get on the train, something was 'up'.

William McMullen, groom, with his bride Margaret, Boxing Day, 1945.

I have been in touch with my Mam's sister (who incidentally is one of the bridesmaids on their wedding photograph) and she said she is sure Mam and Dad met at the Empress Ballroom. They were both keen dancers and Mam went dancing with her girlfriends for many years after Dad was killed. She did remarry but I don't think my stepfather could dance. Another bit of information that I remember being told, a friend or relative of my Dad's (not sure who) left the shift after starting because he was ill, and as he was walking away met someone running to the pit head, when he asked what was up, he was told the pit had 'gone up' he apparently said it couldn't have as he'd just come up. It seemed to happen so quickly.

Mam also said when the three men who survived were found she said that Mac would be saved because he was only little and would find an air pocket like they had. This is the bit that makes me cry as my Dad was only about five feet six inches tall. I remember one of the men who survived went on the compensation trip with us to Czechoslovakia when I was ten. He gave a speech about the disaster and it was very moving, although he could hardly speak for crying.

Billy was what everyone called my Dad but Mam always referred to him as Mac. I have two cousins named after him, one of his sisters called her eldest son Billy and his brother who was only sixteen when Dad was killed also named one of his boys Billy.

You asked what some of the men were like before the disaster, things they liked to do. My Dad played rugby as Mam said he had two false teeth at the front as they were knocked out when he played once - no mouth guards in those days. The men in the family liked to play cards, probably on Sunday afternoons. I know when I was a little girl there used to be a small table with a green baize top. I think this was the card table.

Something that sticks in my mind that my Mam used to say — in Dad's family there were

Billy McMullen's only child, daughter Pauline.

some cousins who died in their teens or early twenties. I think, it was from tuberculosis, which was very common and untreatable at the time. He often told Mam she wouldn't have him long because he always thought he would catch it. He would never have a cup of tea if they went to visit the family in case he caught it. It is quite ironic, he died young, but not from what he dreaded. This is also a memory that makes me cry, and I found it hard to write down.

I am posting the photographs in the morning. I hope you can use them, I am so proud of what my Dad was, but never, ever, would I have let any of my sons become a miner and neither would Mam let my two half brothers.

Pauline Hughes
(née McMullen), daughter

****

Treasured memories of our dear brother Billy,
killed in the William pit disaster August 15, 1947
If you have a loving brother, treat him with love and care
For you never know his value
Till you see his empty chair
Loved and longed for always by Annie, Canny and babies

Treasured memories of our dearest son, Billy, also Daddy of Pauline
Killed in the William Pit Disaster August 15, also his cousins Bob and James
Days of sadness still come o'er us
Silent tears do often flow
Memory keeps our loved ones near us
Though he died one year ago
Loved and longed for always by his Mam and Dad,
Brother and sisters, Mudd, Jimmy, cousins at home and away

VINCENT McSHERRY

Vincent McSherry was 38-years-old and employed as a brusher at William Pit. He lived at 2 Crummock Avenue, Woodhouse, with his wife Catherine and two sons, Wilfred and Vincent. Mr. McSherry was brought to the surface of William Pit on 17 August 1947, at 2.35am, and formally identified by his brother Lawrence McSherry of 53 Bransty Road, Whitehaven. Vincent was the 14th miner located.

****

I was born in 1950 so I didn't know my Uncle Vincent. However I felt as though I knew him because my mother kept him alive with her memories. My mother was the only girl among four surviving brothers and Vincent was the family favourite, everybody loved Vincent. He was fourteen years older than my mother and I think he spoiled her a little.

My grandfather had been a miner and two of his four surviving sons (Michael, had died in infancy) Vincent, and Wilfred went down the pit. Vincent and Wilfred, along with a lot of other miners, were also in the Territorial Army and when the Second World War broke out they went off to war. Wilfred survived Dunkirk and was sent to Burma and Vincent was picked for the 1st Airborne Division where he served as a sergeant and saw action in North Africa, Sicily, Italy and Arnhem. He was taken prisoner at Arnhem in September 1944 and was finally freed by Patton's American Army in 1945.

He came home, but never spoke much about his war experiences; neither did Wilfred or my mother's other two brothers - I think they just wanted to get on with their lives. Vincent went home to his wife and two small sons and back to William Pit. Wilfred went back to Lowca Pit but was laid off and went down to Mansfield in Nottinghamshire, where he later married. My grandmother, who became ill with tuberculosis towards the end of the war, lived just long enough to see her four sons home safe from the war and they all carried her coffin at her funeral.

My mother told me on the day of the 15 August it was red hot. She still lived at home with my grandfather at Bransty, right on the front overlooking the sea.

Grandad had left the pits and was working at the pram factory in the Ginns and was on the afternoon shift. Strangely on the way to work he met Vincent at the bottom of Bransty Brow; Vincent was on back shift and on his way to William Pit. My grandfather later told my mother he had tried to persuade Vincent to give work a miss. They both liked a pint, but Vincent was not himself, he appeared to be in a bad mood which wasn't like Vincent. He said he had to go to work - it was 'bull week' and he needed the money for his family. So my grandfather stood for a while and watched as Vincent walked to the pit and his fate.

Later that day my mother was sitting on the front step after work, having a cup of tea when a young lad she knew, from Parton, ran past.

'Haven't you heard, pit's gone up!'

'Which pit?' asked my mother.

'William,' he replied. She knew Vincent was on back shift and she literally ran from the top of Bransty to the Ginns to tell my grandfather. She told me she couldn't speak when she got there and it took a little while to get the words out. They, like so many other Whitehaven families, made their way to the pit to wait for news.

Meanwhile my mother's brother Lawrence, who was a bus driver, had heard the news and made his way to the pit. Although he had never been down a pit in his life, he volunteered to join one of the rescue parties. I think because he had a close resemblance to Wilfred, and was often mistaken for him, they thought it was Wilfred and let him go down with the search party. Lawrence helped carry his brother out. This act of bravery was reported in the *Whitehaven News* at the time. They laid Vincent in one of the pit buildings beside his marras. Later my grandfather had to go and identify him; my mother went with him and she said she spotted him right away because of his size. She said he only had one small cut on his forehead.

Vincent stood out because he was big lad, over six feet tall, and the doctor remarked on this. My grandfather told him he had been with the 1st Airborne Division at Arnhem and the doctor wept and said, 'What a bloody waste.' My mother told me she didn't know a family that hadn't lost a loved one that day. There weren't enough gravediggers so the miners dug the graves for their marras. Every day there were funerals.

On the day of Vincent's funeral she stood by his grave holding the hands of his two small sons. This was a bad time for my grandfather, John McSherry. He had been elected a councillor in 1932 and had been elected as Mayor of Whitehaven in May 1947 until May 1949. He was the last Mayor to serve for two years. He was later elected an Alderman of the borough. He had to put aside his personal grief because of his position and he was also part of the committee set up to deal with the widows and orphans. He never got over the loss of his beloved son, and he died in September 1954 aged 66 of heart failure. My mother always said he died of a broken heart. All the family kept Vincent's memory alive with stories about him, about his courage, his generosity, and his good nature, but if I can say one thing about him, it is that he was much loved.

I also remember my mother telling me Vincent also loved the social side of the Territorials and loved to be involved with the dances held at the Drill Hall in Whitehaven. I don't know why, I cannot write prose, but I have felt compelled to write these words in his memory,

Do not weep for me
I am at rest
I have crawled deep in the earth
With men who toiled and died to bring warmth to the nation
I am at rest
Do not weep for me

Do not weep for me
I am at peace
I have soared above clouds
With men who have fought and died to bring peace to the nation
I am at peace
Do not weep for me

Do not weep for me
I am eternal
I have walked in the light
With Him who died on the cross to bring love to the nation
Do not weep for me
I am eternal

I am sure the families who lost their loved ones on that day have other poignant stories, this is my family's. My family are Roman Catholics and my mother always believed the Blessed Virgin took those 104 men straight to heaven with her, because the 15 August is the feast of the Assumption of our Lady. My mother died on the 17 July 1994. Only Uncle Wilfred is still alive from that generation. *Eleanor Anderson, niece*

Back, left to right: Lawrence McSherry, John McSherry, Wilfred McSherry. Seated, left to right: John McSherry senior, Vincent McSherry, Eleanor McSherry, Eleanor McSherry

This is the report from *The Whitehaven News,* 21 August 1947, and is being used in these pages as the late Lawrence McSherry's memorial to his brother:

BUS DRIVER CARRIED OUT BODY OF HIS BROTHER

First time down mine - entered explosion area to find brother

On Tuesday there came to light a story which aptly illustrates the daring, initiative, and unselfishness of West Cumberland mining families.

It tells of a man's disregard for his own personal safety: of a man who although he had never been down a pit in his life, not only went underground but entered the explosion area and helped carry to the surface the body of his brother.

On Saturday night, Lawrence McSherry (30), married, with a wife and two young children, and who is a bus driver in Kendal, came through to Whitehaven for news of his brother, Vincent, one of the missing men. At about 8.30pm a call was made for six miners to form a stretcher party. Without a moment's hesitation Lawrence stepped forward and was accepted. He told a 'News' reporter, 'Someone said 'Hello Mack' mistaking me for another brother, Wilfred, who formerly worked in a nearby mine. They asked me how long it was since

I had been down a pit. I was unable to answer them, so I said 'Never mind about that, let's get going."

'All I had with me was my suit, so I borrowed a pair of old pit trousers from the pit top, and with a lamp and a helmet I went down the mine.'

'We went into the explosion area and I helped carry number thirteen body to the shaft, then I learned that number fourteen body was that of my brother, Vincent, so I swapped places with another member of another stretcher party so that I could go back for him. I then helped to carry him to the surface.'

Asked how he felt being down a pit for the first time, especially under such dangerous conditions, Lawrence replied, 'I had no feelings at all, all I was concerned about was getting my brother.'

Lawrence served with the Hampshire Regiment at Dunkirk, but was invalided out in 1941 following an accident. His brother, Vincent, was 37, and leaves a widow and two young children at Woodhouse Road, Greenbank. He had a fine war record. He served with the 1st Borders at Dunkirk, and, after airbourne training, fought in North Africa, Sicily, and Italy.

While fighting at Oosterbrooke, with the 1st Airbourne Division as senior NCO of his battalion, he was injured by the blast from a mortar bomb. While in St. Joseph's Hospital, at Arnhem, he was taken prisoner and was later flown home to England. He returned to William Pit about a year ago and recently joined the Territorials as an instructor.

The younger brother, Wilfred, fought at Dunkirk at the age of seventeen and was wounded in Burma while serving with the 9th Borders. He now trains Bevin Boys at Nottingham. Alderman John McSherry, the father, worked in William Pit for many years before retiring recently; he escaped the 1941 explosion.

****

Vincent was my elder brother. He was a wonderful brother. He had a very sunny nature, always laughing and joking. He loved his garden and I'm sure he kept pigeons like a lot of miners did. He was also very proud of his two sons. We were in the Territorials together and we joined the Border Regiment together at the same time when war was declared. He was in the Airborne and I was with the British Expeditionary Forces rescued at Dunkirk then I was sent out to Burma. We were all devastated when he died, sadly I was away in Mansfield at that time. *Wilfred McSherry, brother*

Vincent McSherry aged 37, was a soldier in the Second World War. He was a Platoon Sergeant in the Border Regiment, seeing action in Dunkirk and Sicily. He then volunteered for the Airborn Division. He was accepted and fought at Arnhem. He was taken prisoner at Arnhem. He was a time served plumber, but work was scarce after the war so he found work at William Pit. On the day of the disaster I remember going for his pay with him as he was always on the back shift and all the men were sitting on the pit top waiting to go down. They were having a smoke and chatting and cracking jokes. After a while I left and came home with my Dad's pay. Later on that day, after being on Wellington Beach, I went home for tea. It was then I was told that the disaster had happened. *Vincent McSherry, Jr, son*

In loving memory of my dear husband, Vincent,
Killed in William Pit Disaster, August 15, 1947
He had a nature you couldn't help but loving
A heart of purest gold
And to those who knew and loved him
His memory will never grow old
From his loving wife and sons

JOHN MILBURN

John Milburn, was 40-years-old and worked as a brusher at William Pit. He lived at 94 Grasmere Avenue with his wife Hetty and children John, Raymond and Mary. In the early morning hours of 16 August 1947 at 4.30am, John was raised to the surface of William Pit and later identified by his oldest son John Joseph Milburn, of the same address. John Milburn was the seventeenth man to be reached by search and rescue workers.

My father was James Milburn, who was born Cleator Moor in 1920. He had a brother John who died in the 1947 mining disaster. I believe he was a brusher. He left a wife and three children.

I am doing my family tree and have traced back to 1800 within the Cumberland/Westmorland areas but always feel that maybe now some of John's grandchildren and great-grandchildren might like to know something about his brothers/sisters/mum and dad, etc. but have not had any luck tracing them as yet. I am hopefully going to Whitehaven within the next few months to visit churchs, cemeteries and libraries for further information.

John's father was Thomas Milburn. His mother was Mary née Kirkwood. He was the first born child and had brothers Thomas, James (my Dad), Joseph, and sisters Katherine (Kitty), Rose, Anne and Theresa. Their father Thomas died around 1923, after being run down by a motor cycle. Today it would be called a hit-and-run as they never found out who was responsible. He died some months later at home, leaving Mary to bring up very small children, as the youngest was only months old.

John, being the eldest son, took on the role of the man of the house until he married and moved to Whitehaven to live. My Dad's second eldest brother, Thomas, had lost an arm in an accident so was never able to work. So, after John married, my Dad took on the role, and left school early to go out to work. The family eventually left and went to live in London, but Dad always remembers going back to see John and his wife Hettie until John's death. Hope this gives you an insight into John Milburn who died in the 1947 mining disaster.

Veronica St Hilaire, niece

****

In loving memory
of a dear husband and father,
John Milburn
killed in William Pit explosion
August 15, 1947.
Always remembered by his wife and family

****

JOHN EDWARD MOORE

Pal

John Edward Moore was a 37-year-old shift-hand and pan puller at William Pit. He was a resident of 3 John Square, Peter Street, Whitehaven. John was survived by his wife Ruby, and three children, John, Margaret, and Mary Elizabeth. Brought to the surface of William Pit on 19 August 1947 at 12.45am, Mr. Moore was formally identified by his brother-in-law Thomas Stewart of 141 Windermere Road, Woodhouse, Whitehaven. He was the 75th miner reached by the search and rescue teams.

I am the daughter of one of the miners who died in the 1947 pit disaster. Although I was made aware about you last year asking for information from any family left, I was very reluctant to put pen to paper. Where shall I start?

It is spring 1946, my Dad is coming home from the war. I can't remember him I was too young when he went away, but my brother and I can't wait. My Dad turned out to be a fine man with lots of love to give but he was firm and fair. The only work available was in the pits. I never knew about the dangers they faced down in that dark, damp, place. I used to go most times with him to bring his wages home to my Mum, and knew that two pence of sweets would be my reward.

It was a fine warm day, I was going down Scotch Street and someone asked, 'Is your Dad at work?'

I answered, 'Yes.'

'Run and tell your Mam there has been an explosion!'

How could I tell her this? Only two weeks before she had given birth to a baby girl whom she had named Dorothy. Dorothy died almost immediately, both Mam and Dad cried a lot. I remember my Dad getting into a taxi by himself with a little white coffin.

I went with my brother John who is older than me, to the pit head gates, and there we waited for news just hoping for Dad to come out. We were eventually taken home by the police, but we went back the following morning. We took turns running back home to give Mam any news. She was being looked after by friends and family.

Each day seemed a lifetime, until someone called at the house and told Mam that Dad had been brought up from the pit. He had not survived. Once again our lives had been torn apart. I had known him for such a short time. He went through the war and all its horrors, came home and died in the mines after such a short time. I was very angry that he was taken so soon.

I am now nearly 70-years-old, and the anger has all gone. I've never spoken much about 1947. I think I felt cheated of a father who didn't see me grow up, wasn't there when I got married, who never lived to see his grandchildren.

I've only got two photographs left of my Dad, so am including copies with this letter. One shows him in uniform before he left home. He went into the army as a Lance Corporal and came out as a Sergeant Major. The second photograph was taken in Burma.

John Edward Moore in Burma during the Second World War.

My mother was only seventeen when she met my father, he was about twelve years older. This was not taken too well by her family as they were all connected to the Orange Lodge, and my father's family were all strong Catholics. The story, from what I have heard, was that my mother's oldest brother was the only member of her family who went to St. James church on the day they wed. My father loved my mother so much, he went against their wishes and turned for the day from his own religion and married in St. James Protestant Church.

I have three children, Ruby, Margaret and Sean; five grandsons; three great-granddaughters and two great-grandsons. I thank God for all we have, a loving family and lots of happy memories.

Margaret Quinn (née Moore), daughter.

****

In loving memory of our dear son, John Edward,
killed in William Pit Disaster August 15, 1947.
Lord take this message to my son
Tell him I miss him and give him my love
Sweet is his memory dear is his name
God bless my son, till we meet again, R.I.P.
Mam and Dad, Margaret and John

In loving memory of my dear brother John Edward,
killed in William Pit August 15, 1947
He had a nature you could not help loving
A heart of purest gold
And to those who knew and loved him
His memory will never grow old
Always remembered by his loving sister, brother-in-law, Mary and Victor

JAMES MOORE

James Moore was 63-years-old and a hewer at William Pit. He was survived by his wife Elizabeth and four daughters. The couple lived at 96B George Street, Whitehaven. Mr. Moore was brought to the surface of William Pit on 17 August 1947 at 6.00am and formally identified by his son-in-law Richard Price of 96 George Street. James Moore was the 63rd miner located by the search and rescue team. Mr. Moore also served his nation as a member of the King's Own Royal Border Regiment.

****

In loving memory of my dear husband James,
killed in the William Pit Disaster August 15, 1947
Life is eternal love will remain
In God's own time we will meet again
Ever remembered by his wife Elizabeth and daughters Ellen, Annie, Mary and Jean

****

JOSEPH MOORE

Joseph Moore was a 39-year-old brusher at William Pit. He lived at 64 Seven Acres, Parton, with his wife Margaret and three children, Annie, Isabel and John. At the time of the disaster, Margaret was expecting their fourth child. Mr. Moore was the 104th, and last, miner to be brought to the surface of William Pit. He was formally identified by his brother, John William Moore of 134 Windermere Road, Whitehaven. Margaret Moore gave birth to a son six weeks later and named him Joseph.

****

I am writing on behalf of my husband Joe. We have tried to find out as much as we can but there is not a lot of information, I'm afraid. Joe was born six weeks after the disaster, and knows very little, except that his father was regarded as a kind man who loved his family.

We believe that his father had swapped shifts that day, and should have been on the first shift. He was only identified by his new boots. His wife and elder daughter, Annie, waited at the pit-head every day morning to night, until the last body, his, was brought out.

His niece was playing on Parton Beach that afternoon, and remembers the whole beach shaking at the time of the explosion. Joe was obviously not included in the family report, as he was not yet born. *Audrey Moore, daughter-in-law*

****

In loving memory of Joseph Moore,
killed in William Pit disaster, August 15, 1947
Loving and kind in all his ways
Upright and just till the end of his days
For all of us he did his best
My God grant him eternal rest
Sadly missed by his wife and family at 64 Seven Acres.

****

Joseph Moore, far left, with unidentified workmates making up a demolition crew.

****

JOHN RICHARD MOWAT

John Mowat was a 26-year-old shift hand at William Pit. He lived at 3 Lowther Street, with his wife Isobel McAdam Mowat and infant son. Mr. Mowat was brought to the surface at 8.35am on 17 August 1947, and later identified by his brother Thomas Mowat of 7 Second Avenue, Ashington, Northumberland. He was the 29th miner located by rescue workers.

****

ROBERT GLOSSON MULHOLLAND

Bob

Cousin of James McMullen and William McMullen

Robert Glosson Mulholland was a 39-year-old pan puller at William Pit. He lived at 67 Windermere Road with his wife Margaret (née Dobson) and five children. Mr Mulholland was one of the last miner's located. He was brought to the surface on 20 August 1947 at 5.55am and formally identified by his brother William Mulholland of 20 Brick Row, Northside, Workington. He was laid to rest in Whitehaven cemetery.

I can't remember too much, as my Daddy was in the army when I was little. He came out in 1945 and was killed in 1947, but I do remember he would take my sister Edie and me, to the pit on a Friday for his pay. And when Mammy and Daddy went out on an evening, they would bring us some chips back. We would all sit at the table and share the bowl of chips. I say bowl as in them days you took a bowl to the chip shop!

Daddy went by the name of Bob. He was the son of Rebecca Glosson (née Adair) and Christopher Glosson. Christopher died before Daddy was born. Rebecca remarried and her second husband, James Mulholland, raised him. He had two brothers, James and Billy, and two sisters, Sarah and Annie.

My brother Robert was working early shift the same day and my Dad was working back shift. When Robert got to the top of the pit he saw my Dad having a smoke before he went down to work. That was the last time anyone saw him alive. My brother Robert was washing the faces of the pit workers who were being brought out after the explosion to identify who they were, but never washed my Dad's. *Kathleen Elliott, née Mulholland, daughter*

****

In loving memory of our dear Daddy,
Robert Mulholland,
killed in William Pit disaster August 15, 1947.
When last we saw your smiling face,
you looked so bright and well
Little did we know that day
We had said our last farewell
Remembered by his loving son and daughters,
and at 67 Windermere Road, and 7 Senhouse Street

Treasured memories of my dear son, Robert,
killed in the William Pit Disaster;
also his cousins James and Billy
What peaceful hours we once enjoyed
How sweet that memory still
But they have left an aching void
The world can never fill
Remembered always by Mother and family

In memory of Bob who died in William Pit August 15, 1947
Remembered by his pal, Pat

FRANCIS MURDOCK

Pica

Francis Murdock was a shift hand at William Pit and lived at 11 Todhunter's Buildings, Queen Street, Whitehaven, with his wife Hetty, and three young children. Mr. Murdock was brought to the surface on 17 August 1947 and formally identified by his brother Michael Murdock, of 16 West Strand, Whitehaven. He was the 58th miner to be found by rescue and recovery workers.

In 1939 Francis Murdock enlisted with the King's Own Royal Border Regiment and became batman to the then Major Stanley Bell, first seeing action in France with the British Expeditionary Force 5th Batallion.

During a week long break in Kent, Francis was asked to pick up a large order of cider on his motorcycle. The following day, after he failed to return, a search party set our to look for him. His motorcycle was found at the side of the road. The boxes of cider intact, and there in the ditch, fast asleep,was Francis. The soldier from the north west, it would seem, could handle West Cumbrian brew but not Kentish cider.

Major Stanley Bell met his future wife while on that leave. Mary Bell spent time knitting her new husband an assortment of socks. It was a great source of frustration to her when she eventually discovered that the over-sized socks she had so lovingly created for her husband, actually ended up warming Francis Murdock's feet as he liked to wear them as slippers and plod around the camp in them. *Michael Bell*

****

Francis Murdock, better known as Pica, (his nickname might have been because he once lived in Pica?) is the man who haunted me for a long time because he took over my job. At the weekends he wore the usual miner's uniform - navy blue double-breasted three piece suit, white collarless shirt, a white silk scarf, and lanky clogs. The brass work was highly polished as was the leather. *A friend and co-worker*

****

In loving memory of Francis,
beloved husband of Hetty Murdock,
killed in William Pit explosion,
August 15, 1947 aged 39 years.
He had a nature you could not help loving
A heart of purest gold
And to those who new and loved him
His memory will never grow old
From his loving wife, daughters and son

****

JAMES MURRAY

Jimmy

James Murray was 36-years-old and a coal hewer at William Pit. He was a resident of 22 Crummock Avenue, Woodhouse, Whitehaven, where he lived with his wife Catherine and four children. Raised to the surface on 17 August 1947 at 12 noon, James Murray was identified by his father-in-law John Wolleyhern of 2 Pipehouse Lane, Whitehaven. He was the 36th man located.

****

In loving memory of James Murray,
killed in William Pit disaster August 15, 1947
Always remembered by his sons,
William and John, and daughters Patsy and Maureen

Treasured memories of our dearest brother, Jimmy
who was killed in the William Pit explosion August 15, 1947
Today brings memories sad to recall
Without goodbye he left us all
Dearer to us than words can tell
The brother we lost and loved so well
From Dad, sisters, brothers-in-law and grandchildren

Treasured memories of my pal Jimmy
who was killed in the William Pit disaster August 15, 1947
Your end was sudden Jimmy pal
You made me weep and cry
But oh the saddest part of all
You never said goodbye
From your pal, Nether

****

WILLIAM MURRAY

Trink

Billy and Mary Murray.

William Murray, known as Billy or Trink, was a 39-year-old pan-puller at William Pit. He lived at 5 Ladypit Terrace, Sunnyhill, Whitehaven with his wife Mary Elizabeth and their three young children, Yvonne, Allan and Margaret. Billy was brought to the surface on 20 August 1947 at 5.30am and later identified by his brother, James Murray, of 43 Common End, Distington. Billy was given the identification number of 'Special 3', and was the 101st miner to be found.

Having just read the *Whitehaven News* appeal today and seeing the beautiful photograph of my Mam and Dad, I would like to thank you for the interest and compassion you are showing in tracing the stories from relatives about that awful day in 1947 when so many of the Whitehaven people lost loved ones in the disaster.

I was only five-years-old at the time so there is really very little I remember of my Dad. I do know from my Mum in the conversations we had of that day, that he shouldn't have been at work. She had tried desperately to persuade him not to go, but he said the extra money would be handy, so I guess that is what I call fate. She wanted him to have a family day at relatives in Maryport. It was on returning home that we were met by Mam's sister, who told her of the accident.

I do not recall much after that until the day of the funeral and although I was only five I can still remember the hearse at the house to take my Dad to his resting place. We were looked after by neighbours, Dorothy and Leonard Graham.

My Mam did an excellent job bringing us up after that fateful day, and I have great admiration for her. She lived until she was nearly 93.

I don't remember much about my Dad except he used to like the hound dogs who raced on the fells and I remember going there with him. *Yvonne Bond, (née Murray), daughter*

****

The following is a transcript of a lesson the late Mary Murray Broatch, presented at a local school. Mrs. Murray was the widow of Billy Murray. Their son Allan submitted this transcript for his father's memorial page:

Thank you for asking me to come and talk to you about the William Pit Disaster of 1947. I come from a mining family - my grandfather, my father and uncles all worked down the mines. They helped to sink mines out near Aspatria and as they were working on one, my father's eldest brother fell down the shaft. He was only nineteen years of age and although the only mark on him was on his temple, he had hit his head on a girder and was killed. They still carried on working in the pits and when they moved to Whitehaven worked at Wellington Pit, where in 1910 there was an explosion at the pit and 136 miners were killed.

My grandfather, father and uncles were all in the rescue teams and King George V sent to Whitehaven for the names of rescuers and my grandfather was selected with others to go to London to be presented with a medal. My father still worked down the mine until 1922 when he left to take up farming near Distington.

I thought I had finished with the mines but it wasn't to be. I met my first husband but didn't know he was a miner at first. He worked at Moresby Pit for years then Lowca No 10. He left Lowca after we were married in 1936 and got work at William Pit, which at the time was lucky for him because an explosion then occurred at Lowca killing twelve miners.

He enjoyed working down the pit which he had done since leaving school. In 1941 he was down William Pit when an explosion occurred and eleven men were killed. They got the rest of the miners out but couldn't find thirteen miners, including my husband, who were so far into the mine.

One of my uncles happened to be with them and he said, 'Don't worry I know another way out, follow me,' and that's how they escaped. Some of the men lost their clothes because it was so hot they would strip down to just shorts, and that's why many miners had black marks on their backs because the jagged coal above them would cut their backs when working.

All went well until 1947. The mine managers made a change in the working hours and the miners would go to work on Saturdays so they could make a bit more money, because when we were first married, my husband was working 48 hours a week for £2 and, after stamp money and other dues taken off, he brought home £1.50p which went on until 1940 when, with the war breaking out, they gave the miners a rise to £3. They started a five day week and if they worked all week they got paid for Saturday free, which helped a little if you had children as you didn't get any family allowance for the first child, but five shillings for each of the others.

As I said all went well until 1947. It was a Friday morning, such a lovely day, and myself and the three children and my sister-in-law were going to see her brother at Maryport, who was ill. Well I don't know whether I had a premonition that something was going to happen, but I begged on my knees for my husband not to go to work that day and come with us to Maryport, but he said, 'If I don't go to work today I will loose my Saturday money.'

I said, 'That doesn't matter we will manage.' We went to the bus station and I still begged him not to go to work.

He said, 'I will go and see your mother and father before I go to work,' and as the bus was leaving he waved to us until we were out of sight and that was the last I saw of him.

The explosion occurred at 5.40pm and all rescue men from different places were called out to help. I arrived home at 7.30pm and was met by two of my neighbours who told me about the explosion. I knew then that he would't be rescued because he worked right at the coal face three miles under the sea as a pan-puller and chocker, which meant he worked on his back or stomach in just one yard height spaces putting in pit props to hold up the roof.

My father and mother came to my house and my mother also told me she too had begged him not to go to work that day and he had said the same thing to her! My father then went to the pit and asked if he could go down the mine to help with the rescue, but they asked how old he was and when he said 62 they said he wouldn't be allowed as he would have forgotten all about the workings of the mines, but my father knew the workings well.

My husband and four other men were not found until the following Wednesday morning. They were the last to be found and were all badly injured. They had found a pay cheque in his pocket which showed he had been given a rise up to £10 a week.

After everything was over we, the widows and mothers of the victims, had to attend the miners' offices in Queen Street where we were asked questions about our savings etc. Well we had very little and according to the size of each family and other things such as rents, insurances, etc they paid a sum of different amounts which was to be paid to us every week. I was allowed £15 per week which was to last about three or four years only. The children were growing up and needed more expensive clothes so eventually I got married again.

When my husband worked at the mine he went in old clothes and had to give in a token for his lamp. He went so far into the mine on a truck then had to crawl in and use a pick and shovel to dig the coal. When they came back to the surface they handed in their lamps and got their tokens back and that's how all men were accounted for. Miners in years gone by did not have a canteen to go to for a meal when they came up after a day's work. They only had an oval shaped bait tin which held two or three rounds of bread and jam and a tin bottle full of cold tea or water.

They only had Christmas Day, Boxing Day, Good Friday, Easter Monday and Whit Monday off, then in August they had a one week holiday. The year after the disaster they had two weeks holiday awarded but there were always special men working down the mines to make sure everything was in working order for the men returning to work. There weren't any pit head baths either - they had to come home all black and have a bath in a long tin bath in front of the fire and every drop of hot water had to be boiled on a coal fire in kettles and pans. So, just imagine boiling water for five of us to get bathed. We had three children - aged five and a half, three and a half and two and a half. I would put the children in the bath first, then their dad and next time I would get a bath. All food had to be cooked on an open fire where pans were hung on a long iron bar with a crook and baking was done in an oven beside the fire. Wood and coal were used to heat the oven; coal was cheaper but I could only afford one bag per week. I still have a coal fire today and have to pay £5 a bag! All miners get cheap coal now.

You know the workings of the pits are very different now. One can walk upright in them, all lit by electric light and all coal cut by machines and brought to the pit bottom by conveyer belt. Miners go to work in good clothes and are able to have a bath and a meal before they go home.

We never had a holiday, and we were trying to save up to have a week in Blackpool because holidays were cheap then, so my brother and his wife said they would look after the children. While we were walking down the Promenade a young couple passed us by and I said 'that couple is from Whitehaven.' A few weeks after the disaster I was attending my husband's grave and I saw a young woman at a grave crying. I went up to her and asked if she had lost her father or mother and she said 'no my husband.' It turned out to be the young woman we had seen in Blackpool. They had been married a fortnight and he was only 27. The eldest man killed in the disaster was 66. Black Damp killed a lot of the miners.

Thank you for asking me to come and talk to you about being the wife of a miner and what it was like after my husband was killed. I will just explain to you how I came to talk about this subject. A teacher from Whitehaven School came to see my next door neighbour and they were talking about exam time at school which was to be about industrial history such as iron and steel works, brick works, gas works, etc. but they could not find out about mining. So my neighbour told her about me being a miner's wife and the teacher came to see me and asked if I would talk to the scholars. I said if it would help them with their exams I would.

I talked to three classes the first time I went, then went for three days the following week and talked to six classes. They couldn't understand why we didn't have electric or gas cookers, washing machines, hoovers, fitted carpets, etc. in those dark days after the war! *Mary E Broatch, wife.*

Billy and Mary Murray at Blackpool on their first ever holiday, two weeks before the disaster.

****

Treasured memories of my
dear husband William (Billy)
killed in William Pit disaster
August 15, 1947
When last I saw your smiling face
You looked so bright and well
Little did I think that smile
Would be your last farewell
Loved and longed for by his loving
wife Mary and children
Yvonne, Allan, Margaret

Loving memories of Billy
Killed in William Pit, August 15, 1947
Sadly missed
Longed for always
Mother, Father and Hilda

Memories of Billy, our dear brother-in-law,
died in William Pit August 15, 1947
We will remember when others forget
Jen and Bill

Treasured memories of our dear brother-in-law, William (Trink)
killed in William Pit disaster, August 15, 1947
A sudden blow which we were never to expect
Dear William we shall always truly expect
Ever remembered by George, Ethel and children, Freda and George

****

LAWRENCE H. P. MURTAGH

Laurie

Brother of Patrick Murtagh

Lawrence Murtagh with his wife and children

Lawrence Hatfield Patrick Murtagh was a 41-year-old deputy at William Pit. Known as Laurie, he lived at 73 Buttermere Avenue, Seacliffe, Whitehaven, and was survived by his wife Kathleen and three children, Kathleen, Maureen and Anthony. On 19 August 1947 at 11.35am, Mr. Murtagh was brought to the surface and identified by a family freind, Mr. Joseph Beck of Old Woodhouse, Whitehaven. He was the 83rd miner located by search and rescue teams. Lawrence Murtagh's younger brother Patrick, was also killed in the disaster.

Tony Murtagh remembers his father as a great family man. He enjoyed taking Tony and his sisters to the beach, and any other children who wanted to go as well. He was an avid outdoors man who loved walking, and also sang in the choir.

as told to Tom Scott

****

In loving memory of my dear husband, Laurie, also his brother Patrick,
both killed in the William Pit Disaster August 15, 1947
We often sit and think of you
And think of how you died
To think you could not say goodbye before you closed your eyes. R.I.P.
Lovingly remembered by his loving wife Kathleen,
also Dad and Mam.

In loving memory of our darling Daddy, died August 15, 1947
God's greatest gift, remembrance
From his three loving children, Kathleen, Maureen and Tony
R.I.P. dear Daddy

****

PATRICK MURTAGH

Pat

Brother of Lawrence Murtagh

Patrick Murtagh was 28-years-old and worked as a pan puller at William Pit. He was survived by his wife Margaret and two little boys, Michael and Brian. The family lived at Old Woodhouse, Whitehaven. Raised to the surface on 19 August 1947 at 10.15pm, Pat was later identified by family friend Joseph Beck of the same address. Patrick Murtagh was the 97th miner located by rescue workers. His older brother Lawrence also died in the disaster.

On the back of this photograph is written, my lovely Pat, aged nineteen.

Thank God for my good memory as I knew practically all the men including the deputy (Lawrence), Pat's brother.

My lovely Pat shouldn't have been at William Pit as, previous to the war, he worked at Haig Pit and when he returned after serving in the war abroad, he was sent to William Pit where we lost him. His friend Wilf Farrer died with him, also William Nicholson, who was known as Red Nicky.

One man was told at the pit top that his wife had just had a son. His name was Jimmy Reed, he went back home instead of the pit.

I went every day to Pat's resting place until last year when I was ill. So now I only get there twice a week, when one of my family takes me. I am now 86-years-old so can't do everything I would like to do, so please excuse the scrawl. Pat and Wilf, and Red Nicky were pan men.

I know it sounds selfish but we lived for each other and the children and I still feel the same as Pat and I were soulmates, and still are.

Sadly Harry Maddison's new baby was buried with him having died, a few days later.

I have loads of beautiful memories, but would rather have Pat. We were married on the 21 October 1939. It would have been 68 years this year. I have some lovely poems written by Phil Tait but sadly I just can't find them.

We will never forget that fateful day
As we walked along the wagon way
Bait bottles by the side on our way
To catch the ride...

That is all I remember...

It was very, very, hard to manage as my youngest Brian was just six-weeks-old so I got a job at the workhouse and was able to work until I was 62-years-old – thanking God because the bonus coal was stopped right away and we could only afford to light a fire at week-ends.

Pat and I loved the Lake District, and cycled every part of it. My family, my two sons, Michael and Brian, do the same, and so do my grandsons Craig and Michael and my great-grandson Jackson. Pat would have been so proud, as I am. God bless,

Margaret Murtagh, widow

****

Mrs. Murtagh was interviewed for the 1997 Border Television documentary, *The Cost of Coal*, in commemoration of the 50th anniversary of the disaster.

****

Patrick Murtagh's resting place, photograph courtesy of Ray Devlin.

Treasured memories of Pat,
a dear husband and Daddy
Killed in the William Pit disaster
August 15, 1947 aged 28 years
St. Anthony pray for him
Grant unto him and his comrades
Eternal rest Oh Lord, and let
Perpetual light shine upon them
Forever in the thoughts of his loving wife Margaret, and two little sons, Michael and Brian and all at Old Woodhouse

****

Treasured memories of a dear nephew Pat,
who lost his life in William Pit, August 15, 1947
Always remembered by his Aunt and Uncle
and all at Yeathouse Road, Frizington

RICHARD MUSSON

Dick

Uncle of Ronnie Musson

Richard 'Dick' Musson was a 36-year-old trainer at William Pit. He lived at 22 Brisco Crescent, Parton, with his widowed mother, Mary Elizabeth Musson. Brought to the surface of William Pit at 5.20pm on 19 August 1947, Dick Musson was formally identified by his brother John Musson of 44 Seven Acres, Parton. He was the 90th miner located by search and rescue workers. Mr. Musson was laid to rest in Moresby Churchyard on 21 August 1947.

****

In loving memory of my dear son, Richard (Dick)
also my grandson Ronnie,
who lost their lives in William Pit disaster August 15, 1947.
We loved them in life they are dear to us still
But in grief we must bend them to God's Holy Will
We miss them and mourn them in sorrow unseen
And dwell in the memories of days that have been
Dearly loved and sadly missed by his mother, sister and Elizabeth,
little John, and all at Seven Acres

In memory of my brother, Dick, and nephew Ronnie,
killed in William Pit disaster August 15, 1947
We miss them because we loved them
They were dearer than riches or gold
No treasure on earth can replace them
Their memory will never grow old
Ever remembered by Bill, Jane, Margaret, Chris and Helen
at Arnside, Westmorland.

In loving memory of our friends
Who lost their lives in the William Pit Disaster August 15 1947
We open and close , but we still remember you all
From Mr. and Mrs. Musson, family and customers at The Rose and Thistle, Whitehaven

****

WILLIAM RONALD MUSSON

Ronnie

Ronnie Musson was 22-years-old and employed as a brusher at William Pit. He was survived by his wife Catherine, and lived at The Rose and Thistle, 21 West Strand, Whitehaven. Mr. Musson was brought to the surface of William Pit on 19 August 1947 and identified by his father James Musson of the same address. Ronnie Musson was the 72nd miner reached by search and rescue workers. Mr. Musson was laid to rest at Moresby churchyard on 21 August 1947.

****

In loving memory of our dear son Ronnie,
who lost his life in the William Pit disaster
August 15, 1947;
also his Uncle Dick.
We miss their smiling faces
Their voice we long to hear
Each day and night we pray that God
Will keep them ever near
Always remembered by his Mam, Dad,
brothers and sisters and pals

Treasured memories of my dear husband
who lost his life in the William Pit Disaster
August 15, 1947; also his Uncle Dick
Oft times we sit and talk of you
Of things you used to say and do
And wonder why you had to die
Without a chance to say goodbye
Always remembered by his wife
and all at Bransty

****

THOMAS NELSON

Thomas Nelson was a 36-year-old brusher at William Pit. He lived at Summer Grove Cottages, Hensingham, Whitehaven, with his wife Sarah Jane, and three young children. The family may have moved to 13 Senhouse Street as this address is handwritten on the original documents. Mr. Nelson was the first man brought to the surface of William Pit at 7.30am on 16 August 1947 and was formally identified by his brother-in-law William Boyle of Calthwaite, Penrith.

In loving memory of a dear husband and father,
Thomas Nelson
who lost his life in the William Pit disaster August 15, 1947
No more to see his smiling face
Nor hear him say hello
It came as a shock we didn't expect
A hard and bitter blow
Ever remembered by his wife and children.

****

WILLIAM NICHOLSON

Red Nicky

William Nicholson was a 33-year-old deputy employed at William Pit. He lived at 1 Temple Terrace, Catherine Street, Whitehaven, with his wife Julia Theresa Marie Nicholson and their two-year-old son David Allan. On 17 August 1947 at 6.55am, Billy Nicholson was raised to the surface of William Pit and formally identified by his father-in-law, James Edward King of the same address. Mr. Nicholson was the 21st miner located by rescue teams.

I was ten-years-old when the disaster occurred. It was a scorching summer's day. I was playing with my best friend, Margaret Hanlon (who was later to marry Ray Devlin, co-author of *The Most Dangerous Pit in the Kingdom*). A small boy, came running up Lowther Street shouting something about the pit, but we couldn't make out what he was saying. We strolled up to my Gran's in Catherine Street, where we knew we would get a welcome lemonade. A few minutes later, an urgent knock came to the front door, and my Auntie Julia came in looking very shocked and crying. The pit had indeed gone up, and my Uncle Billy (William Nicholson) her husband, and father to their adorable two-year-old son Allan, was one of the missing. The rest is history.

Julia was my father's only sister and she, Billy and Allan were living with my Gran and Grandpa until they could get their own house. They met in the Fire Service, where Julia worked, and Billy was an auxiliary (part-time) fireman. He was a deputy in William Pit, but still wanted to do his bit for his country, and tried to enlist. However, because he worked in the pit and for the Fire Service, they would not accept him. He was very upset about it at the time. Little did he know he would indeed give his life for his country. One of my abiding memories is of Uncle Billy in a large zinc bath in the living room (no bathrooms or showers at the pit head) having the coal dust washed off him by my Auntie. His modesty was preserved by his pit shorts! He had red, wavy, hair and was a very shy, unassuming man. I think he was just about 33-years-old.

My Uncle Eddie, the eldest of the family, travelled overnight on the train from Bath, where he lived with his wife and family. Everyone was in a state of total shock, but in the beginning Julia was filled with hope that he would be rescued. Eventually, his body was found and identified, and the coffin laid to rest in the front parlour. There was a peculiar smell emanating from it, which my Grandpa said was the gas.

My Auntie never married again, but continued to live with my grandparents whom she nursed until they died, many years later. Their little boy grew up to be the image of his Dad and now has a son and grandchildren of his own.

Billy's death left a large void in her life and she never really got over it. She and her son, and grandson, were very close until she died, and she had the pleasure of seeing them every day, as she lived just across the road from them. My pre-disaster memories are of a happy, normal, loving family whose lives were forever changed by this disaster.

Theresa M. Cowley (née King), niece

In loving memory of my dear husband, William,
killed in William Pit disaster, August 15, 1947.
Always remembered by his loving wife and son Allan.

JOSEPH NORMAN

Joe

Joseph Norman was 41-years-old and employed as a borer at William Pit. He was survived by his wife Sarah Ann and children, Josephine, Joseph and Victor. The family lived at 1 The Close, Bransty, Whitehaven. Mr. Norman was brought to the pit surface at 10.30pm on 19 August 1947 and was formally identified by his brother W. Norman of 41 Seven Acres, Parton. Joseph Norman was laid to rest at Moresby Churchyard.

****

My maternal grandfather Joseph Norman was killed in the the disaster aged 41 years. My mother will be eighty-years-old in June this year, and she has often told us of the events before and after the disaster.

Grandad was the oldest son of nine children – four boys and five girls – from Briscoe Crescent, Parton. One of my Grandad's brothers, William (Billy), was also killed a few years after my Grandad at the Lowca Pit. His brother Isaac (Ike) also worked down the pit and died in his early 60s of the coal dust disease.

He married my grandmother Sarah Mulholland at St. Bridget's Church, Moresby, on Easter Saturday, 6 April 1926. The vicar said he had not yet married one so dark and one so fair. They lived at 1 George Street, Whitehaven. My mother, Josephine, was born in June 1927, the oldest of four children. John, their second child, died aged only one year, of pneumonia. Joseph was born in 1934, and Victor in 1938.

They all moved to 1 The Close, Bransty, when my Mam, Josephine, was thirteen-years-old. Grandad was a devoted dad and husband, and he enjoyed gardening and fishing. He liked growing his own vegetables, and marguerites and roses were his favourite flowers. He also fished for lobster. My Mam said they often had lobster to eat (can't be bad eh?)

The winter of 1946/47 was really harsh, really cold, and heavy falls of snow lay around for days. Then summer came and apparently it was the hottest one on record.

My Mam says she recalls her Dad being in the 1941 explosion at William Pit and he got

Sarah Ann Mulholland and Joseph Norman.

all his eyebrows and the front of his hair burned off, also his left hand was burned. Mam said Granna had begged him then not to go back down the pit.

She's not one hundred per cent sure, but Mam thinks her Dad had swapped shifts that day, he should have been on the first shift, but went in on the back shift. On his way to work a neighbour shouted, 'Too nice to be going to work today Joe.'

'Aye,' he answered, 'but someone's got to go,' and went on his way.

My Mam was going out that afternoon and was waiting at the bus-stop, and her grandmother stepped off it (her mother's mother). Mam said she knew right away there was something wrong. Her grandmother looked awful and still had her full length pinny on.

'Have you not heard lass?' she asked, 'William Pit's gone up!'

And that was it. Mam went straight home and my grandmother (we called her Granna) did not move out of the chair for days. My Grandad's body was one of the last to be brought up. Mam said due to the summer heat, wreaths were placed in baths to keep fresh. Grasses in the fields were burning, it was so hot.

I didn't know Grandad, as I wasn't born until 1956, but from his photographs, he was a very handsome man. My Granna was 38-years-old when he was killed and she never remarried. She lived her life for her family. Granna died 12 April 1991, aged 82 years, and was buried with my Grandad. *Anne Wilson, granddaughter of Joseph Norman*

****

Joe Norman at Blackpool with his daughter Josephine and wife, Sarah Ann.

****

In treasured and ever present memory, this day, tomorrow, and always,
of my dearly loved and loving husband Joseph,
who died so tragically as the result of an explosion
in William Pit on August 15, 1947, aged 41 years
With a loving smile he left the door
We never thought we'd see him no more
But beautiful memories will never fade
Of the best Daddy God ever made
Links of steel rust can sever, but links of love last forever
Linked with a love no parting can destroy
Inserted by his loving wife and children, 1 The Close Bransty

In loving memory of our dear son, Joseph Norman
who lost his life in William Pit Disaster, August 15 1947
Always in our thoughts
Ever remembered by his Mam, Dad and Bell, Briscoe Crescent

In loving memory of our dear brother Joseph, who lost his life
in William Pit Disaster, August 15, 1947
Without farewell he fell asleep, with only memories left to keep
From Billy, Mary and family, Seven Acres Parton

In loving memory of my dear brother Joseph Norman, also our dear friend Henry Gibson
accidentally killed in William Pit explosion, August 15 1947
Always in our thoughts
From his brother Jimmy, and May, Seven Acres Parton

****

SYDNEY O'FEE

Corporal Sydney O'Fee

Sydney O'Fee was 34-years-old and employed as a coal hewer at William Pit. He lived at 62 Windermere Road, Woodhouse, Whitehaven, with his wife Eva and infant daughter Yvonne. Mr. O'Fee was also survived by his children Celia and Sydney. At 7.35pm on 19 August 1947, Sydney O'Fee was brought to the pit surface and formally identified by his brother William George O'Fee of RAF Biggin Hall, Kent.

****

My father, Sydney O'Fee was a good man. My stepmother, Eva, always used to say to Yvonne he was 'the best Daddy in the world.' I did not know him very well as he was away in Europe and France during the Second World War until his discharge in January 1946.

He was one of the last to be evacuated from Dunkirk and he fought at Arnhem. My Father's military number was 3595591 and he was a corporal in the Catering Corp. He had very flat feet (which I inherited) and could not march.

I remember when we left England to live with my aunt in South Africa my Gran gave all his cookery books away. They were mostly handwritten and the recipes had huge amounts of ingredients. Before he married Eva he lived with my grandparents and myself and worked down William Pit. He never worked on a Friday until that day in August 1947. I remember I was in the bath and my Gran was washing my hair when we felt the explosion. My Gran immediately said 'the pit's gone.'

It was almost a week before he was found. Often when I am lying awake in the early hours of the morning I can hear him whistling as he walked up the road after his shift. My Grandmother once told me that my Mother always refused to clean his 'clarty' boots. My Dad was a greyhound racer. His dog's name was Peggy and sometimes he would take me with him when he walked her.

After my mother died he married Eva and went to live at Windermere Road. Sometimes the family would meet at the local pub on a Saturday night and Dad used to ask Eva if she was going to the first 'house' or the 'second' the next morning.

My father was the fourth of my Grandmother's children to die. He had two brothers and a sister die of tuberculosis, as well as my mother, Muriel (née Wright).

Funny how things come back when one starts thinking. He and I were walking down

King Street and he had bought me a peach which to me was so big and juicy and he said, 'You had better eat it all it cost me 1/6d (7½p).'

Celia (née O'Fee) Barnes, daughter.

****

Treasured memories of Sydney O'Fee
Beloved husband of Eva O'Fee
I lost my sole companion
A life linked with my own
And day by day I miss him more
As I walk through life alone
Never a day forgotten by his Wife,
Eva and darling baby Yvonne

****

In memory of our dear cousin, Sydney
killed in William Pit August 15, 1947
Gone but not forgotten
Always remembered by all in London, Blackpool,
May, Canada and Raymond, Germany

****

JOHN ALLAN PARAGREEN

Jack

John Allan Paragreen was 30-years-old and an engine fitter at William Pit. He was survived by his wife Margaret (Peggy), and lived at 9 Bransty Row, Whitehaven. Jack was brought to the surface of William Pit on 20 August 1947 at 1.45am and identified by his father, John Henry Paragreen of 104 Station Road, Douglas West, Lanarkshire, Scotland. John Allan Paragreen was the 94th man located.

Jack and Peggy Paragreen

I read with keen interest your article in my local paper the *Lanark Gazette*. John Allan Paragreen, known as Jack, was my uncle on my mother's side of the family. John Henry Paragreen, my grandfather, was chief engineer in the Douglas West Colliery. Uncle Jack was killed in the William Pit disaster the year before I was born.

I know little of him but remember my father - an engineer in the William Pit at that time - speaking of Uncle Jack changing shift with another man on that fateful day. His wife Peggy moved back to Douglas and remained there until her death some five years ago - they had no children. Sadly none of the Paragreen family of that generation are alive. However, I will get in touch with my eldest sister who will perhaps have more information.

Andrew Paragreen Fowler, nephew.

****

I live in Douglas and read how you would like information about the Paragreen family. The most information I have is that John Paragreen had only been married about two years when he was killed. His widow, Peggy, came to live with the Paragreen family at Douglas West. She lived and worked in the Douglas area until she retired.

She stayed in sheltered housing until she died aged 84 in 2004. John was also known as Jack. I showed an interest in Peggy and helped her as she suffered greatly from arthritis. She had a great sense of humour and was very popular. Some of the family still survive but since Peggy died I have had no contact. Probably you may have heard from them. I have a wedding photograph of Jack and Peggy.

Peggy did speak about how she met Jack. Peggy was born and lived in Leith (which is a part of Edinburgh) and as Jack was in the forces he was stationed near Leith. They met, and after they got married, she came to live with his parents at Douglas West. Later he went to work at Whitehaven and they had a house there until the disaster.

Then of course she returned to Douglas West to be with his family. I keep trying to remember what she told me over the years but memories fade. If I find anything important I will let you know. I hope this has been a little help.

Betty McFarlane, Lanarkshire, friend of the family

****

From the *Hamilton Advertiser*, Lanarkshire, 30 August 1947:
Douglas West: Pit Disaster Victim – It is with regret that we record that one of those who lost their lives in the disaster at Whitehaven had a local connection. One of the sons of Mr. Paragreen, who is an engineer at Douglas Castle Colliery, and who has lived at Douglas West from some time, was a victim. He was a married man and had only recently started work at Whitehaven.

****

In loving memory of my dear husband
John Allan
Who was killed in the William Pit Disaster August 15, 1947
The blow was hard the shock severe
We little thought that death was near
Only those who have lost can tell
The loss of a loved one without farewell
Always remembered by his loving wife and family at Douglas West, Lanarkshire

In loving memory of John Allan
Who died in the William Pit Disaster
August 15, 1947 aged 30 years
Time may pass with many changes
Fresh with every coming year
But his memory will be cherished
In the hearts that loved him dear
Inserted by all at Douglas West, Lanark.

****

WILLIAM LEWIS PICKERING

William Lewis Pickering was 24-years-old and a pan puller at William Pit. He lived at 28 Haig Avenue, Bransty, and was survived by his wife Margaret and infant daughter. He was brought to the surface of William Pit on 17 August 1947 at 2.45pm, and formally identified by his father-in-law, Nathan Murphy, of the same address. William Pickering was the 46th miner recovered by the rescue team.

I never met William Pickering. I never even knew of his existence until recently. I live two hours drive from the place where he lived and died. Yet he shares the surname which my Mum had until 1951. He is kin.

In the early days of the 20th century, in much of Lancashire, it was normal for the boys to go down the pit and the girls to work in the cotton mills. Yes, that's right, boys and girls. Not even teenagers. At the age of twelve they would start to work what was called a half day, starting at seven in the morning and working until one, then off to school for the rest of the day. Not many years before it would have been a full day working at that age. My Mum was lucky in this regard – she stayed at school until fourteen, even though her father had died seven years earlier and another wage would have been very useful indeed.

My Mum had always wanted to find out more about her family's origins, having been told many tales as a young girl. So I started digging.

Her mother's side proved relatively easy. The family never moved far. The men were coal miners; the women worked in the mills - Howcrofts, Bulloughs, Marshes - few escaped the pits and the mills. The job titles in censuses changed a little – collier, coal miner, hewer, drawer, dataler – all underground.

Her father's side, however, was a problem. She had been told that her granddad, Edward Pickering, had been born at Lancaster Castle. After some investigation, it turned out that the town was right, but the location much more lowly, and his age was way out. He had knocked a good few years off his age when he married, and after that his better half had been keeping track for the rest of his life.

Edward Pickering was no pitman. He was one of the reasons for others to go underground. He was a firebeater, a stoker of some of the thousands of boilers which drove the machinery keeping Britain rich. He stoked boilers on ships which took supplies to South Africa during the Boer War. He stoked boilers at the linoleum works in Lancaster. He stoked boilers at cotton mills in Bolton. He lost an eye to a flying cinder. His wife lost her fingers to mill machinery.

Edward's father Jacob was not a miner either, but a stonemason - still there was a connection with the rocks. Jacob died young, of tuberculosis, the same disease that took my Granddad over 60 years later. He appeared with his children in only one census, and there he gives his place of birth as Hensingham, Cumberland.

Never having heard of the place, I looked it up. It is on the outskirts of Whitehaven.

Well, I looked for Jacob's family round Whitehaven. I found his father William, stonemason, his grandfather William, stonemason and brother William, stonemason. His brother John, was weigh clerk at an iron mine. Nephews were iron ore miners and drivers of stationary engines at the mines. All connected with the ground, either working under it or using its products. There are few other Pickering families around Whitehaven, but all gravitated towards the mines. Children of shoemakers and agricultural labourers, all ended up working underground.

The earth does not give up its products easily. The work is hard, even when things go well. When things go badly, people die. On the 21 December 1910, at the Pretoria Pit, Westhoughton, an explosion of firedamp killed 344 miners. At least four of them were related to my Mum. The disaster was still being discussed many years later.

The Pickerings did not escape. In 1900 James Pickering, nephew of Jacob, was killed outright when a small section of roof came loose at an iron mine in Frizington. He left a wife and two children, at least two other children having died before him. His total effects were worth £18.

Another nephew, Thomas, was also a coal miner. His son, John Robert, followed him into the pits. He probably fought in the Great War – he and his wife Jane (née Lewis) had no children between 1915 when Tom was born, and 1920, when he boarded the *Carmania* in Liverpool, en route for the new world. His occupation was given as miner. His wife Jane boarded the same ship with Tom the following spring, to join him in Plains, Pennsylvania, a great coal mining area.

Things must not have worked out, because there is no trace of them in the 1930 US census, but before they left, William Lewis Pickering was born.

William, like his father and grandfather, went down the mines around Whitehaven and, like too many of his friends, his neighbours and his relatives, he paid the ultimate price. William died in the William Pit. *Andrew Alston*

****

In loving memory of my dear husband,
William Pickering,
who died in the William Pit disaster August 15, 1947
God takes our loved ones from our home
But never from our hearts
Always remembered by his wife and daughter, Ann,
and Mam, Dad, John and Gordon of 28 Haig Avenue, Bransty.

****

WILLIAM PILKINGTON
and his sons
JOHN PILKINGTON
and
THOMAS PILKINGTON

William Pilkington was 66-years-old and employed as a brusher at William Pit. He lived at 60 Windermere Road, Woodhouse, Whitehaven, with his wife Ann Jane. He was the oldest man killed in the disaster. William was survived by his wife and four children, James, Mary (O'Fee), Margaret (Peggy) and Eileen. Two sons, John and Thomas, were also killed in the disaster. Mr. Pilkington was brought to the surface of William Pit on 17 August 1947, at 10.15pm and was formally identified by his son-in-law Edward O'Fee of 82 Fleswick Avenue, Woodhouse, Whitehaven.

William Pilkington, senior, on his allotment

****

John Pilkington was 32-years-old and was also employed as a brusher. John was survived by his wife Eleanor, and four young children, Eleanor, John, Annie and Eileen. He was brought to the surface of William Pit on 18 August 1947 and identified by his wife. John was killed with his father and his brother Thomas.

****

Thomas Pilkington, aged 27 years, like his father and brother, was also employed as a brusher at William Pit. He lived at 60 Windermere Road, Woodhouse, Whitehaven. Thomas was survived by his mother Ann Jane, and four siblings. At 6.30pm on 17 August 1947, the body of Thomas Pilkington was brought to the surface of William Pit and identified by his brother-in-law Edward O'Fee of 82 Fleswick Avenue, Whitehaven.

****

The following story is of Mrs Margaret (known as Peggy,) O'Neill (née Pilkington), as told to Joseph Ritson:

On August 15, 1947, Peggy and her sister Eileen, were working on a farm at Crofton Hall near Wigton. After they heard the news on the radio that there had been an explosion at William Pit, Peggy and Eileen returned home to Whitehaven as their father and three brothers worked at the pit. Peggy's father, William Pilkington, and two brothers, John and Thomas, were in William Pit at the time of the explosion, as well as her Dad's cousin, also called William Pilkington (known as Buff). Another of Peggy's brothers, James (Jim) Pilkington had swapped shifts at the pit with his brother because he wanted to go to the pictures. Jim had not been at home very long after working on the first shift when the explosion happened. Jim went straight back down to the pit. Peggy, her mother, and sisters, went to the pit gates every day for almost a week for news until they brought out the bodies of their relatives. Jim was never the same again after the explosion. William Sr. was a keen gardener and had an allotment. John had worked at the pit all the way through the war. He was buried on his birthday. Thomas Pilkington was in the army during the Second World War and went all the way through Burma, the Far East and the Middle East, only to die at home.

My name is John Pilkington and my father and uncle and granddad were killed in the William Pit explosion. My granddad's cousin was also killed, but I didn't know much about him. I was four-years-old when the explosion happened so I remember very little about what happened. On the day of the explosion I was sitting on the street when my uncle, Mr Samuel Curry, picked me up and took me to my grandmother's house and said, 'Yes, you're stopping there!'

Thomas Pilkington, back right.

We lived up at the Ice Works on Queen Street at the time and I never lived at my mother's again. There was an archway at the top end of Queen Street and we lived in a court off there. Sam Curry was my mother's brother. He wasn't a miner as he was disabled. He took me to what was his mother's house then - which was my grandmother's - on Crummock Avenue at Woodhouse, and I lived there afterwards.

I was brought up with my grandparents, and went to school from there, firstly to Monkwray Junior School and then up to Kells School. I never went on any of the trips the William Pit families had to Czechoslovakia. I was going to go with one of the families off Buttermere Avenue, but then they weren't allowed to go so I didn't go either.

I remember seeing my Granddad William Pilkington but I couldn't really say I remember a lot about him. I've seen his photograph at my aunty's house. I used to go and see my other grandmother (Pilkington) on Windermere Road, and her daughters Peggy and Eileen. There was another daughter, Mary, who has since died on the corner of Fleswick Avenue, and Coniston Road. They called her O'Fee. Then there was my Dad's brother Tom, who died in the explosion as well.

I have never been to any of the William Pit memorial services. I don't think anyone has really known I am related to those who were in the explosion. They erected a monument for the William Pit men down at the pithead and I didn't hear of it until sometime later. My sister, Eleanor Walsh, who lives in Leeds, went to the service. We were four in our family. I had three sisters - Eleanor, Eileen and Anne. They moved to Leeds with my mother Eleanor after she married my step-dad, Arthur Rodgers, who came from Leeds. I would like to go to the services if someone lets me know when they are.

I haven't got a single photograph of my Dad. The only one that I have seen was one that my Aunty Mary O'Fee had up in the house. This photograph had Tom and John on it and I think it was the only one there was of them together. They had been to Blackpool and brought this photograph back from the trip and were wearing a greatcoat or a 'Mac' and a cap!

John Pilkington, son, as told to Joseph Ritson.

****

In loving memory of my dear husband,
William Pilkington,
also of my two dear sons, John aged 32
years and Thomas aged 28 years,
who all lost their lives in the William Pit
Disaster, August 15, 1947
Always in our thoughts
From a loving wife and mother and all
at 60 Windermere Road

In loving memory of our dearest Daddy
(and son-in-law),
John who lost his life in
William Pit Disaster,
August 15, 1947
Gone but not forgotten
Remembered always by his three little
daughters, son John,
and all at 63 Crummock Avenue,
Woodhouse.

In loving memory of my dear father,
William Pilkington,
also of my two dear brothers,
John aged 32 years, and Thomas 28 years,
who lost their lives in the William Pit
disaster August 15, 1947.
Loved and remembered always, by
Mary, Eddie and family
at 82 Fleswick Avenue, Woodhouse.

****

James Pilkington, the only surviving son.

WILLIAM PILKINGTON

Buff

William Pilkington was employed as a brusher at William Pit. Known as Buff, he was survived by his wife Cecilia. The couple lived at 3 Woodhouse Road, Greenbank, Whitehaven. Mr. Pilkington was brought to the surface of William Pit on 19 August 1947 at 4.45pm and formally identified by his brother Patrick Pilkington of 42 The Green, Bransty, Whitehaven. He was the 88th miner located.

In loving memory of William (Buff),
beloved husband of Cecilia Pilkington,
killed in the William Pit disaster August 15, 1947.
St Anthony pray for him
Give unto him and his comrades who lost their lives
Eternal rest O Lord
And let perpetual light shine on them
In the midst of life we are in death

****

GEORGE PORTHOUSE

Sandy

Sandy Porthouse was a 54-year-old brusher at William Pit. He was survived by his wife Elizabeth and several adult children. The couple lived at 16 North Road, Bransty, Whitehaven. Mr. Porthouse was brought to the surface of William Pit at 9.45am on 17 August 1947 and was later identified by his son, William Porthouse, of the same address. George Porthouse had also been seriously injured in the 1941 William Pit disaster.

In loving memory of George (Sandy) Porthouse
who was killed in the William Pit explosion August 15, 1947
Always remembered by his loving wife and sons, 16 North Road, Bransty

In loving memory of George (Sandy) Porthouse
killed August 15, 1947 in the William Pit Disaster
Always remembered by Jack and Kitty.

In loving remembrance of a friend George Porthouse (Sandy)
who died in the William Pit disaster August 15, 1947.
Memories
Fondly remembered by Mr. and Mrs. Messenger, 15 North Road, Bransty

****

JOHN QUIRK

Jack

John (Jack) Quirk was 38-years-old and employed as a brusher. He lived at 23 Victoria Road, Whitehaven, with his wife Lottie, and two sons, fifteen-year-old Chris Hinde, and Miles, aged ten. On the morning of 17 August 1947 at 6.45am, John Quirk was brought to the surface and identified by his brother-in-law, John Miles Hinde of Brakeside Villa, Monkwray, Whitehaven. He was the 22nd of the 104 Men.

Lottie Quirk withdrew her application for compensation after she commenced work in the months following the disaster.

****

I am the only surviving descendent of John Quirk, who was one of the 104 pitmen. I know he was a 'brusher' in the pit. I'm sure there is not much I can help you with, but I will do what I can. I have only one photograph of my Granda, some newspapers from that time, a bowler hat (size 7⅛ that cost seven shillings and six pence from Birketts in Whitehaven), some Masonic regalia and a photograph of my Dad (Miles Quirk - who was also a pitman) when he visited the Czech Republic on a visit for survivors, widows and orphans of the disaster, paid for by the Czech miners.

My Granda wasn't supposed to be in the pit that day but he wanted to earn a bit extra and went in for another shift. My Dad told the story that when they brought his Dad out, there wasn't a mark on him - as my Dad said, 'It was the gas that got him.'

My Dad was only eleven when his Dad was killed. My Grandma (Lottie Quirk) had two boys to bring up and worked in the Beehive store in Whitehaven, so my Dad spent a lot of his time with his aunt (his Dad's sister, Sadie Cowman at their farm in Eskdale).

Some years later, my Dad, by then a joiner at Haig Pit, went into William Pit and was able to get near the spot where his Dad was found, unfortunately, the actual spot was bricked up, so he could only stand on the other side of the wall and wonder. My Mam, despite them being together almost 50 years, knows absolutely nothing about her father-in-law.

My Dad hardly spoke of his Dad, hardly surprising really, these days a boy of eleven who sat on the banks above the pit watching them bring out the bodies, waiting for one of them to be his Dad, would have support, counselling and years of therapy. In 1947, it was a different story!

The only other things I can tell you... Dad recalled his Dad sitting in a tin bath in front of the fire, while my Grandma took the segs off his back with a razor blade (nice!) and that the miners were always so thirsty when they came back at the end of the shift, they had to call into the Shipwrights' Arms for a pint on their way home (at least that was his excuse!!!) Home, by the way, was Victoria Road in Whitehaven.

Sadly, my Dad is no longer with us, so there lies the end of the story. I have no family either - so I guess his memory dies with me. I hope you will be able to include a reference to John Quirk in your book so that others will be able to read about him.

Sal Calvin (née Quirk), grand-daughter

****

Dear Lottie,

I have seen Mr Charles today and he has arranged for you to come back permanently. I mentioned the date as September 29th but Mr L thinks if you can possibly manage, he would like you in not later than September 8th, or through the week. He thinks if you get into the company of the assistants it will perhaps help you a little.

I did admire you on Saturday evening. I think you are so brave. I'm afraid I wouldn't be half so brave. Mrs Quirk senior too, I thought was wonderful.

If I can do anything possible for you Lottie, in making you jam or anything I'll be only too pleased to help you. You have always been a very good friend to me and I'd like to help you if I can. Before you start work again, you must come for a few afternoons and bring Mrs Quirk with you. It will be a change for you both and I'll be very pleased to have you. I hope Chris is successful in getting a temporary post on Wednesday.

My kindest thoughts to you,

Miss Nicholson *PS Mr Charles says will you call and see him sometime.*

[Letter dated 25 August 1947, from The Beehive Litd, Drapers and Furnishers, Whitehaven]

****

In loving memory of Jack
killed in William Pit explosion August 15, 1947.
When last I saw your smiling face
You looked so bright and well
Little did I dream that day
Would be our last farewell
Ever remembered by his wife and two sons

Treasured birthday memories of my dear son
John (Jack) on his 40th birthday,
August 18th, who lost his life
in the William Pit disaster August 15, 1947.
So dearly loved, so dearly missed.
Always in the thoughts of his loving mother, Adelaide, Sadie, Ted and all at Eskdale.

In treasured remembrance of dear Uncle Jack
who was accidentally killed August 15, 1947.
In the midst of life we are in death.
Remembered by all at Stirlings Infirmary.

****

ADAM RABY

Adam Raby was 25-years-old, a brusher, at William Pit. He lived at 45 Fleswick Avenue, Woodhouse, Whitehaven with his new bride Winifred Raby (née Thompson). Mr. Raby was brought to the surface of William Pit at 3.10pm on 17 August 1947, and was the 49th miner recovered. He was identified by his father Adam Raby M.M.

Adam and Winnie Raby

Adam Raby married my Mum's sister Winnifred (Winnie) Thompson, two weeks before he was killed which makes the photographs really sad. Unfortunately, he didn't live long enough to see the wedding photographs. In the group photograph, the bridesmaid to the bride's left is my Mum, Betty, and I believe that the other two bridesmaids are Uncle Adam's sisters.

I was always brought up to know who my Uncle Adam was and my Mum always said what a quiet and gentle person he was. I can always remember her telling me that on the day of the disaster, he was waiting to go into work when a little girl who lived nearby came to the house. Apparently, she was quite shy and had never bothered Uncle Adam before (probably because she didn't know him because he'd only been living at my Grandma's for a couple of weeks) but she flung her arms round his neck and sat on his knee.

I think all the adults were quite surprised because it was out of character and afterwards, they thought she must have sensed that something bad was going to happen to him. I think my Auntie Winnie was comforted by this happening as it was quite a positive last memory of him for her. My Mum and Dad weren't married at the time, they were just courting but my Dad helped with the rescue and helped to bring Uncle Adam up from the pit.

It's hard to believe what the families must have gone through then and I'm sure that the families who are left will be so grateful that you've taken the time to do this book.

Hazel Ridley, niece

****

My Dad has asked me to email you following your article in the *Whitehaven News*. I had an Uncle Adam Raby who was killed in the pit disaster he was the 49th body to be pulled out of the disaster. It was quite sad as Adam had only been married for thirteen days when he died. The best man at the wedding was also killed in the disaster. His name was Harry Maddison he was the 52nd body to be pulled out. My Dad can remember it as if it was yesterday he said it happened at 5.40pm on the 15 August and both his Father and Uncle helped with the rescue.

Dad has finally got the birth certificate and his date of birth was 21 August 1921. He was only 25-years-old when he died, and was buried on his 26th birthday. Hope this is of some help. If you need any more information I am sure Dad will try and find out more - it's good to remember the loved ones people have lost. *Anne Marie Rogan, niece.*

A beaming Adam Raby with his bride Winifred Thompson. Best man Harry Maddison is on Adam's right; Adam's parents Adam Raby senior M.M. and Frances Raby (née Ross), also sisters Betty and Catherine Raby. The flower girl is cousin Elsie Fox.

In loving memory of my dearly beloved husband Adam Raby,
killed in the William Pit Disaster August 15, 1947
He had a nature you could not help but loving
A heart of pure gold
But to one who loved and lost him
Your memory will never grow old
Always remembered by his loving wife Winnie

In loving memory of our dear son, Adam,
who was killed in William Pit Disaster August 15, 1947
It's only a grave that needs our care
For the one we love is resting there
The flowers we place upon his breast
Are from the ones who loved him best
Never one day forgotten by his sorrowing Mam and Dad, brothers and loving sister Betty

In loving memory of our
dear brother Adam,
who was taken from us in
William Pit Disaster
August 15, 1947 aged 26 years
We loved him so we miss him
Yet our hearts still ache
We can't forget. Years will not darken
Or shadows dim the loving
memories we have of him
Never one day forgotten by his sorrowing
sisters, Kathleen and Lillian

In loving memory of my
dear son-in-law, Adam,
also my dear brother-in-law
Joseph Wilson Hewer,
and his brother Ronnie,
who all lost their lives in the
William Pit explosion
Oh Lord grant unto them that which
they dearly earned
Eternal rest in thy heavenly home
From all at 45 Fleswick Avenue
Woodhouse; also Ted, Bransty

****

In loving memory of our dear nephew Adam,
killed in William Pit Disaster
August 15, 1947
Deep in our hearts his memory is kept
We loved him too dearly to ever forget
The tragic way he had to die
We shall always remember and wonder why
From Aunt Lizzie, Uncle Sam,
Mother Ross and family

In loving memory of a dear pal, Adam,
who lost his life in the William Pit Disaster
August 15, 1947
We fought together side by side
And both shared every fear
But when God called you to Himself
I lost a pal sincere
Ever remembered by Smutts and
his wife, 2 Scotch Street
(Smutts was Adam's friend
William Smurthwaute)

In loving memory of dear Adam
Accidentally killed in William Pit,
August 15, 1947
In our home stands a beautiful picture
Of one who was dearer than gold
To us who loved him dearly
His memory will never grow old
Ever remembered by George and Nora

EDWARD R. RAY

Edward Ray was 33-years-old and employed as a shift hand at William Pit. He was survived by his wife Minnie Ray and six-year-old daughter. The family lived at 1 Front Row, Northside, Workington. Mr Ray was brought to the surface of William Pit on 17 August 1947, and formally identified by Joseph Crone Green of 4 Brick Row, North Side, Workington. He was the 37th man reached by rescue workers.

****

JOHN J. RENWICK

John Joseph

John Joseph Renwick was a 39-year-old coal cutter. He lived at 12 Gameriggs Road, Greenbank, Whitehaven, with his wife Mary Jane and two children, Jackie and Margaret. He was brought to the surface of William Pit on 18 August 1947 and identified by his brother-in-law Matthew Wilson of 61 Greenbank Avenue, Greenbank, Whitehaven.

John Joseph Renwick
Who never ate his bread in sorrow,
Who never spent the midnight hours
Watching and weeping for the morrow
He knows ye not ye heavenly powers *Goethe*

Even though I live two hundred miles away in the Midlands, and wasn't born until the late fifties, I have always known about Whitehaven and the William Pit Disaster. I didn't know about it in the academic, learned way of a history lesson; I just knew that it hurt my grandmother very much. I knew about the deathly silence, the waiting, the churning stomach and the endless cups of tea. Of the women, too sick with fear to move, or eat, or even wash, as they waited and dreaded what news must surely come. As a child I would sit with my gran and listen to the stories – for such they were to a small child – of her brother, John Joseph Renwick, who was killed in the William Pit Disaster.

I live in a mining town and grew up hearing the occasional wail of the pit siren. To my knowledge, our local siren never cried for the death of a miner and we didn't have any family in the pit - but I can still see the way that siren affected my gran and my mother, even though it was not calling for us. The fact was, every time it rang in the 1960s, in a small town in the Midlands, it was Whitehaven 1947 all over again.

First, my mother's hands would begin to shake. Like most women in those days, she always seemed to be at the sink, cooking or washing for a huge family. The kitchen window looked onto the colliery and pit wheel about a mile away. There would be this awful, deathly silence where everyone in the house seemed to be paralysed by the wail gathering momentum. As small children, we'd stare at my mother, as her face turned white, head slowly rising to look out at the wheel. Then my mother would dry her hands, fill the kettle… panic, really.

I don't think it was a case of my mother or my gran consciously giving us a history lesson; but the memories that siren brought were so strong that they could not help but re-live it, telling us about the events of that week in August 1947. Besides, the topic was never 'what happened' in the pit but what happened to those who were left behind.

My grandmother was born in 1898 in Whitehaven. She went into service when she was thirteen and after her marriage she moved to Brampton, but she adored her family and in particular, her only brother, John Joseph. She always said that her mother 'couldn't rear boys' and had lost three sets of twins either at birth or prematurely. These were all boys so it is easy to see how such a superstition grew. Easy too, to see how John Joseph was so precious to them. John Joseph (and she always gave him his full name) was born on the 10 March 1908 when my gran was already ten so she had been a 'little mother' to him. They grew up in 4 Front Row, Newhouses, along with sisters Sarah-Jane and Margaret. They went to Trinity School.

This was a close family even after marriage, perhaps because their mother had died young. John Joseph was only fourteen when Mary Ann (née Kirkbride) died of pneumonia. Family history research shows that the Kirkbrides were very close-knit and Mary Ann lived all her short life within a street or two of her married siblings and the Renwick brothers.

Jack Renwick, John Joseph's dad, must have kept the family together after Mary Ann's death for they remained at Front Row, Newhouses.

John Joseph married Mary Green in 1932, aged 24. His married sisters, Sarah Jane Rogan and Margaret Wilson, were their witnesses. He was a colliery shiftsman, according to his marriage certificate. By 1934 he had two children, Jackie and Margaret.

One of his nephews, (Bella's son) Ralph, says he remembers him like it was yesterday. 'Your gran used to take us to Whitehaven for our holidays. John Joseph used to pay me tuppence to look after old Jack's goat. He used to make nets of willow then he'd catch finches on St Bee's wasteland. He'd sell them for 2/6. I had to keep lookout and it was not easy with that goat.' This would have been in the late 1930s before the war, when Ralph was only twelve. Seventy years on, he laughed throughout the telling of this tale.

John Joseph was a smart, slim, 'wiry' man, about 5'8" tall with dark hair. Like many a Whitehaven lad, he joined the 5th Battalion of the King's Own Royal Border Regiment for the war but was released to go back to the pit.

In 1947, he and his family lived on Gameriggs Road in Whitehaven and he was a coal cutter aged 39. For my gran, Bella, celebrating her 49th birthday on the 13 August, she was about to undergo the second of three harrowing events in four years. In 1943 she had received a 'missing, presumed dead' telegram when her eldest son, Jackie, was shot down over Pilsdon. She later found he was alive and in a prisoner of war camp in Germany. Jackie returned unscathed but now it was her brother for whom she would wait. In two years' time she would re-live it all over again when the same son would be killed in a peacetime mid-air collision.

It is impossible to even begin to imagine what those three days were like, waiting for John Joseph to be found, number 109, and if there was cruel solace in having so many other wives, mothers, sisters, daughters, waiting too. Or what it was like for Jack, 77-years-old, waiting for word of his only son. Jack had been a miner so he would have known what was going on underground.

John Joseph was raised at 6.40pm on 18 August 1947. Margaret's husband, Matt Wilson, identified him. He died of carbon monoxide poisoning. It must surely have been a blessing that his mother, Mary Ann, was not alive to suffer the long wait along with his sisters.

History has a cruel way of repeating itself. John Joseph was only fourteen when he lost his mother. Now his children were aged thirteen and fifteen. His daughter Margaret lived only another three years before dying of meningitis, still a teenager.

Jackie, John Joseph's son, grew up, and became a bath attendant. He married and had only one child. They called him John Joseph. This child died when he was about eight months old and is buried with his grandfather. John Joseph has no widow or children or grandchildren alive to write this memorial. There is no direct descendant.

However, his sisters Bella Simpson, Sarah Jane Rogan and Margaret Wilson adored their brother so much, they ensured that his memory lived on through their children and grandchildren. And not just through the tears of remembrance of August 1947, of sunny days chasing finches, of a man who could cause a grown man to chuckle away at the re-telling of a seventy-year-old memory.

Compiled with the kind help and memories of Marjory Henny, Ernest Rogan and Ralph Simpson, niece and nephews. All errors are mine. Jackie Ostle, 29 April 2007.

Memories of a dear husband and Dad, John Joseph,
killed in William Pit August 15, 1947
'Tis sad but true we wonder why
The best are always first to die
While I earth I gave you the best
Thank God I have no regrets
Always remembered by his wife, son, daughter,
Mother-in-law, Brother-in-law Ben

In loving memory of a beloved only son and brother
John J. Renwick
Who lost his life in the William Pit disaster
August 15, 1947 aged 39 years
Without farewell he fell asleep
With only a memory for us to keep
A cheery smile, a heart of gold
He was one of the best this world did hold
Sadly missed by his Dad and all at 61 Greenbank Avenue

In loving memory of my brother, John J.
Killed in William Pit August 15, 1947
We had a brother with a heart of gold
He was more to us than wealth untold
Kind and unselfish a brother so true
Our proudest possessions are memories of you
From his loving sister Sarah and all at 21 Thwaiteville
also Bell and Jack, Brampton

****

THOMAS RICHARDSON

Thomas Richardson was 40-years-old and employed as a brusher at William Pit. He lived at 150 Queen Street, Whitehaven, with his wife Josephine (née Maderick) and seven children. Mr Richardson was brought to the surface of William Pit at 9.55am on 17 August 1947 and later identified by his brother-in-law James Madrick of 10 Bransty Row, Bransty, Whitehaven. He was the 32nd man discovered by search and rescue teams.

Thomas Richardson's son, Harry, appeared in the 1997 Border Television documentary *The Cost of Coal.*

****

JAMES RIGG

Jimmy

James Rigg weds Ellen Cruddock

Jimmy Rigg was 28-years-old and employed as a brusher at William Pit. He lived at 12 Marlborough Street, Whitehaven, with his expectant wife Ellen, and their ten-month-old son, James. On the morning of 17 August 1947, James Rigg was brought to the surface of William Pit and identified by his brother, Harold Rigg of the same address. Mr. Rigg was the 25th man located by search and rescue personnel. Ellen later gave birth to a daughter she named Denise.

My grandfather was among the men killed in the disaster – his name was James Rigg (Jimmy). My Mam, never met her father - my Nana had just found out she was pregnant with my Mam. My grandfather was not due to go to work that day, but he said he needed the money as they had another baby on the way. My great uncle had asked him not to go to work – my great uncle was a psychic and he used to see things in the flames in the fire – he had seen the disaster happening – he had begged him not to go to work, but Jimmy just told him to stop with his silly ways and that he was going to work.

My Nana passed away nearly ten years ago – she remarried later in life – but Jimmy was always her soul mate. As far as I can recall they met and courted during the war years – my Nana served abroad driving five ton wagons (they put blocks of wood on the pedals so she could reach them – she was only five feet tall).

My grandfather also served abroad – he had quite a distinguished service - including the chinditz – where he saved a few men and was mentioned in dispatches back to his country – he was awarded an honour for this on his return home.

My Granda was with the Border Regiment from 16 May 1938 to 7 November 1945. He was released from service to the reserves on grounds of national importance to be a miner for the Cumberland Coal Company. He was awarded the following medals:

The Burma Star — *The Africa Star*
The Defence Medal — *The 1939-1945 Star (WWII Campaign Medal)*
Efficient Service Medal — *Oakleaves for Bravery*
Service Medal

He served in Norway, Egypt, Ceylon, India and Burma (Chinditz). He would speak of his war service in all the countries except for Burma. He would never mention Burma and the atrocities that happened there.

He was born in May 1918 in Egremont and went to Bookwell School. He was from a large family - his parents had been married several times each. His immediate siblings are brothers: Harold, Herbert, (Jackie Rigg and Tom Morris are half brothers); sisters Gladys, Mary and Doris and June (half sister). His own father was called Jimmy and he was killed at a young age in the mines in Africa. His mother was called Sarah (née Trohear). She was known as Moo Moo to her grandchildren (my Mam and uncle). This is the information I have from my memories of talking to my nana about Jimmy.

Andrea Curwen (Miss), grand-daughter

****

Loving memories of James, beloved husband of Ellen Rigg,
killed in William Pit disaster August 15, 1947
I was not there beside you to hear your last faint sigh
To whisper just one loving word
Or even say goodbye
Some may think I have forgotten
When at times they see me smile
But no one knows the heartache
That's hidden beneath that smile
From his loving wife and babies Jimmy and Denise

In loving memory of my dear son Jimmy who was killed in William Pit August 15 1947
We never heard his last faint sigh
We never saw him die
We only know he passed away
And could not say goodbye
Ever remembered by his Mam, Bill , Herbert, Mary, Gladys, June

****

In loving memory of my dear brother, Jimmy,
who was killed in William Pit August 15, 1947
Deep in our hearts the memory is kept
We loved him too dearly to ever forget
The tragic way he had to die
We shall always remember and wonder why
Always remembered by his four brothers, and sister-in-law, away

In proud and everlasting memories of my brother James,
killed in William Pit Disaster August 15, 1947
On the sideboard there's a picture
More precious than silver or gold
It is of you dear Jimmy
And it's memories will never grow old
His duty doubly done
From his sister Doris, Tom, Nieces and Nephew, Devon Road, Hensingham

In loving memory of my dear brother, Jimmy, killed in William Pit, August 15, 1947
I wonder why the best are always the first to die
From Maggie, Joe and family, Lincoln

In loving memory of my dear brother killed in William Pit Disaster August 15, 1947
He never failed to do his bit
His heart was true and tender
He toiled so hard for those he loved
And left us to remember
From his sister Alvina, Jack, Nieces ad Nephews Cumberland Road

****

JOHN ROBBS

John Robbs was a 56-year-old brusher at William Pit. He was survived by his wife Constance Adelaide and nine children. He lived at 6 Brayton Road, Whitehaven. Brought to the surface of William Pit on 19 August 1947, Mr. Robbs was identified by his son John Robbs of 6 Low Harras Moor, Whitehaven.

In loving memory of John, the beloved husband of Connie Robb
killed in William Pit disaster August 15, 1947.
God's greatest gift remembrance
Always remembered by his wife and family, at home and away

In memory of Dad, killed in William Pit disaster August 15, 1947
Not forgotten by all at Harras Moor

****

Memoriams in 1948 *Whitehaven News* have the spelling as Robb.

ALBERT E. SAULTERS

Albert Edward Saulters, aged 40, was a coal hewer at William Pit. He lived at 12 Meadow View, Castle Croft, Egremont, with his wife Margaret and daughter Muriel. On 17 August 1947, at 2.15pm Albert was brought to the pit top and identified by his brother Baden Powell Saulters of 24 Annie Pit Lane, Workington. Albert Saulters was the 43rd man reached by rescue and recovery teams.

****

My great-grandfather Albert Saulters was the son of Alex and Hannah Saulters, and one of eight children —two daughters and six sons. The sons were called John, Alex, Hans W, James and Baden P. and of course Albert. The daughters were named Eleanor and Margaret.
Jason Hill, great-grandson, aged 12

****

Treasured memories of a dear
husband and Dad,
Albert Edward
who died in the William Pit disaster
August 15, 1947.
His heart was kind his friendship true
Loved and respected by all he knew
To a happy life came a sudden end
He died as he lived, everyone's friend.
Sadly missed by his loving wife, daughter
Muriel, all at home, and Deal

****

LEONARD SEWARD

Leonard Seward was a 36-year-old brusher at William Pit. He lived at 7 Pasture Road, Rowrah, Cumberland. He was survived by his wife Marjorie and two young children. On the evening of 19 August 1947 at 8.25pm, Mr. Seward was brought to the surface of William Pit and identified by his brother Walter Seward of Haile Farm, Beckermet. Leonard Seward was the 91st miner located by the rescue team.

****

In loving memory of Leonard, dearly loved husband of Marjorie Seward,
killed in William Pit explosion August 15, 1947
Beautiful memories are all that are left
Of one we all loved and will never forget
Sadly missed by your loving wife, Pat and Leonard

In loving memory of our dear son, Len,
who was killed in William Pit disaster August 15, 1947 aged 36 years
We miss your smiling face
Your kind and loving ways
God thought it best to call you to eternal rest
From his loving Mam and Dad

****

THOMAS SHACKLEY

Thomas Shackley was 40-years-old and worked as a pan-puller in William Pit. He lived at 76 Low Church Street, Whitehaven, with his sister, a Mrs. Gertrude Waggett. Raised to the surface at 2.25pm on 17 August 1947, Mr. Shackley was formally identified by his brother-in-law John Waggett of the same address. Thomas Shackley was the 47th miner to be recovered.

****

In affectionate remembrance of my
loving brother, Thomas
who was accidentally killed in the William Pit Disaster Friday August 15, 1947
Happy smiling always content
Loved and respected wherever he went
Helpful winning thoughtful and kind
What beautiful memories he left behind
Always in our thoughts
At rest
From his loving sister, Gertrude Waggett, also his nephews and nieces

****

MARK JACKSON SHAW

Quiet Mark

Mark Jackson Shaw was 45-years-old and employed as a general shift hand at William Pit. He was survived by his wife Martha and seven children: John, Robert, Dorothy, Clifford, Doreen, Annie and Margaret. The family lived at 30 North Road, Bransty, Whitehaven. At 2.45pm on 17 August 1947, Mark Shaw was brought to the surface and later identified by his uncle, Whitehaven Miners' Agent, James Martin of 22 Lowther Street, Whitehaven. He was the 50th man located by rescue and recovery teams.

Mark and Martha Shaw had a family of eight, I was the third oldest. My eldest brother William Edward, died at the age of twelve in 1937. On the day of the disaster, John my other older brother was on active service in Burma. I was eighteen and on farm service, the remainder of my brothers and sisters were at home, the youngest child being four-years-old. My father was at work down the pit.

Mark Shaw with his wife Martha.

In the late 1920 and 1930s he was unemployed, so there was never much money available, but his first concern was for his family, and any treats he could provide he did. To keep the house warm, along with many others, he went to the pit waste heaps to collect coal to keep the fires going.

In 1938/39 he did get work in William Pit. This continued until 1941 when there was an explosion at the pit. He was at work that day as well and fortunately he managed to get out safely. During the time the pit was closed he was able to get some casual work, but when the pit reopened he went back.

In August 1947 just prior to the

explosion Mam and Dad took the younger children to Fleetwood for a holiday staying at my Grannies (that is where our Mother originated from). When it was time to come home Dad had suggested that Mam stay another week with the children, but he had to return to go to work. I saw my Dad on the Tuesday and he told me the rest of the family were staying another week at Fleetwood. For some unknown reason Mam decided to return on the Wednesday before the week was up. If she had stayed until the end of the week she would have returned on the day of the explosion.

Front, left to right: Robert (me), John, and Edward. I think the photo was taken by my mother circa 1935.

The first I knew about the explosion was when I saw the girl I was courting (now my wife) with her friends waiting for the local bus. On asking where they were going they told me about the explosion and were going to the pit to see what was happening so I decided to go with them. At the pit there were crowds of people looking for information, but at that point there was none available. I made my way home to my mother's which was about ten minutes walk away. She was busy ironing and was unaware of the accident at the pit. I did not tell her, and after a short while I went back to the pit. I stayed there until it was dark but there was no news so I went back home.

When I got home, friends and neighbours, were with my mother offering support after breaking the news of the accident at the pit. I remember sitting up all night in chairs waiting for news, none came that night. Early the next morning I went back to the pit, still no news of my father. It was twelve noon when it was reported that three men had walked out and there were others to follow. No more men walked out. Saturday went into Sunday and I returned to the pit where I met Jimmy Martin, who was my Dad's uncle and also the miners' agent. He told me that they had recovered my Dad's body and that he had already carried out the identification. At the time I did not mind that he had identified my Dad's body but as time went by I wished it had been me to confirm his identity.

I made my way home and found that the Salvation Army people were giving my mother the news. This was not surprising as the family were members of the Salvation Army. From that point on natural progression took over. My brother John was on his way home from Burma, but did not arrive in time for the funeral.

After the inquest my mother was means tested and was awarded £3,000 in compensation, but was only allowed a fixed amount each week. She got the news that the concessionary

coal which miners' families enjoyed would be stopped. Now 60 years on and looking back I realize what a hard time Mam must have had raising the family. My eldest brother and one of my sisters have since died. There are five of us left, we are all proud of what our mother achieved. *Robert Shaw, son*

****

I have attached a picture of my grandfather Mark Jackson Shaw who was killed in William Pit in 1947. He was a Salvationist and played in Whitehaven Salvation Army band. He left seven children, my father was the oldest. My Uncle Clifford was five-years-old at the time and was on William Beach when the disaster happened. My father was 21 and serving in Malaysia in the British Army. He received the news by reading a newspaper. He didn't make it home in time for the funeral.

I am named after my grandfather. My Dad said he was known as quiet Mark, and used to develop his own photographs as a hobby.

My Grandma moved to 23 Haig Avenue, Bransty, Whitehaven, and lived there until she died on 7 February 1972. Most of my uncles and aunties still live in Whitehaven all except Annie who lives in Mansfield. She moved there with her husband when the mines closed.

The Shaw children.

My Aunty Doreen who died in 1994, left home and became a Salvation Army officer. My uncles Robert and Clifford went to work at Sellafield along with my Dad and were there until they retired. My Aunty Dorothy is still in the Salvation Army at Whitehaven and I am a fourth generation salvationist. *Mark Shaw,grandson*

****

In loving memory of a dear husband and father,
Mark Jackson,
who fell asleep in William Pit Disaster, August 15, 1947.
Never one day forgotten by his loving wife and children.

****

HENRY SHILTON

Henry Shilton was a 44-year-old brusher at William Pit. He lived at 23 Main Street, Parton, with his wife Lilian and four daughters. Brought to the surface on the morning of 17 August 1947 at 9.10am, Mr. Shilton was identified by his brother Joseph Shilton of 18 Main Street, Parton. He was the 24th man located of the 104 men who lost their lives in William Pit. Henry Shilton was laid to rest in Moresby Churchyard on 19 August 1947.

****

In loving memory of my dear husband
Henry Shilton
Killed in William Pit disaster August 15, 1947
Sweetest of memories are all that are left
Of one we loved dearly and shall never forget
Loved and longed for always by his loving wife
and four little daughters,
Joyce, Marian, Lillie and Valerie,
23 Main Street, Parton.

****

THOMAS B. SMITH
and his sons
THOMAS T. SMITH
and
HAROLD SMITH

Thomas Barnes Smith was 62-years-old and employed as a brusher at William Pit. He lived at 2 Torrentine's Place with his wife Mary Ann born 30 April 1885. Thomas Smith had three sons: Harold, Thomas, and Cyril, and a daughter Evelyn. At 5.50am, on 19 August 1947, Thomas was brought to the surface of William Pit and later identified by his son, Cyril Smith of 9 North Row, Kells, Whitehaven. He was the 79th miner located by rescue teams.

****

Thomas Thompson Smith was a 36-year-old brusher. He was survived by his wife Eleanor, born 23 September 1913 and three children Thomas (born 21 June 1938), John (born 15 March 1941) and James (born 26 November 1943). The family lived at 7 South Row, Kells, Whitehaven. Thomas was raised to the surface of William Pit at 6.10am on 19 August 1947, and identified by his brother Cyril Smith of 9 North Row, Kells, Whitehaven. He was the 80th miner located.

****

Harold Smith was 41-years-old and employed as a brusher at William Pit. He lived at 31 Solway Road, Moresby Parks, Whitehaven, with his wife Jane. The couple did not have immediate family. At 9.35am on 19 August 1947, the body of Harold Smith was brought to the pit surface and identified by his cousin William Edward Thompson of 10 Woodhouse Road, Greenbank, Whitehaven. He was the 82nd miner to be located by search and rescue teams.

****

I'm trying to find out about Norman's grandfather Thomas Smith. Norman can't remember anything, but on our Christmas visit to Norman's aunt Mary Smith, who married Cyril Smith, the son of Thomas and brother of Harold and Tommy, I asked her if she could help. The only thing she could tell me was Norman's grandfather left the pit and went to work at the ammunition's depot at Drigg. However the miners worked so many men in a band (as they were called) or a team, and sons Tommy and Harold persuaded him to come back to William and work in their band. *Joyce Haile (née Hewer)*

I would like to recall an instance referring to the 1947 William pit disaster. I remember my late father Robert Lavery (an ex-miner at Walkmill Colliery, Moresby), saying that he was out for a walk that morning with a Mr. Harold Smith who had sadly changed shifts with one of his workmates. On that day Harold said to my father, 'It's such a beautiful day Bob, I think I'll have the shift off!' However, unfortunately he went to work and was killed in the disaster. *Robert E. Lavery*

No. 1 and No 2 Torrentine's Buildings off Tangier Street, Whitehaven. Sketch drawn by ex-pat Les McKenna of Washington State, USA, and given to author in 2001. It shows the home of Thomas B. Smith. Mr. McKenna said, 'I can still hear the sound of their clogs as they made their way to the shift that day.'

Harold Smith was one of the 104 men. He lived at 31 Solway Road, Moresby Parks, next door to where I was brought up (my Mum, now aged 92, still lives there.)

She remembers Mr Smith sitting on the back step and putting on his clogs on the day of the disaster. My sister Susan was about nine-months-old and was outside in the sunshine in her pram. He was chatting to her as he got ready for his shift - of course, he never came back.

Mr Smith and his wife Jane didn't have any children. She looked after me a lot when I was small and was at our wedding. She had a hard life as a widow. One of her jobs was doing the washing for the boys at St Bees School - there were often hundreds of blue woollen knee socks hanging on her line (the boys wore shorts there until they were eighteen in those days). I think that sometimes she even walked to St Bees and back. I don't think she ever got over the tragedy. *Gill Kerrush*

****

In loving memory of my dear husband and two sons, Harold and Tommy,
killed in William Pit Disaster August 15th 1947
Death did to them short warning give
So now be careful how you live
Their weeping friends they left behind
They had no time to speak their mind
Sadly missed by a sorrowing wife and mother; also Evelyn and Harry, Tangier Street

In loving memory of my Dad, Thomas,
and two brothers, Harold and Tommy
killed in William Pit Disaster, August 15, 1947
We are always together in memory lane
Not just today tomorrow the same
Wherever we are; whatever we do
Our thoughts dear father and brothers are always of you
Sadly missed by Cyril and Jessie, Kells

****

In loving memory of my dear husband Harold,
who lost his life in William Pit disaster August 15, 1947
When last I saw your smiling face
You looked so bright and well
Little did I dream that day
Would be our last farewell
Never one day forgotten by his loving wife Jane and little Harold
31 Solway Road, Moresby,
his loving sister-in-law and brother-in-law 13 Selby Terrace, Hensingham,
also all his dearest cousins and friends, Carlisle and Newcastle on Tyne

****

Treasured memories of my beloved husband Tommy Smith
killed in the William Pit disaster August 15, 1947 aged 36 years.
He lived for those he loved
We who loved him remember
Loved and longed for always by his wife and sons
Also our dearest Granda and Uncle Harold killed in the same disaster
Age shall not weary nor the years condemn
Ever in our thoughts, Eleanor and children

****

THOMAS TURNER

Tom

Thomas Turner, a shift hand, was 46-years-old when he lost his life in William Pit. He lived at 17 George Street, Whitehaven, with his wife Mary. Mr. Turner was brought to the surface of the pit on 17 August 1947, and identified by his only child, his son, 23-year-old Charles Turner of 16 George Street, Whitehaven. Thomas Turner was the 27th man located. He was laid to rest in Whitehaven Cemetery.

****

After reading your article in the Whitehaven news I thought I might be able to add a little to your story as my grandfather, Thomas Turner, was killed in the disaster, aged 46. I did not know my Granda as I was not born until 1953 but my only brother William was born in 1946 so was an infant at the time of Granda's death.

Thomas and his wife Mary had one child, my father Charles Edward. My Nana never married again and died in 1981. She is buried with my Granda in Whitehaven cemetery.

Both my parents are dead now, my Dad at the age of 48 when I was only nineteen, so I didn't have the chance to talk much about my Granda. I do remember my Mam telling me he was a lovely kind man and she thought he must have sensed something was going to happen on the day of his death because he was restless and on edge all morning, and after leaving for work, returned to the house to once more say his goodbyes, before finally going to work, not to be seen alive again. *Michael Turner, grandson.*

****

In loving memory of my dear husband Thomas,
killed in William Pit Disaster August 15, 1947.
When last I saw your smiling face you looked so bright and well
Little did I dream that day would be our last farewell
Always remembered by his loving wife Mary

In loving memory of my dear father Thomas Turner,
killed in William Pit disaster August 15, 1947
We cannot bring the old days back
His hand we cannot touch
But we treasure happy memories of the one we loved so much
Ever remembered by his loving son, daughter-in-law and grandson.

Thomas Turner, back left, at the wedding of his son, Charles to Miss Alice Cowling.
Also pictured are Mary Turner (née Mather) and John and Violet Cowling.

Happy memories of a loyal pal, Tom,
who was accidentally killed in William Pit Disaster August 15, 1947.
May the winds of God blow softly
O'er a sweet and hallowed spot
Where the one we love lies sleeping
And shall never be forgot
From Fred, Mabel and Monica, Grange-over-Sands

****

ALBERT TWEDDLE

Albert Tweddle was 41-years-old and employed as a brusher at William Pit. A resident of Woodhouse, he lived at 6 Fleswick Avenue, with his wife Jane (Jennie). Mr. Tweddle was brought to the surface on 17 August 1947, and identified by his brother Thomas Tweddle of 122 Moresby Parks, Whitehaven. He was the 60th miner to be located. Albert Tweddle was laid to rest in Moresby Churchyard on 21 August 1947.

Further details about his life may be found in the pages dedicated to Thomas Allan.

In loving memory of my dear husband,
Albert, also my dear brother Thomas,
who were killed in the William Pit
explosion, August 15, 1947
Precious are their memories
Treasured are their names
Dear to my heart they will always remain
*Always remembered by a loving wife
and sister, Jennie.*

*Albert Tweddle with his nieces
Frances and Mildred Allan*

****

In loving memory of my dear son, Albert,
who lost his life in the William Pit disaster August 15, 1947.
Resting where no shadows fall
In perfect peace he awaits us all
Always remembered by Mother and Sarah, Lowca

In loving memory of my loving brother, Albert
who was killed in the William Pit Disaster August 15, 1947
No more to see his smiling face
Or hear him say hello
It came as a shock we didn't expect
A hard and bitter blow
Always remembered by his sister Maggie, brother-in-law Billie and family

****

WILLIAM A. WALBY

Willy

William Arnott Walby was 46-years-old and employed as a shift-hand at William Pit. He lived at The Lodge, Ewanrigg Hall, Maryport, with his wife Leah. William and Leah Walby did not have a family. Mr. Walby was brought to the pit surface on 20 August 1947 and identified by his wife.

****

Willy Walby was a little fellow from Maryport, who worked putting tubs across behind the loader end. He always had a big chew of bacca and with no teeth looked funny when he was chewing. Most of the time when the coal was coming, only the tubs coming down, indicated he was still there. *A friend and co-worker*

****

RALPH WALKER

Ralph Walker was a 34-year-old shift-hand. He lived at 16 Valley View Road, Greenbank, Whitehaven, with his wife Elizabeth (Betty) and two little girls, Alice and Elizabeth. Mr. Walker was brought to the surface on 17 August at 7.25am, and later identified by his brother James Henry Yates of 66 Buttermere Avenue, Seacliffe, Whitehaven. Ralph Walker was the 56th coal miner located by rescue workers.

Ralph and Betty Walker

****

I have read your appeal in the *Whitehaven News* (December 28) my father was also killed in the William pit disaster, 1947.

I just about remember the day it happened. I was nine-years-old, my sister Betty was four. We had only been home about two weeks. We had been on our holidays to the Isle of Man. I remember it was a red hot day. My father should have been on the front shift, but changed shifts with someone. So he went on the back shift.

My father had only been home from the army about two years. We lived on Greenbank then. We were only getting used to him being home. My sister doesn't remember our father very much. We went to the pictures every Saturday night. My Dad then went for a couple pints. The pub was called the 'Canteen.' It was on Low Road. He also liked to smoke. My mother never really got over it. My Dad was only 34.

TO: 5683248
PTE. R. WALKER
SOM. L. I. DEFENCE COY.
H.Q. 15TH ARMY GROUP
C. M. F.

I have enclosed a photograph taken when we went to Czechoslovakia. At the front is my mother Elizabeth Walker, Albert Farrer and John Allan. The one who has his back to us is Joe Norman. The woman in the black dress is Mrs. Calvin. Albert Farrer was later killed in an accident in the Haig Pit.

Miss. Alice Walker, daughter

Pictured left, Betty and Alice Walker, Ralph Walker's daughters.

Below, Agnes Allan, Alice Walker, Jean Allan, Betty Walker and Betty Walker, Skegness, 1948.

****

Treasured memories of my darling
husband and our dear Daddy,
killed in William Pit,
August 15, 1947
The flowers we place
upon his grave
May wither and decay
But the love for him
who sleeps beneath
Will never fade away
You are always in our hearts
Ever remembered by his loving
wife; good night and God Bless
Daddy, Alice and Betty

Pictured left, Mrs. Walker, Albert Farrer, John Allan, Joe Norman and Mrs. Calvin Czechoslovakia, 1956.

****

Loving memory of our dear son
and brother, Ralph, who was killed in
William pit disaster, August 15, 1947
Your end was sudden dear son
And as oft times we sit and talk of you
Of things you used to say and do
And wonder why you had to die
Without a chance to say goodbye
Always in the thoughts of
your loving Mam and Dad
Brothers away, and sister at home, and
Robert, Malta.

****

WILLIAM WILLIAMSON

Billy

Billy Williamson, aged 27 years, was employed as a brusher at William Pit. He lived at 14 Hilton Terrace with his wife Muriel and the couple's young son, David. Mr. Williamson was brought to the surface of William Pit on 17 August 1947, at 11.45am and later identified by his father-in-law, Thomas Wilson, of 60 Victoria Road, Whitehaven. Billy was the 35th miner located by rescue teams.

****

Treasured memories of a dearly
loved husband and Daddy, Bill,
killed in the William Pit disaster
August 15, 1947 aged 27 years.
Silently the shades of evening
Gather round my lonely door
Silently they bring before me
That dear face we'll see no more
Ah! Not lost but gone before us
Let him never be forgot
Sweet his memory to the lonely
In our heart's he'll perish not
Loved and longed for by his wife Muriel,
and small son David

In ever loving memory of William, killed in
William Pit disaster August 15, 1947
No more to see his smiling face
Or hear him say hello
It came as a shock we didn't expect
A hard and bitter blow
Always remembered by Mam, Dad,
Sisters and Brothers

In loving memory of our dear son-in-law
William (Billy) Williamson,
who was killed in William Pit explosion
August 15, 1947
So deeply mourned
Remembered by all

GEORGE H. WILSON

George Henry Wilson was a 29-year-old brusher, residing at Douglas Burn, Market Place, Whitehaven. He was survived by his wife Jean Veronica Wilson and a two-year-old daughter. George Wilson was brought to the surface of William Pit on 17 August 1947 and identified by his wife. It is possible that Mr. Wilson was a native of South Shields, as documentation has a further address of 158 Roman Road, South Shields, listed. He was given the identification number of 30.

****

MATTHEW WILSON

Matt

Matt Wilson was a deputy at William Pit. He was 46-years-old, single, and living at 27 South Row, Kells, Whitehaven, with his widowed mother and sister. Brought to the surface of William Pit on 16 August 1947 at 9.40pm, Mr. Wilson was identified by his brother-in-law, Thomas Gainford, of 8 Basket Road, Prospect, Whitehaven. Matthew Wilson was the eighth man located of the 104 men who lost their lives.

****

My Uncle Matt (Matthew Wilson) was killed at the age of 46, and his body was brought home. He never married, and lived with his widowed mother, my grandmother, and his invalid sister Elizabeth. He was their everything, and one of the few men left in the family, after the deaths of his three uncles in the Wellington Pit disaster in 1910.

When we went into the silent house — the clocks were stopped and the curtains were closed, in accordance with tradition — it seemed to be filled with women all in black. They spoke softly and resignedly as they made preparations for the funeral. Someone asked my mother if she was going to take me upstairs to see Matt. My mother said she wouldn't, because his body was affected by the gas. No-one seemed to cry, they were just staunch and solemn.

Matthew Wilson as a boy.

Uncle Matt had recently bought a car, and had a garage built outside the house. The car was his pride and joy, and he was looking forward to taking my grandmother and his sister out for trips. The car sat in the garage for some time before it was sold. My grandmother never really recovered, she had a stroke and died the following year. But I remember how strong she was, and how she would sing *The Old Rugged Cross* to keep her going.

Margaret Walsh, (née Gainford) niece

****

In loving memory of my dearly beloved son Matthew
who was killed in the William Pit disaster, August 15, 1947,
son of Elizabeth and the late William Wilson who died August 24, 1924:
Had he asked us well we know
We should cry 'oh spare the blow!'
Yes with streaming tears should pray
Lord we love him, let him stay
Sadly missed by his mother and sister Elizabeth, 27 South Row, Kells;
also remembered by his Aunt and Cousins, Vancouver, BC, Canada,
also his pal John.

Treasured memories of Matthew,
who was killed in the William Pit disaster August 15th, 1947,
also Dad, August 14, 1924.
He was such a wonderful brother
He played life's battles square
No matter when we needed him
We always found him there
And on this day our hearts go out
To the dearest and best of brothers
Who never had time to think of himself
But always remembered others
Never forgotten by Isabel, Harry, little Hazel and all at 13...
(rest cut off)

****

JOSEPH WILSON

Joseph Wilson was a contractor at William Pit, and 38-years-old. He was survived by his wife Susan and two sons. The family lived at 72 Valley View Road, Greenbank, Whitehaven. Mr. Wilson was brought to the surface at 3.40am on the morning of 17 August 1947 and formally identified by his brother, Thomas James Wilson of 6 Addison Street, Whitehaven. He was the 55th man found by the rescue team.

****

Treasured memories of a devoted husband and Dad,
Joe killed in William Pit disaster, August 15, 1947.
What would I give to clasp his hand
To hear his voice, to see him smile
That means so much to me
He did not fail to do his best
His heart was true and tender
He did work hard for those he left
That's something to remember
From his ever loving Wife and two sons, Raymond and Arnold, Greenbank.

****

In loving memory of a dear son and brother, Joseph
who was accidentally killed in the William Pit disaster August 15, 1947
Quick and sudden was his call
His sudden death surprised us all
Only those who have lost can tell
The bitter parting without farewell
Fondly remembered by his loving mother, brothers and sisters
at home and sister in Manchester.

****

THOMAS WOODEND

Tom

Thomas Woodend was 64-years-old and a shift-hand at William Pit. He lived at 11 South View Road, Bransty, with his wife Elizabeth. His son Thomas Woodend of 12 Addison Street, Whitehaven, identified his father after he was brought to the surface of William Pit on 19 August 1947.

My Uncle Tom Woodend was a victim of that tragic event. Evidently he had told his wife that he didn't want to go that day, as he didn't feel very well. He went anyway as he liked to be known as a reliable worker, who only took time off when he was really ill. My father's brother Robert Kenmare was due to go on that fatal shift but swapped at the last minute. When he heard of the disaster he went immediately to the pit top to help with the rescue operations. He was the son of John Edmund Woodend and Martha Watson Woodend. His daughter was called Jessie, and his sons were Tom and John. *Eddie Kenmare, nephew.*

Treasured memories of a dear husband, Dad, Granda, Thomas (Tom) Woodend
who lost his life in the William Pit disaster August 15 1947, aged 64 years.
We were not there beside you
To hear your last faint sigh
To whisper just one loving word
Or even say goodbye
Sadly missed by his Wife and son John; Good night Granda and God bless
from Barbara, Diana, Michael and Peter

In loving memory of a dear father, Thomas Woodend,
accidentally killed in William Pit disaster August 15, 1947.
Always in our thoughts, Tom and Ella, Jessie and Jim also grandchildren

In loving memory of Thomas Woodend
who lost his life in the William Pit Disaster, August 15, 1947
Worthy of remembrance
From his step-daughters Margaret, Annie, Elizabeth; sister-in-law, brother-in-law,
Louie, Tot, niece and nephew, Lilian, Tommy

****

WALTER WYLIE

Walter Wylie was a 26-year-old brusher at William Pit. He was survived by his wife Catherine, and two daughters. The family lived at 36 Fell View Avenue, Woodhouse, Whitehaven. On the afternoon of 17 August 1947, Catherine Wylie identified her husband after he was brought to the surface at 2.50pm. Walter Wylie was the 41st miner identified.

****

LETTERS FROM THE PAST

When I first learned of your interest in the William Pit Disaster, it was only with difficulty that I managed to restrain myself from contacting you and continued to do so when I read of your progress in the *Whitehaven News*. However, the write-up in the paper for 22 March, stating that the deadline for correspondence was 30 April, finally prompted me to relate to you my participation in those events.

I didn't know any of the miners involved, so I do realise, from the point of view of the records you are collating, my story isn't really relevant but, possibly as the only person still alive who had been closely involved in the events of those days, I felt it was permissible to contact you. I was, at that time, nineteen-years-old and undoubtedly the youngest person present.

In August 1947 I was employed as a clerk in the National Coal Board offices. I do not remember whether or not the pit horn was blown announcing to the town that there had been a disaster but at about 6.20pm on Friday, 15 August 1947, our next door neighbour, Dick Coyles, who was in charge of the St. John's Ambulance service and knew where I worked, knocked on our door to say there had been a disaster at the William Pit.

Because I knew how to work the telephone switchboard in the office, I decided to go down there in case I could be of help. I rang William pithead and spoke to Joe Roe, the land sales manager, who gave me permission to open up the switchboard. After working there a couple of hours, the official telephonist was brought in to take over and release me to take the press calls that were coming in from all over the world. Later that evening I remember my sister brought me some food and then a taxi was sent to collect me and take me round to the pit.

Quite a crowd had gathered at the pit gates and I remember a policeman being on duty there. I was on duty all night and when I was relieved in the morning by Peggy Sharpe (later Clark) I went straight to work. I received a message during the day to get some sleep and go on night duty again for a while. Peggy worked a day shift for two weeks.

I think there were two sources of rescue teams involved - Dearham and Ashington, County Durham - and originally my work was typing the lists of men on the rescue teams. The RAF were also involved. I remember airmen bringing Alsatian dogs which had been trained to track bodies under debris. One dog was a beautiful black one named Jet. Years later I learned that a black Alsatian named Jet had been awarded the Dickin Medal for rescue work and wondered if it was the same one.

I don't remember how long elapsed before the three survivors - James Weighman, John Edwin Birkett and Daniel Hinde - managed to make their way to safety. Until then there had been a fleet of ambulances parked in the pit yard but, as the time passed, it became obvious that it was unlikely there were going to be any more survivors.

There was a heat wave that August and the smell of disinfectant was everywhere. Allisons the Chemists had made up the disinfectant and I didn't like going in the shop for ages afterwards as it still reeked of it. I believe an engine house was used as a mortuary and the post mortems were done by Dr Faulds and Dr Inglis from the Cumberland Infirmary, Carlisle. I typed the pathologist's reports but these were just done as lists, not on official post mortem report forms.

A couple of days or so after the survivors were rescued, a debriefing meeting was held to record their experiences. There were probably only eight (or maybe nine) people present - Bill McAllister, J. G. Helps, Mr G. Nussey (H. M. Inspector of Mines), the three surviors, Peggy and I. Now Peggy and I were only youngsters and had no previous experience of taking shorthand records during a meeting such as this, and we decided that both of us would record everything and then between the two of us make a combined transcript. Presumably we managed OK - we never heard otherwise! (I remember Mr Nussey obligingly kept sharpening pencils for us!)

I remained seconded to the pit for a further six weeks during which time I continued working on the rescue lists and, as bodies were found and identified, Inspector Bell of the Whitehaven Constabulary gave me names, and lists of the deceased and next of kin were compiled. Several widows were pregnant and, as happens in a mining community, some families lost more than one member. I typed the letters of condolence that Bill McAllister dictated to each family and I noticed that, as he signed them, he added a personal remark on the foot of each one. Permission was kindly received from the town hall for me to use their electric duplicator to copy work I had been doing, as at the Coal Board we just had an old hand-driven Roneo. I did not attend the official inquest.

Freda Gowan and Peggy Sharpe

A number of years later, there was a commemorative service at St. James's Church, for the dedication of a miner's lamp for the sanctuary. Bill McAllister, who had by then moved to Fife returned to Whitehaven for that service and at the end people, presumably relatives or employees, queued to shake his hand. I was the last in the queue and, as I took his hand I said, 'I don't suppose you'll remember me.' But he said, 'Oh, I do, I do. It's my little secretary!' and tears rolled down his face.

Years later a memorial was built in St. Nicholas's Church grounds. I attended the dedication service and we later proceeded from there to the pithead site for the installation of a plaque. Fifty-six years after the event BBC 2's *Timewatch* had plans to produce a programme about it and, as I had been in touch with Helen Partridge, the researcher, she eventually wrote to me to say it had been shelved.

I remember, of course, that a mining community in Europe offered holidays to the bereaved familes and that two miners who lost their lives just a few miles away at William Pit, Camerton, on 15 August, are usually associated with the Whitehaven disaster. Needless to say I feel privileged to have shared in such an important event of my home-town's history.

Freda Howson (née Gowan).

****

In 1947 I was ten-years-old and lived in the big house next to William Pit. The house is on the Parton side of the pit. At 5.00pm I used to go to the bus station for an evening paper for my Dad. I also bought a paper for the haulage driver of the steam haulage which was at the pit top. The reason for waiting to 5.00pm was to make sure the last racing result was in. The name of the haulage driver was Tommy Ellwood. When I came back with the papers I would talk to Tommy for a few minutes. At 5.40pm the underground phone rang. Tommy answered the phone and he told me to run up to the manager's office and tell Jim Graham to phone the manager that there had been an explosion underground and for him to also phone the rescue brigade.

The first people to arrive at the pit were the police and the rescue brigade. The police closed the wooden gates on the town side of the pit. When the doors to the rescue brigade van were opened at the back, there were rows and rows of small cages with canaries in them. I was standing outside the manager's office when a policeman came up and told me to go home. There wasn't a gate on the Parton side of the pit, so two policemen were posted there.

When I got into our house my Dad asked me where I had been. I told him about the explosion. He grabbed his jacket and ran up to the pit. My Dad, Jimmy Semple, had been retired about a year. He was the back shift senior collier overman. He retired at 66 years of age. My Dad was one of the first men to go underground with the rescue team. It was not long before people started to gather at the pit as the night went on. My Mam and the old lady next door made teas for the women in the crowd. My Dad came back from the pit at about 1.00am, and I heard him tell my Mam that there would not be any hope of any survivors as it was a bad explosion. I remember this as if it was yesterday.

When I left school I went down the William Pit. I worked there from 1952 until it closed at the end of 1954. Then I was sent to work at the Haig Pit until it closed in 1986. I was then a collier senior overman. *Tommy Sempie, Glasgow, Scotland*

****

I am sending this newspaper cutting, hoping it will help you in your search for information on the William Pit disaster. I came across this paper while searching for a photograph for a nephew. I have lived at Parton all my life. I am now 91-years-old and was friends with the Parton men killed in the disaster especially Joe Hewer. He used to go fell racing in the summer at sports meetings. My father went with him several times but just as a spectator. Joe also played the violin and I used to go to his home and he gave me lessons. That was before he married. There were seven brothers.

I often see and talk to Henry Gibson's sister down town. She married John Fisher, brother to Bill Fisher. The tale in dialect (in the newspaper) was about how lucky he was to have missed work that day. Henry Gibson's sister was called Eva, and as a matter of fact I spoke to her this very morning. I was in Dixon's Café down town with my daughter when she came in to be served, so it was just a matter of waving to each other as we were ready for coming out.

I started work at number 10 Colliery in East of 1929. I had just left school at fourteen years of age and went to service my apprenticeship as a boiler smith. At 22 years of age I became the boiler smith at number 10. Just before I reached forty, I had a severe accident and two dislocated lumbar discs, which kept me off work for two years. Eventually I got the job of weighman at number 10. I could only do light work.

However on the day of the explosion, my Muriel with our young son, along with several other mothers with their young families, were down on the Parton Beach, on the grass part above the shore. It was a lovely summer day, and I went there to give them the bad news. It was a very sad time for all the people of Parton; it seemed to affect everyone. This was the second pit disaster that affected Parton, for on Monday 9 December 1946, there was an explosion at number 10 colliery which affected both Parton and Lowca. I had neighbours and friends killed in that disaster too. I had worked at that district a fortnight before, on the night shift repairing a metal shunt. I am sorry if I have bored you with all this, I still think about it. My father had his spine fractured down the mine. I was only eleven-years-old at the time. I think it was a good job that the mines were closed down. It was slavery and left so many people injured, and scarred for life. *Mr T. B. Robinson*

I don't know if I can be of any help in your William Pit project, but perhaps my memories of the event may be of interest. I was eleven-years-old at the time and, like everyone else, I was totally shocked and saddened. At the time, I was on holiday at Blackpool with my parents where we were having a grand old time - or as grand a time as you could have with the rationing of nearly everything. The news came over the radio and we were all struck dumb, and tears rolled down my Mum's face. The holiday was curtailed and we returned home to a stunned Whitehaven.

As a Whitehaven lad you could not be unaware of William Pit especially where I lived on Bransty. From my bedroom window I could look out at the tall chimney sited at the top of the colliery. Many of the miners lived on Bransty and I saw them every day tramping to work with their bait tins, swinging by their sides. Many of them had pigeon lofts on Bransty Brows. I guess they liked to think of the pigeons flying free while they were scrambling in blackness, miles out under the sea. I seem to remember that three men escaped the disaster by finding a way further into the mine. I believe one of these men lived on Bransty and immediately returned to the coal face when he was able. This is not uncommon for miners. An uncle of mine worked at Lowca Pit and was killed along with thirteen others. He had a young son who was deaf and dumb, and when he was old enough, he too went down the same mine where his Dad had died.

Mining was traditional in Whitehaven and many of my school chums followed their fathers and brothers 'down the pit'. After the disaster there were many desks empty at my school, and many tears were shed and many prayers offered. The newspapers were full of it of course - including a special glossy edition of the *Picture Post*. My sleepy town of Whitehaven was in the news for all the wrong reasons. It is now 50 years since I left Whitehaven, but it is my heritage, it is all my childhood memories, and the sad fact of William Pit is the saddest of them all.

Leonard Watson

****

I came across your appeal quite by chance when I was searching for family members who were killed in the 1910 disaster - three brothers died in the incident together. The account from my Grandmother, Hannah Ferguson, née McCourt, of Low Corkickle was that her brothers were found together apparently gassed whilst on a break.

I wanted to tell you that my sister, Edris Ferguson, who was thirteen at the time of the 1947 disaster, was on holiday with our Grandmother and happened to be in the vicinity of the docks when the explosion took place. She along with everyone to hand, were formed into lines to pass buckets of water. When she returned home very late and very dirty, our worried and infuriated Grandmother did not believe the reason behind her being so late and in such a filthy state. Edris was put to bed with the customary cuff round the ear for making up such a tale.

When news spread around the town, our Grandmother had to eat humble pie. Someone who was also on the dock, told Gran how ceaselessly Edris had worked along with everyone else. Unfortunately neither are still with us, but we often smile about my sister's rough justice. But now, reading the reports on the 1910 disaster, all those terrible memories came flooding back. The memorial picture of her three brothers was always at the house but unfortunately it did not make it back to Yorkshire after my Grandmother's death, but I do sincerely hope it has pride of place in one of her descendant's homes.

Ann Dowson (née Ferguson)

****

EPILOGUE

Thirty four years have passed since my childhood encounter with the ghosts of William Pit, and in a few months God willing, I will return to Whitehaven, and make my way once more to the old wagon road.

I venture now with eyes wide open, the mystery of my summer day is no more. How many times had I asked myself about this great love affair? What was it that had kept me captive over the years? Had I never left the field? I smile and again lift my eyes to Heaven. For it is not the fear of the dark place that has endured these many seasons, but the heart-beats of men. It is not their deaths that have kept me hostage, but their lives; and lives abundant - generations upon generations of Whitehaven's royal families, the coal miners of the ages past. Not the blue-blooded, but the blue-scarred. I am at last, among my people.

I hear them. I see them. Billy Fisher dancing with Stella. Harry Allan training Lady. Pica Murdock modelling socks. Joe Norman tending roses. Tosh Lancaster with Lanc and the pigeons. Pal Moore's homecoming. Henry Gibson on Foundry Road; practical joker Dicky Grearson with his face pressed against a glass window pane. James McMullen proudly holding his little son's hand. Jacob Bridges and *Three Little Fishes*, Patrick Murtagh with his beautiful wife. Ike McAllister shopping for sweets. Billy Lee at Buckingham Palace and John Joseph Renwick catching finches. All of them. One hundred and four men, living, loving, laughing, being.

And finally down Parton way, I see the boy, a six-year-old mischief maker, attempting to hide from a group of miners as they make their way to a final shift at William Pit. One of them stops and slowly turns to face his son, and with a command and a single hand motion chases him home.

If only. If only Ronnie Hewer could have looked down through the years and smiled at his now adult son; a son who had known the goodness of a father and mother, of hard work and sacrifice.

When the time was fulfilled, he would reach out to the girl in the field and whisper the first story. He would ignite the spark of love and remembrance, and create a flame more powerful than the destroyer of life fathoms below my feet.

And now, united with a gathering of storytellers, as the sun sets on Whitehaven's coal mining history, we, the pit families, offer that for which we were born - the lives of men.

****

But you have gone now, all of you, that were so beautiful when you were quick with life.
Yet not gone for you are still a living truth inside my mind. So how are you dead, my
brothers and sisters, and all of you, when you live with me as surely as I live myself?
How green was my valley then, and the valley of them that have gone.

Richard Llewellyn

****

The three survivors, left to right: John James Weighman, John Edwin Birkett and Daniel Hinde.

****

Treasured memories of all our workmates

Who lost their lives in the William Pit Disaster

15 August 1947

Remembered always by their three workmates

****

GLOSSARY OF MINING TERMS

Airways Repairman: His duty was to repair any falls in the return airways of the pit.
Borer: His duty was to bore holes in the coal face for shot firer to blast down.
Brusher: The brusher was responsible for advancing and enlarging the roadways.
Coal Cutter: A coal cutter undercut the coal at the face in preparation for machine blasting.
Chocker: A miner who builds the chocks (wooden in 1947) between stone packs to support the roof of the coal face
Contractor: A miner who was paid by the coal owner to complete a task of work at an agreed price e.g. coal tonnage, roadway advancement.
Deputy: This man was a colliery official assigned to the shift management within a specific district of the coal mine. He was responsible for the safety of the men and day to day operations. He was subordinate to the Overman.
Deputy Overman: Acted in a temporary capacity as an overman. He would deploy the miners to their working positions, oversee production, and haulage, in one or more of the mine districts.
Engine Fitter: A mechanic responsible for the maintenance and repair of underground machinery.
Fan Man: The fan man closely monitored the underground booster fans and filed reports.
Haulage Hand: He was responsible for the movement of the tubs of hewed coal, equipment and supplies.
Hewer: The hewer/hagger was employed to fill the coal from the coal face on to the conveyor belt.
Machine Man: He was also a coal cutter, or any man who operated a coal cutting machine.
Occupations Development: This person worked in developing new areas of the pit.
Pipe Fitter: He was employed to extend and repair pipes carrying compressed air and water.
Pan Puller: This job title was given to the team working on the preparation shift who dismantled, advanced and set-up the conveyor for the transportation of the coal.
Shift hand: General pit labourer, he performed a variety of tasks.
Stoneworker: The stoneworker drove tunnels through the stone strata.
Trainee: Usually a younger miner learning a new job.
Trainer: Often an experienced miner teaching a new job to a trainee.

****

ABOUT THE AUTHOR

Author Amanda Margaret Garraway was born in Whitehaven, Cumbria, in 1965. The discovery of her own ancestral ties to the coal trade explained a life-long fascination with the collieries and pitmen of her hometown. She resides in Cambridge, Ontario, Canada with her husband David and three children. *104 Men* is her first book.